THE PRACTICAL STEP-BY-STEP GUIDE TO
PATIO, TERRACE, BACKYARD
& COURTYARD GARDENING

AN INSPIRING SOURCEBOOK OF CLASSIC AND CONTEMPORARY GARDEN DESIGNS, WITH
IDEAS AND TECHNIQUES TO SUIT ENCLOSED OUTDOOR SPACES OF EVERY SHAPE AND SIZE

INCLUDES OVER 60 STAGE-BY-STAGE CONSTRUCTION AND PLANTING SEQUENCES, GARDEN
CASE STUDIES, A COMPREHENSIVE DIRECTORY OF PLANTS AND OVER 850 PHOTOGRAPHS

JOAN CLIFTON AND JENNY HENDY

HERMES
HOUSE

This edition is published by Hermes House, an imprint of Anness Publishing Ltd, Blaby Road, Wigston, Leicestershire LE18 4SE; info@anness.com

www.hermeshouse.com; www.annesspublishing.com

If you like the images in this book and would like to investigate using them for publishing, promotions or advertising, please visit our website www.practicalpictures.com for more information.

Publisher: Joanna Lorenz
Editorial Director: Helen Sudell
Project Editor: Emma Clegg
Designer: Abby Franklin
Practical photography: Howard Rice
Illustrator: Robert Highton
Production Controller: Wendy Lawson

© Anness Publishing Ltd 2012

A CIP catalogue record for this book is available from the British Library.

Part of this book was previously published as *Courtyard and Terrace Gardens*

PUBLISHER'S NOTE
Great care should be taken if you include pools, ponds or water features as part of your garden landscape. Young children should never be left unsupervised near water of any depth, and if children are able to access the garden all pools and ponds should be fenced and gated to the recommended specifications.

Although the advice and information in this book are believed to be accurate and true at the time of going to press, neither the authors nor the publisher can accept any legal responsibility or liability for any errors or omissions that may have been made nor for any inaccuracies nor for any loss, harm or injury that comes about from following instructions or advice in this book.

Above left: *A path of bricks and encroaching planting with a purple/yellow theme lead to a classical-style bench – acting both as a focal point and a place to enjoy the garden.*

Above centre: *The bright colours of pelargoniums make them ideal candidates for wall-mounted containers, especially as they require little care, once established.*

Above right: *A terracotta pot soaks up the sun, its green foliage stealing the lavender hues from the bed behind.*

Page 1: *This design combines the traditional materials of red brick and stone with a formal pool, a stepped fountain and a natural planting style.*

Page 2: *The sights and fragrance of a Mediterranean courtyard are created with a mock hanging basket, warm orange paving broken up with creeping herbs, an orange tree and lavender.*

Page 3: *Evergreen plants give a strong architectural dynamic, creating enclosure and protection for this paved seating area.*

CONTENTS

INTRODUCTION

In recent years the courtyard has seen a reincarnation. The small, enclosed garden is the natural result of the need to maximize our urban spaces. It also offers a sanctuary from the noise and pollution around us. The design potential of these private areas, as extensions to our homes and as places of relaxation, is strongly evident in the work of modern architects and designers.

Above: *Flooring details are juxtaposed to accentuate the curves of the garden.*

The design that you choose for your courtyard will depend on many factors, from its aspect and soil quality to your own style preferences. This book sets out to unravel all the possible options for a contained outside area, with design hints, useful plants, practical features and ways of making it your own.

Following a brief history, a chapter called Planning Your Courtyard explains how to assess your site, freshen up a neglected courtyard and then plan a more permanent design. The following six chapters focus on different visual styles. Traditional Lines is the natural choice of those who respect orderly proportions and classical features. Mediterranean Moods offers charming patios, bright colours, overwhelming scents and the promise of long, sunny days outside. Outdoor Rooms explains a concept that makes your courtyard a real-life living space, with interior styling, and a place to cook, eat, relax, welcome friends, bathe and sleep. Productive Spaces shows the potential of a decorative kitchen garden in which to cultivate fresh vegetables as well as fruit and flowers for the table. For those who would like to escape the urban bustle, Contemplative Retreats demonstrates how to create a calm, private paradise. The final chapter on Modern Zones looks at minimal,

streamlined spaces using contemporary and experimental materials, or traditional materials used with a modern twist.

Each chapter examines the key elements – flooring, walls and screens, plants and containers, structures and furniture, decoration and water features, and lighting – and each one concludes with a case study that brings an individual location to life, and offers two step-by-step methods of how to create key features. The techniques are chosen for their relevance to the chapter, but many of them are interchangeable – such as laying random paving, painting a rendered wall, lighting a pathway – and useful for any courtyard.

Plants are the reason we create a garden and to help you make your choice there is a Plant Directory identifying suitable types by their form and function, appearance, seasonality and growing requirements. Finally, a section on Maintenance shows how to keep your courtyard at its best, ranging from plant upkeep and pruning and training to watering techniques and seasonal jobs.

The courtyard is a garden in miniature. It gives you the opportunity to enact any decorative or horticultural fantasy, classical or romantic, spare or productive. So use the ideas in the chapters that follow to create something special.

Left: *Interior meets exterior; a chequered floor has dappled shade spilling down through a stylized tree canopy.*

Right: *Mediterranean floral delights jostle with each other in a container-filled patio.*

A BRIEF HISTORY

Courtyards are known to have existed before 3000BC and are described in the Bible as protected, walled enclosures. They are spaces that have always provided many benefits: somewhere to live and work, a source of warmth, shade, food, protection, privacy, and even spiritual nourishment. This short history traces the highlights of the style, from Egypt and Persia to Japan and Spain.

Above: *A traditional Chinese courtyard, or* siheyuan, *with surrounding houses.*

The First Courtyards

An inventive and cultured people, the ancient Egyptians developed the concept of the courtyard well over 5,000 years ago, with their tomb paintings and hieroglyphs showing walled gardens open to the sky. Skilled in utilizing land for cultivation, they created lush oases that were decorative and productive, protected by walls from the harsh desert environment outside. These gardens frequently featured trees, such as the fig, sycamore and jujube, and other ancient plants and flowers would have included convolvulus,

cornflowers, mandrakes, myrtle, jasmine, celosia, lychnis, sweet marjoram, henna, poppies, papyrus and grapes.

Another early civilization that used the courtyard was Persia (modern-day Iran, Iraq and Syria) in the period 3000–2000BC. The Persian word for 'enclosed space' was *pairi-daeza*, a term later used to describe the Garden of Eden. This style used the spiritual idea of the garden as a protected paradise away from the sun. Their courtyards often used a *chadar bagh* design, meaning 'four gardens', with an area dissected by pathways or rills symbolizing the four rivers of Paradise referred to in the Koran. Apart from the spiritual symbolism, these water features gave relief from

the dry heat, alongside elements such as trees, trellis, pavilions and walls that gave cooling shade. The unmistakeable style of these Persian gardens remained strong even after the Muslim invasion in the 1st century AD, and the influence is still clearly seen in the gardens of the Indian Moguls who invaded Persia in the 13th century and took their garden makers back to India.

China has a courtyard tradition dating back to the Han dynasty (206BC–AD220). Chinese urban domestic architecture comprised individual houses, usually lived in by members of a single family, overlooking a shared square of rectangular form. Referred to as a *siheyuan*, the central inner courtyard was a place of privacy and tranquillity

Below: *Garden with an ornamental pool, part of a wall painting from the Tomb of Nebamun, Thebes, New Kingdom (c.1350BC).*

Below: *The Court of the Lions in the Alhambra Palace in Granada, Spain, is a classic example of the* chadar bagh.

Above: *Reconstruction of a peristyle in a Roman house in Pompeii. This is a courtyard with a covered walkway all the way around.*

Above: *This dry garden at Ryogen-in, Japan, is an example of the* tsubo-niwa, *or courtyard garden. A dry garden was the most commonly used style in a courtyard of this type, and the various elements of gravel, rocks and mounds were symbolic of Japanese mythology.*

away from the hectic city, almost always featuring a garden with decorative plants and a water feature.

Interestingly, because the Silk Route enabled a trade pathway for both the communication of design ideas and the transport of plants, Chinese and Persian courtyards have many common characteristics, including the concept of gardens that look inward and the use of similar plants such as peach, pomegranate, apricot and rose.

The Roman Courtyard

In Roman times (*c*. 146BC–AD476) many ordinary houses were one-storey terraced homes with mud-brick walls and no windows, which took in light from the entrance and from a central atrium. These would have kept them cool during hot weather. They often had an open-air area surrounded by colonnades, and sometimes an internal garden called a peristyle. This formula was later adapted for church courtyards, called cloisters.

Open courtyard areas became a standard feature in large Roman country houses, where formal display and lavish entertaining were intrinsic to everyday life. Their urban garden, *hortus*, was used not only as a garden but also as a space for living, and usually incorporated a roofed walkway around the courtyard, with murals depicting agricultural life. Their courtyards used chalice wells, wall fountains, central water basins (or *impluviums*), water stairs and water couches for cooling wine, as well as carved marble and stone shrines, grottoes, columns, seating and tables. Evergreen box was used as bed perimeters and as topiary. Other plants would have included cypress, rosemary, mulberry, fig trees, hyacinth, violets, saffron and thyme. Kitchen gardens and small orchards or vineyards were popular to secure plentiful produce for their banquets.

The Japanese Courtyard

In Japan, the garden has, from the Nara period in AD712 right up to the present, had its own set of traditions, with a design philosophy based on the ancient religion of Shintoism. The Japanese garden, including the *tsubo niwa*, or courtyard garden, was seen as expressive art of the highest order. The symbolism is paramount, with rocks representing mountains and islands, gravel expanses of water, and gateways and pathways the spiritual journey of man. The *tsubo niwa* became commonplace in 15th-century Japan when the economy was strong and merchants had large houses with surrounding storage buildings. These gardens, often as small as 3m(10ft) square, provided a transition between the house and the other buildings. Plants such as azaleas, moss, ferns and bamboo were chosen for their form and architectural structure, along with fruit trees for their profuse spring colour. The traditional temple 'viewing garden' created a miniature landscape designed to be seen from a terrace, and this was adapted to be overlooked from the house, bringing the outside view inside. The Japanese courtyard still remains a powerful source of inspiration within the urban garden, with features that are easy to maintain and that suit small outside spaces.

Right: *The Patio de Monteria in the Alcazar Palace in Seville, Spain (c. 14th century), shows a symmetrical design.*

The Spanish Courtyard

After the Muslim invasion of Spain in AD711 the Spanish-Moorish culture that evolved amalgamated the European influences of the homeland and that of the Islamic invaders. They used patios to control their heat requirements – thick walls that were resistant to heat and cold meant that the Spanish patio or inner court was cool in summer and warm in winter. Because they adjoined the living quarters these areas were typically paved. These gardens sectioned off areas within them with shorter walls, often adorned with vines to create enclosure and privacy.

Formality and geometry underlined the style, part of the Moorish influence. Water features abounded, as well as a delight in flower scents, especially the white blooms of jasmine and lilies. Other trees and plants included palms, cyprus, orange trees, pomegranates, cactus, daisies, rosemary and lavender. The inheritance of this flower, sunshine and shade-filled style can still be seen in the Festival of Patios, held annually in Cordoba, Spain.

Late Medieval Courtyards

The gardens of the 11th and 12th centuries in Europe were inspired largely by the courtyards of the Spanish Moors, with the idea of outside spaces as a protected refuge for relaxation.

A typical garden was designed within castle walls for security in times of conflict. Called an ornamental garden or *herber*, it was usually blocked off with partitions from the rest of the castle, and features included a lawn with grasses and wild flowers, bowers with climbing plants such as clematis and jasmine, fruit trees, trellis panels, wattle fencing and raised beds. These combined all kinds of planting to create an ornamental look. More practical gardens would have been kitchen courtyards with vegetables and herbs, these typically surrounded by a thicket to keep animals out. Produce would have included turnips, onions, peas, beetroot (beets), squashes and strawberries.

Left: *An illustration of a walled town garden, from* Ruralia Commoda, *a medieval treatise on agriculture by Pietro de Crescenzi (c. 1306).*

Renaissance Escapes

The gardens of early Renaissance villas in Europe in the 14th century aimed to create an escape from the pressures of public life. These protected spaces were used for entertaining, and literary and political debate. While these spaces were rarely walled, using terraces on sloping sites as points of relaxation and contemplation, they included various garden features associated with the courtyard vocabulary, including classical statues, grottoes, topiary and sundials. The knot garden was a popular form, with low hedges forming an enclosed pattern that was then filled with gravel, flowers and herbs. It offered a useful way of introducing intricacy and colour in a limited space.

The Courtyard Today

As we have seen, many early examples of courtyards had a specific practical purpose or style that reflected the needs of a location, its people and a point in history. The modern courtyard can follow a set style or purpose in the same way. But most importantly it should offer you a personalized and private space. You might choose simply to reinvent lawns, backyards and side passageways, or you might have a more significant budget for a swimming pool and jacuzzi. Whatever resources you are working with, a private enclosed paradise surely awaits you.

Above: *The Cordoban patio is a central fixture in the home, and is a gathering space during warm summer nights.*

PLANNING YOUR COURTYARD

The first stage when starting work on a new garden, or renovating an old one, is to assess its condition, make some plans and smarten up the framework. This chapter shows how to assess a courtyard's good and bad points critically and how to deal with any shortfalls imaginatively. With the knowledge gleaned from carrying out a site survey, you will be able to make practical building and planting decisions, and adapt the appearance and setting of the courtyard to suit your needs.

There are plenty of things you can do quickly and easily to improve a space, and this chapter also shows you how to begin the process of applying basic techniques to smarten up a neglected courtyard area before committing to a visual style, and how to draw up paper plans for a complete design makeover. The more thorough your preparation, the easier it will be to realize your design. Plants will have the best possible start and you are then able to make your courtyard garden a really special place.

Left: *Bold planting, a fresh coat of paint and stylish new floor tiles have transformed this basement garden into an urban oasis.*

ASSESSING THE SITE

Before beginning work, it's important to carry out a thorough site survey. Key points to consider are the amount of sunlight various parts of the garden receive, relative degrees of shelter or exposure, the acidity or alkalinity of the soil, and drainage. If you are new to the garden and can wait a season before starting, you will be able to map out where plants are and what you would like to keep.

Above: *Aim to create a pleasing balance between hard landscaping and greenery.*

Above: *Courtyards can be sheltered from wind but may sacrifice light as a result. Use plants that will thrive in your courtyard's specific microclimate.*

Soil Type and Drainage

Many courtyard gardens will already be paved or covered with solid concrete. Alternatively, you may want to put fresh paving down. In these cases the soil is buried and therefore its quality is of no consequence.

However, in courtyards that need soil, a healthy soil structure requires air exposure. So compacted soil without air spaces or soil that is too wet will support only a limited range of plants, earthworms and microorganisms. At the other end of the spectrum, very dry soil that drains rapidly, such as sandy or stony soil, also poses problems. Nutrients are washed from the rooting zone of plants and the lack of moisture means that only drought-tolerant types, such as succulents and hardy herbs, thrive.

Light and Aspect

In more open gardens, the points at which the sun rises in the morning (east) and sets in the evening (west) are easy to calculate through simple observation. This gives you an idea of which are the sunniest and warmest areas of the garden (south- and west-facing parts) and which are the cooler, shadier regions (north- and east-facing parts). However, in small and enclosed courtyards and on terraces, using compass points may not be helpful, since walls, buildings and large specimen plants or trees may block out the sun during the main part of the day, even if the garden faces due south.

Make a sketch of your garden and mark on it the rough distribution of light as it moves throughout the day, in particular the sunniest areas and the shadiest areas. These findings should inform your planting decisions more than any other factors.

Reducing Wind Turbulence

Wind turbulence caused by the position of surrounding buildings can be damaging to plants and structures. It can also make sitting out in the garden less than pleasant. Map where these vortices are so that you can plan natural or artificial windbreaks to reduce wind speed and create sheltered oases. Robust trees and deciduous shrubs as well as hedges make efficient wind breaks because they filter the air. Solid barriers, such as fences, can create even more turbulence. In addition to plants, try fixing windbreak mesh on to the back of trellis screens or use loose woven screens, such as wattle hurdles.

Above: *Overcome a lack of planting space or poor soil by using large planters.*

ESTABLISHING YOUR SOIL TYPE

You need to know the soil characteristics of your garden so that you can choose the appropriate cultivation technique. Divided into three types – clay, sand and loam – each soil has a specific visual and handling quality.

Loam is the easiest soil to manage, but you can work on both clay and sandy soils to make them just as productive. Remember, too, that some plants actually prefer sand or clay.

Clay soil This can easily be formed into a ball shape. Your soil will be clay if water pools on the soil surface, or it sticks to your boots in winter and dries hard in summer. Clay soil is the most fertile, but can have drainage problems. To improve poorly drained clay, dig in grit and bulky organic matter, such as well-rotted manure or spent mushroom compost (soil mix).

Sandy soil This disintegrates when you try to form it. A light-coloured, free-draining soil, it is constantly thirsty in summer and is the poorest quality soil. Mulch sandy soil with manure to make it more moisture retentive and fertile. Do this by covering the surface of the damp soil with a thick mulch of well-rotted manure.

Loam or silt You can form loam into a ball that crumbles under pressure. A mixture of sand and clay, this is the best balanced soil and poses few cultivation problems. Loams are usually dark because of their high humus content (decayed organic matter), but lighter soils can be improved by digging in manure.

TESTING YOUR SOIL PH

All plants prefer soil that has a particular level of acidity or alkalinity, measured on the pH scale. Therefore, soil pH is an important factor when deciding which plants will thrive in your garden. Expressed as a scale ranging between 1 and 14, 1 is highly acidic while 14 is extremely alkaline. A soil reading at 7 is neutral. Test pH meters are available at most garden centres (see Useful Suppliers on pages 250–1). Some plants, such as azaleas, rhododendrons, conifers and blueberries, prefer acid soils,

whereas vegetables, grasses and most ornamentals like a slightly alkaline soil. The sequence below shows you how to measure the pH.

Having established the soil pH, depending on the plants you want to include, you can increase or, less successfully, decrease the soil pH. To make the soil less acidic (and raise the pH), apply a material containing lime, such as ground agricultural limestone or calcified seaweed. Don't try acidifying soil for rhododendrons.

1 After loosening several different areas of soil, moisten using rainwater (tap water could give false readings) and allow this to soak through the ground for a few minutes.

2 Using a trowel, take a sample of the wet soil from the first patch only and place it in a clean, dry jar, adding more rainwater if necessary ready for the reading.

3 Always clean and dry the probe on the pH meter first to eliminate the risk of an incorrect reading. It is important to do this between each soil reading.

4 Push the probe into the moist soil sample and wait a few moments until the needle stops moving. The readout will show how acidic or alkaline each sample is.

UPGRADING THE SITE

It is amazing how effective spring cleaning a site can be. Small, enclosed gardens often end up as repositories for junk, including left-over materials from home renovations. So, start by clearing out the rubbish, followed by cleaning, weeding and pruning. This is also the time to check basics, such as garden drainage, as well as the integrity of walls, fences, paving and any existing structures.

Above: *Attach a discreet support framework of wires for climbers such as clematis.*

Far left: *Consider replacing tiny lawns with easy-care planting and surfacing.*

Left: *Building raised beds with sympathetic materials creates new planting opportunities.*

Simplifying Floors and Boundaries

If your garden boundaries are made up of mismatched fencing panels or walls with different paint or trellis coverings, the space may not be showing itself to its best advantage. An inexpensive yet effective way to hide mismatched surfaces is to cover them with a roll of brushwood or bamboo screening. You can quickly attach this to existing fencing using a heavy-duty staple gun.

To simplify the garden floor, to create a feeling of space and to smarten its appearance, treat it as you would a room in the home and have the space decked, paved, tiled or covered with gravel to hide any uncoordinated surfaces.

Flooring Fixes

Unloved paving or concrete can be effectively rejuvenated using a pressure washer to remove all surface grime and algae (see also page 246). And if you can't match up broken paving slabs, try filling the gaps with bricks, setts or cobbles rather than repaving the whole area. This is also an excellent way to add texture and interest to plain paving.

Areas of concrete are often problematic, as removing thick slabs of this material is both difficult and expensive. A suggestion for camouflaging concrete is given below. Another option is to pave the concrete over with slabs – however, if the slabs are abutting a house or garage wall keep them well below the damp-proof course (usually two bricks depth). Other surfacing ideas include thin, non-slip ceramic, slate or limestone tiles, or gravel and slate chippings. You could also suspend a deck over the concrete, leaving a gap with the house wall.

CAMOUFLAGING CONCRETE

Use gravel to hide areas of concrete. There are many types and grades of gravel, from limestone chippings, peagravel (a well-rounded gravel) and hoggin (a mixture of clays, sand and gravel), to the more decorative and expensive aggregates. Loose surfaces laid over concrete may pose a slip risk, so add a solid pathway of slabs, decking tiles or stepping-stones.

1 Lay your gravel to a depth that is thick enough so that the concrete does not show through when the gravel is walked on.

2 Rake the gravel over until it is level. You may need to do this regularly depending on the foot traffic it receives.

RENOVATING PAINTED WALLS

Painted walls start to look neglected after a few years and so need repainting from time to time. As structural elements of the courtyard, renovated walls provide you with a canvas on which to apply various design ideas.

Before repainting a wall, first carry out all necessary repairs and surface preparations, including repointing any brickwork where the mortar is crumbling or replastering any damaged areas of rendering. Be aware that algal growth on walls, which can show up prominently on whitewashed surfaces, is not only unsightly, but it may also point to an underlying problem with drainage – this could be a leaking gutter, or the accumulation of surface water due to a blocked or collapsed drain.

1 A patchy wall with peeling and blistering paint will be a constant distraction, so it is worth taking the time to prepare the wall properly to lessen the risk of the problem recurring.

2 First, untie any climbers or lax shrubs from their support wires or trellis and carefully lay them down on the ground, or draw them to one side. Most will have sufficient flexibility.

3 Using a soft nylon hand brush and a bucket of water containing detergent, scrub off dirt and algae to leave a clean surface. Excessive algal growth may indicate drainage problems.

4 With firm strokes and a circling movement, remove any flakes of loose paint and surface salts with a wire brush. If left behind, these will bubble up and cause the fresh paint to lift and drop off.

5 For more stubborn areas of flaking paint, use a paint scraper to lift away the loose layers. Afterwards, go over the surface with a soft, dry brush to remove dust and any remaining small particles.

6 Seal the wall with a diluted coat of PVA. Apply it liberally. This will help to prevent moisture and salts in the brickwork from lifting the new paint and also acts as an undercoat.

7 Cover the ground with protective sheeting. Then, using a wide brush, paint the wall margins on the top, bottom and sides. This leaves the middle, which you can fill in easily with a roller.

8 A roller and tray designed for applying thick or textured masonry paint will speed up the job. Use a roller with an extension handle, like the one shown here, to avoid using a ladder.

9 You may need to apply a second coat or to touch up the paintwork once the first coat has dried. When dry, reattach the climbers and wall shrubs and review any pruning needs.

Disguising Unattractive Walls

As the most visible surfaces, it is vital to make walls and boundaries as attractive as possible. Having ensured your walls are smart and cared for (see page 17) think about using climbers and wall shrubs to green up and camouflage stark expanses of wall. Learn the requirements of each wall plant so that you can keep them in good condition. Be wary of vigorous climbers such as wisteria, *Clematis montana* and Virginia creeper as these quickly get out of hand.

When planting in front of walls and windows, allow access for window cleaning, painting and pruning. You can use hinged decorative treillage panels to allow access for painting the wall behind. Trellis and bamboo or brushwood screens and panels transform the look of a lacklustre wall or fence. Take care when applying paints, trellis and other decorative façades, as poorly applied elements quickly become eyesores.

Above: *The decorative tile border, tile wall panels and frame of clipped wall shrubs create a dramatic area where otherwise there would have been white walls.*

TRAINING PLANTS AGAINST WALLS

Where space is limited, training plants upwards is an obvious way of maximizing what space is available. It is also a classic way to camouflage less than attractive existing walls and boundaries. Climbers and wall shrubs will usually need some form of strong support, such as trellis panels. These, however, may not always be suitable for certain styles of garden, as they can sometimes look too heavy in a small or confined area. A more discreet option is to use galvanized training wire. A large 'mesh' of horizontal and vertical wires is ideal for climbers with tendrils or twining leaf stems such as passion flower and clematis.

1 Hammer a horizontal line of wedge-shaped vine eyes into the mortar joints (as long as the mortar is sound enough to offer support). Alternatively, for screw-fixings that can be used on walls, fences or posts, first drill the wall with a masonry bit and then plug the holes.

2 Thread the galvanized wire through the hole in the vine eye and wrap it around itself to tie it off. Then thread the wire through the intermediate eyes – set at no more than 1.8m (6ft) intervals. Fasten the wire off firmly after taking up the slack.

3 Set lines of wires around 45cm (18in) apart and attach vertical wires to form a grid-like mesh for climbers to use. Curve long stems along the wires, securing them with soft twine at several points. The closer to the horizontal, the more you encourage flower buds to develop.

ERECTING TRELLIS PANELS

Consider creating a rhythm around your garden room by fixing a repeating pattern of trellis panels. This can have both a decorative and practical purpose. For a secure finish, it is important to fix trellis panels or any climbing mesh on to battens. This also creates a space behind the support, allowing plants to climb more easily. The weight of a mature climbing plant can be substantial, so don't skimp on materials.

1 Mark the position of the spacer battens or lathes. Drill holes in the brickwork (not the mortar joints) using a masonry drill bit. Use wall plugs and galvanized screws.

2 Mark and predrill the battens to fit the holes. Tap in wall plugs until they are flush and screw the battens in. They must hold the trellis at least 2.5cm (1in) away from the wall.

3 Mark and predrill the trellis panel, selecting a cross piece to correspond with the battens. Use galvanized wood screws long enough to fix the panel to the batten.

4 Repeat the previous steps to fix further trellis panels around your garden room. Ensure that they are all at an equal distance from each other and at the same level.

Using Decorative Trellis

Plain and decorative trellis panels make an ornamental addition to the courtyard garden, helping to create depth, texture and colour, and distracting from any less attractive features. Trellis has potential in many styles of garden, and is a classic feature to give a new dimension to a neglected space. The quality of trellis varies. If you can, choose wood that is attached to battens and raised off the ground, which is less likely to rot.

Use a colourful outdoor wood paint or stain to add vibrancy to brick or painted walls, both low-maintenance solutions for colouring wood. It is easier to do this before fixing them, leaning panels against a wall with a protective plastic sheet underneath.

Leave a gap between a planting hole and trellis attached to a wall, to avoid the rain shadow. Use stakes to train your climber up to the base of the panel and then attach the plant stems to it with soft garden twine. Don't use coated wire or rigid plastic ties as these can cut into the plant stems, restricting the flow of sap and causing dieback.

Weaving plant stems in front of and behind the trellis makes pruning more difficult. So, it is better to tie the plant stems only to the panel front.

Above: *Diamond trellis panels have an old-fashioned charm, especially when coupled with posts topped with decorative finials. This trellis panel gives depth and structure to the perimeter of the courtyard.*

PLANTING BASICS

Using plants imaginatively is key to transforming a courtyard. They can disguise or distract from less appealing features, such as lacklustre walls or areas of paving, or just add creative focus. You'll need to identify the plants that thrive in your locality, which soil different plants prefer, how to plant them to maximum effect and overcome problems such as shallow soil.

Above: *Clipped shapes and topiary features add style and a touch of theatre.*

Above: *Tender plants and bedding are high-maintenance options but displays are often the most colourful and eye-catching.*

Plant Preferences

Having identified your soil type and pH range (see page 15), as well as the sunniest and shadiest parts of the plot, you can begin to select which plants to use. So-called *ericaceous* plants require acidic soil in order to thrive. Examples include many woodland shrubs, such as rhododendron and azalea, pieris, camellia and gaultheria, all of which are also useful in shady sites. Some plants enjoy neutral-to-acid soil with a high humus content, but won't die if they don't have acid conditions. These include skimmia, hydrangea (acid soils needed to maintain the blue colouring of some cultivars) and Japanese maple (*Acer palmatum*). Many Mediterranean-type shrubs and herbs, including lavender, prefer alkaline or limy soils, usually coupled with sharp drainage and full sun. Certain vegetables, such as brassicas, also prefer an alkaline soil. In the productive garden you can add lime to raise the pH of the soil.

Above: *Climbers and wall shrubs make the most of available border space.*

PLANTING THROUGH LANDSCAPE FABRIC

For gravel gardens, which are traditionally only sparsely planted, you could consider covering the soil with porous, heavy-duty black landscape fabric topped with a coating of decorative gravel. This has the advantage of suppressing weeds already in the soil, while weed seeds blowing in fail to get their roots down into the ground.

1 Lay the landscape fabric over the prepared soil and peg down all around the edge. Make cross-shaped cuts at each point where you want to locate a plant, shrub or tree.

2 Fold back the four points of the fabric to give you a square large enough to plant in. Dig out the soil until the planting hole is deep enough for the plant's rootball.

3 Set the watered plant in the hole and backfill with soil. Water the plant in well. Ease the black liner back a little, leaving enough space for plant growth.

4 When the planting is complete, clean off the fabric surface and then cover the whole area with gravel to a depth of about 5cm (2in). It is easy to add more plants later.

Pots and Raised Beds

If you don't have borders or exposed soil, you will need to make raised beds or plant in pots, troughs and wall containers. For economy and to ensure long-term success, fill raised beds with good-quality topsoil rather than bags of potting mix, and make sure that any perennial weed roots and seeds have been removed.

Planting up a few pots instantly transforms a dull space. Choose large containers, where possible, as these allow greater planting scope. In addition, use soil-based potting mixes for hardy perennials, shrubs and trees as these will be in their pots for several years.

Busy homeowners with little time to look after a garden planted in containers or with free-draining raised beds should consider installing an automatic irrigation and feeding system to keep their plants in tip-top condition.

Below: *Large planters, the one below made from an old barrel, require less maintenance and offer more scope for imaginative planting than small pots.*

Below: *Even vegetable and herb gardens can be given a contemporary feel, this example showing crisp, timber-walled beds and modern planters.*

PLANTING INTO PAVING

Optimize space by adding plants among paving stones. Low-growing and creeping aromatic herbs and alpines are suitable as they can colonize narrow cracks and crevices. Treading on, or brushing against, the foliage of plants such as thyme and chamomile releases a wonderful fragrance. When laying new areas of paving, set some of the stones at a greater distance apart to create planting areas and fill the gaps with soil rather than mortar.

1 Lift a paving stone in an area where you want to introduce a plant. Against a wall, you have the option to plant climbers and wall shrubs. Avoid planting close to thoroughfares, as plants may grow too large and cause an obstruction.

2 Dig out any cement and hardcore or sand and gravel and replenish the soil by digging it over with a fork and working in some garden compost (soil mix) or an organic soil improver together with some slow-release fertilizer granules.

3 After soaking the plant, excavate a hole large enough to accommodate the rootball and plant, backfilling with soil. Mulch with decorative gravel or grit as a foil for the plants and to keep the foliage dry, or use small cobbles.

CHOOSING A DESIGN

Because of the small scale, and the link to an interior space, a courtyard or terrace can be styled in a similar way to a room. Finding a style or theme is a good starting point and then you need to put together a colour and materials palette. Your reference can include paving catalogues, magazine images, sketches, written notes, as well as a wish list of desired plants and features.

Above: *The neo-classical plinth and treillage are perfect 'period' props.*

QUESTIONS TO ASK YOURSELF

- *Do you want to grow fruits and vegetables, or just ornamentals?*
- *Will you garden in borders or in containers? If you choose the latter, how will you water them?*
- *Would you like a pool or fountain, an outdoor lighting feature or a sculptural focal point?*
- *How about a summerhouse or overhead pergola for privacy?*
- *Might you want to include a barbecue, fire pit or informal seating with tiered decking or terracing?*
- *How will you create access around the garden?*
- *Will you need to camouflage utility areas or section off parts to create secluded corners for entertaining and outdoor dining?*

Above: *The whitewashed wall and potted herbs combined with vibrant purples and pinks create a Mediterranean flavour.*

Above: *A crisp, rectilinear layout perfectly reflects the surrounding architecture.*

Architectural Influences

Aspects of a home's design may form the perfect backdrop for a specific style of garden, but the design of the building and its garden don't have to match slavishly. If, for example, you prefer contemporary looks over Victorian charm or you want your courtyard or terrace to be more country cottage than city chic, try some theatrical stage setting. Cover or camouflage the walls, introduce furniture items, pots and plants, and pick an appropriate colour scheme.

To follow an architectural theme, research the art, architecture and garden styles of the period. You could then select from a number of key features. Don't try to cram in too many visual references, and don't be afraid to mix contrasting styles, for example, combining traditional architectural details and decorative touches with ultra-modern elements.

Evoking a Style

Painting walls and timbers in a co-ordinated colour scheme is an inexpensive way of creating a specific mood or character. Areas used for entertaining and outdoor dining benefit from warm, energizing shades, such as oranges, reds, and vibrant pinks. Use these colours

Above: *If you require a low-maintenance solution, focus on decorative flooring and wall features or other plant-free elements such as sculpture or pebble fountains.*

Right: *Design raised beds and steps to double as impromptu seating or commission bespoke, all-weather furniture.*

sparingly, however, as they will make the garden room feel smaller. Gardens for quiet contemplation should be painted in more muted tones, such as soft blues, greens or pale amethyst, to create a sense of space.

Colour is an essential element of any design theme. When using, perhaps, an Italian Renaissance motif, you might choose tints found in faded frescos – verdigris, dusky rose and aquamarine. In a minimalist setting, consider dove grey, willow green or aubergine. For a Mediterranean feel, try teaming Moroccan blue, ochre or dusty terracotta with limestone or sandstone paving. To create a contemporary spa-style backdrop for a Scandinavian hot tub, you might use eau-de-Nil walls alongside bleached wooden decking, a cream canvas sail awning, pale cobbles and zinc planters filled with grasses.

Right: *The painted decking and wall plaque of the raised seating area give this courtyard the distinct flavour of an interior.*

DRAWING UP A DESIGN

Making a scale plan of the garden will allow you to superimpose any changes to the existing design as well as giving you the ability to try out new features. This is easier than you might think, especially if the courtyard, terrace or patio is composed of rectangular shapes. If you are bringing in contractors, give them a copy of the plan to help with calculating amounts of materials.

Above: *Your design should dovetail with existing features and architectural elements.*

Stage 1: Gather the Data

1 Draw a rough, bird's-eye view sketch of the garden to write measurements on and to help you keep track of progress.

2 Buy a long, flexible measuring tape. Work in metric or imperial, not a mixture of the two. Keep the tape taut by ensuring that one end is firmly fixed. This process is quicker and easier if you have a helper.

3 Record all measurements of the ground area/boundary, including the shape of any wall recesses, bay windows and so on. In addition, mark on the position of drainpipes and drain and manhole covers.

4 Mark the position and dimensions of windows, doors and access points. This will help decide the best place to position features and pathways.

Above: *A scale drawing of the site with the new design in colour helps to visualize the garden and calculate materials.*

5 Work out the location of plants and features that are away from the boundaries.

6 Record diagonal measurements across the site to help correct the orientation of walls and fences that are not fully perpendicular. The site may not be a perfect rectangle.

Stage 2: Draw the Plan

1 Working with a sheet of graph paper, calculate the scale to fit the longest horizontal and vertical dimensions on the sheet. Make the plan as large as possible so that you have room to try out your ideas. A convenient and typical scale might be 2cm to 1m (or 1in to 3ft).

2 Transfer the measurements to the plan, checking the position of the corners and the angle of boundaries with the diagonal measurements.

3 Mark on the compass points or the extent of shade at different times of the day. Also mark the edge of any

overhanging tree canopies or how far a hedge juts out from the boundary line. In addition, mark the position of doors and gates and where they open out into the garden.

4 Draw in points where the garden is overlooked by neighbouring windows and sight lines to focal points outside.

Stage 3: Create a Design

1 Ensure that the lines and subdivisions of your design are in scale with the overall size of the plot and that they link to key architectural points. It helps to superimpose a faint grid of squares on to the plan that relates to points on the house or boundary. For example, the width of the grid squares might be taken from the

DESIGN TOUCHES

• *Try setting paving on the diagonal to create a modern look.*

• *Use contrasting paving in adjacent areas to signify the start of a new section of garden.*

• *Use trellis panels to divide the courtyard into discreet spaces without cutting out light dramatically.*

• *Add overhead beams for an enclosed, interior feel.*

• *Repeat walling, paving, construction and colour features to create a linking theme throughout the space.*

• *Create sightlines to focus the eye on a particular feature, such as a piece of sculpture.*

Planting notes

1 A small, ornamental tree such as *Prunus subhirella* 'Autumalis Rosea'

2 Evergreen underplanting for shady patch here

3 An exotic evergreen climber for a hot wall, such as *Clematis armandii*

4 *Phormium tenax* as a lush backdrop to the water feature

5 A shade climber for the pergola, such as *Humulus lupulus* 'Aureus'

6, 7 and 8 A selection of large pots, including *Buxus* (clipped box ball) and a Japanese maple

9 Wall-mounted pots with bedding will create a pretty view from the kitchen

10 A self-clinging climber over the wall recess, such as *Hedera*

11 Espalier-trained fruit, such as pear or plum

12 Colourful, easy summer herbaceous plants, such as *Agapanthus*

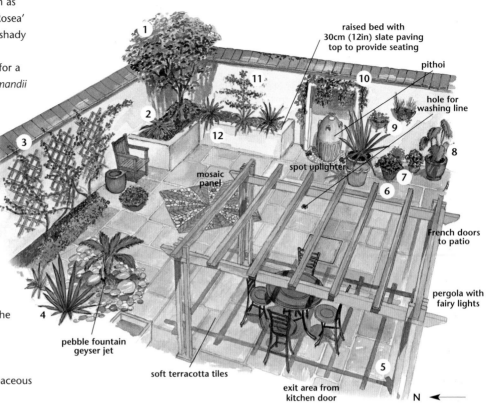

raised bed with 30cm (12in) slate paving top to provide seating

pithoi

hole for washing line

French doors to patio

pergola with fairy lights

spot uplighter

mosaic panel

pebble fountain geyser jet

soft terracotta tiles

exit area from kitchen door

N

width of French doors or the distance apart of wall pillars. Rotate this grid on to the diagonal to produce a more dynamic feel.

2 Try out various shapes and patterns within the grid – you can subdivide the squares or superimpose arcs and circles on to it. You need to create a footprint for the garden that relates to the different areas of activity and to the features it will contain, such as an outdoor dining area, a herb garden, an ornamental pool, raised beds or areas of decking.

3 To avoid redrawing as your design changes, cut out the shapes of the key elements in coloured paper and move them around the plan. This will help you find a pattern that both looks in proportion and flows harmoniously.

Right: *Plants, furniture and sculpture are the final touches, added once the hard-landscaping phase has been completed.*

Stage 4: Develop the Plan

1 Once you have the basic shapes, draw on the position of specimen plants as well as the width of retaining walls, the pattern of paving and decking and any changes in level.

2 Use a correspondingly large piece of tracing paper to copy the design from the graph paper, along with any notations. Photocopy it several times. Pick one copy to colour in, or to superimpose a planting plan on. This will be your master copy. Keep the spares for contractors, or to work with out in the garden during the construction and planting phases.

TRADITIONAL LINES

A courtyard using a traditional approach will suggest a garden of formality, elegance and serenity. Taking as its inspiration the classical French and Italian gardens of the 17th and 18th centuries, this style feels familiar and reassuring. Composed of clean, symmetrical lines, this outside space is laid out with care and evokes calm and order. Fine specimen plants, elegant ornaments and imposing architectural features reinforce the theme, bringing their own distinct finishing touches.

The restricted space in a courtyard lends itself to this formal approach, the style working effectively within the contained boundaries. In contrast with the demands of larger gardens, its manageable scale permits a scheme that can be both impressive and dramatic, without being overly expensive.

Left: *The interlocking lines of this box-edged parterre perfectly complement the elegantly executed paving design. The complex lattice pattern is achieved by contrasting differently coloured pavers against a stone and textured gravel background.*

FORMALITY AND FAMILIARITY

To create a conventional style in your courtyard you can draw on historical architectural influences and simple, reliable materials, such as red brick and natural stone. Classical references play their part in decorative elements made from hand-forged steelwork and cast lead and iron. Planting forms a framework of clipped, dense evergreen, complemented by soft bursts of subtle colour.

Above: Boxwood (Buxus sempervirens) perfectly sets off the pure white roses.

Styles and Approaches

A traditional courtyard style can be inspired by different historical periods. A medieval-inspired space, for example, could include a stone folly, masonry with a gothic arch, a simple stone fountain, herbs, and old-fashioned blooms such as musk roses, violets, hollyhocks, larkspur, monkshood and foxgloves. An Arts and Crafts garden could be brought to life with a Lutyens-style bench seat, a bronze resin statue, a stone-paving rill, flaky limestone pillars and paving, clipped topiary and a white and pastel cottage-flower scheme.

To create a Regency style, think of an elegant wirework gazebo with a rambler rose, curving treillage and an antique portico. To conjure up the feel of the Italian Renaissance, choose large, ornate terracotta lemon pots with bay trees, low-clipped box hedging, mellow-coloured gravel and

Above: The circle of lawn and its curved retaining wall create an intimate seating spot.

stonework. A loggia and formal rectangular pool, classical statuary, wall masks and architectural plants such as cordyline are more ideas to complete the look.

The visual intention may be a formal, even classical, tableau, but its function should still be considered in terms of contemporary living. Relaxation and entertaining space are all-important features of our lives, and the courtyard garden needs to fulfil differing roles. The inclusion of a dining terrace and a secluded corner dedicated to quiet contemplation will extend the use of the garden and help it to enhance the enjoyment of every day. A classical gazebo or garden folly would create an important architectural element, while also providing cover and privacy for entertaining. A fountain or formal pool can help to cement the design, whilst providing a lively focal point.

Combining Elements

A well-established approach offers reassurance to the novice gardener by setting out a formal layout within which to operate. The manageable scale of the courtyard makes it quite easy to plan, maintain and budget, and it can be created in stages. Hard landscaping is the structural mainstay and its success will depend on the quality of the design detailing and workmanship. Without a strong, basic framework to anchor the design, any subsequent planting will not be completely successful. Clipped evergreen topiary plays a vital part in holding the green structure in place,

while mature trees and shrubs can be included to convey an immediate sense of substance. Incorporating carefully selected planting containers and imposing architectural elements will supply the finishing touches.

A traditional approach does not mean that the garden has to use authentic materials. Newly made and reconstituted pieces that impressively represent the originals can be practical and lightweight, and they are easier on the budget than the real thing. Faux-lead planters made from resin are easy to handle and a blessing for the roof terrace; cast aluminium furniture is a fraction of the weight of cast iron; and tinted cement paving blocks cast in moulds made from old pavements are much less expensive than York stone slabs. The trick in using these products is to retain the integrity of the traditional design thesis and to select the materials with a view to their appearance, quality of manufacture and long-term endurance.

The courtyard can equally support the demands of discerning gardeners who are looking to create a significantly impressive, classical garden. The traditional theme provides the formalized framework in which to indulge a particular interest, whether this is placing rare specimen topiaries, setting out a collection of elegant planting containers or indulging a passion for water.

Right: *Oversized corkscrew stemmed bays (Laurus nobilis) complement this gracious, walled courtyard parterre, both in their scale and ordered alignment.*

FLOORING FOR TRADITIONAL SPACES

The hard landscaping of a courtyard will form the structural elements of the design. In a traditional-style garden, flooring might range from cobbles and flagstones to timber and brick, and each of these materials acts as the consistent element on to which all the other details are imposed.

Above: *The random shapes of smooth, washed pebbles are used in a curved path.*

Matching the Style

A successful courtyard design must reflect its surroundings. To create an intelligent, elegant and well-executed scheme you should consider the architectural qualities of the setting together with the character and scale of the adjacent landscape. Therefore, your design approach should take into account the type, colour and texture of surrounding materials. If buildings are constructed from brick, is it coloured red or yellow? Is it bright and new or old and worn? If the buildings are made from stone, is the tone predominantly yellow or grey? Are wall finishes rendered with cement or are they painted? Are there any significant elements of colour or material that could be picked up on or mirrored in other selected features?

Above: *Low brick retaining walls allow planting to integrate naturally into this shallow flight of steps.*

Choice of Materials

It is important to understand what your options are and the qualities of different materials. Traditional designs tend to utilize natural materials. Stone, which is a fundamental element of landscape work, varies hugely in colour, texture and durability depending on its composition. In addition, its appearance can be altered dramatically by how it is cut and finished. Stone pavers, for example, can be 'sawn' to produce a crisp, square edge and smooth finish, resulting in a fresh, new appearance. An order for 'riven' flags will produce an uneven surface and edges, which suggest age.

Put simply, the way different stones have evolved can be described in three textural types: soft, hard and flaky. Soft stones include sandstone, which normally occurs in yellowish tones and the

Above: *Wooden planks are cut into short lengths and used to create an informal deck that follows the intersections of the garden and creates a seating area.*

more whitish/grey-toned limestone. Reference is frequently made to 'York stone', a type of sandstone that comes from the north of England. It has a beautiful honeyed colour and a smooth texture that blends well with brick-built surroundings. It is one of the most superior paving materials.

The hardest stone of all is granite. It is supremely hardwearing and completely non-porous. But, as a result, it is difficult and time consuming to work, and thus expensive. The highly polished finish frequently seen in corporate settings is seldom appropriate in a domestic situation. Textured surfaces, achieved by hammering or burning the surface,

fit better with nature and are much easier on the eye. Granite should be employed with care because its somewhat 'aggressive' appearance can look too harsh in a garden.

Granite is perhaps most useful in the form of small cubes, or 'setts', which are extremely effective in making paths and steps. Order them with a textured, non-slip surface. They are easy to handle and lend themselves well to curvy designs. They are also very well suited to edging details for paths and steps and they make an effective device for forming a border around a tree or planting bed.

Limestone, which frequently contains fossils that add immensely to the beauty of the stone, is more fragile, or flaky, than granite. Most crucially, it is porous and has a tendency to stain, often from the feet of furniture or other objects placed on it. Tannins can leach from insufficiently matured timber

furniture, especially oak, while steel, even though protected, will rust sooner or later. It is therefore perhaps best used in locations used exclusively for foot traffic, such as paths and steps.

Below: *Moulded paving slabs in complementary honeyed tones.*

Above: *Pale-coloured materials introduce a calm, tranquil ambiance. Natural limestone slabs occur as plinths to the retaining walls and as contrast elements of texture and shape in a path of small paving setts.*

Below: *Gentle flights of steps descend to an elegant courtyard of pale granite paving, the central detail using contrasting dark stone.*

LAYING BRICK PAVERS

If they are chosen with care, concrete pavers that have been formed to look like house bricks are a practical and attractive choice for the traditional garden. Look for rustic, brindled or antique-effect bricks. It is not always necessary to lay them in a bed of concrete. They can be simply laid in a sand base with sand-filled joints – these allow rainwater to percolate, reducing the risk of flooding after a heavy shower.

1 Excavate the area to be paved and prepare a sub-base of about 5cm (2in) of compacted hardcore or sand-and-gravel mix. This prevents sunken areas developing at a later date. Set an edging along one end and side first. Check that it's level and then mortar it into position, laying the pavers as shown.

2 Lay a 5cm (2in) bed of sharp sand over the compacted hardcore. Then, using a straight-edged piece of wood notched at the ends to fit over the edging bricks, scrape off surplus sand. This method provides a consistently level surface on which to bed the remaining bricks.

3 Position the pavers in your chosen design, laying about 2m (6ft) at a time. Make sure they butt up to each other tightly and are firm against the edging. Mortar further edging strips into place as you proceed. On a slope, work upwards from a solid edging to prevent slippage.

4 Hire a flat-plate vibrator to consolidate the bricks on the sand base. To avoid damage, do not go too close to an unsupported edge with the vibrator. Alternatively, especially in small areas, tamp the pavers down with a club hammer used over a piece of wood to prevent chipping.

5 Brush loose sand into the joints of the pavers with a broom, then vibrate or tamp again. It may be necessary to repeat the vibrating process once more to achieve a firm, neat finish. The patio is then ready to use. Brush in more sand later to prevent moss and weeds growing.

GETTING CREATIVE

• *You can lay bricks, brick pavers or cube-shaped setts (terracotta/clay, granite or the cheaper concrete reproductions) in a wide range of patterns and designs. If you are working on a larger area, which could become monotonous if paved using just a simple pattern, it is best to try new combinations.*

• *Smaller, square-shaped setts are the most versatile to use, but both bricks and setts can be worked in as panels between stone or reproduction paving slabs, or to form a smart edging or border.*

• *Because of their small size and proportion, setts and bricks are useful for creating complex formal designs for curved paths, circular patios and focal point details.*

Visual Dynamics

The physical qualities of building materials play important sensory and directional roles in the design process. A rise of granite steps could provide a solid ascent to a terrace above a soft grassy lawn, while narrow borders of black slate would emphasize the route of a pale flagstone path. This balance of soft and hard, dark and light can be used to create exciting visual and tactile effects. Avoid polished surfaces, which are less suited to domestic landscapes, appearing overly formal. The subtler character of textured finishes is easier on the eye and more in tune with the qualities of foliage and stems.

Having terrace areas for seating and dining is important in a courtyard, offering a space for relaxation and entertainment. To develop the full potential of a plot, look at incorporating three-dimensional devices, such as an above-ground fountain. It may be possible to create a secondary garden level beyond the terrace. Raised planting beds contained within retaining walls are a good way to achieve this.

Above: *Random shaped slabs make it easy to deal with curved paving features.*

The walls create a background for the terrace, and provide support for the upper garden. You would also need to have a flight of steps. Such works are not minor, but the bonus of working on a relatively small area is that your budget can go further.

Juxtaposing Materials

When designing flooring, a simple approach is best. The use of lots of different materials and textures results in a visual chaos that reduces the feeling of space. So select one main material to create a neutral background and use it throughout. To reinforce the layout and bring the design into focus, use a contrasting material to create the finishing details. Border edgings prevent paths appearing to 'drop off' into the garden and can play an important safety role on steps.

You could use reclaimed handmade bricks (normally too soft and crumbly to be used as paving in its own right) as detailing. Combined with the warm tones of a sandstone path, it would make an excellent visual connection with a brick-built house. Alternatively, engineering brick is durable and well suited to paving. While it looks most at home in a modern setting, it has its place in certain types of traditional gardens, especially urban ones.

Slate is a beautiful, soft-looking stone; it ranges in colour through soft greens and mauves, and almost to black. Slate is elegant when used as detailing in combination with cool-looking limestone surfaces. Its texture and colour varies and the brighter shades can be used as inserts to liven up plain paving.

Environmental and social factors to do with the choice of materials can result in a dilemma between the constraints of budget and the concerns of conscience. Because the quarrying and finishing of stone is highly labour intensive, it is sourced from regions where labour costs are low. So when ordering materials find out if the source is sustainable and that fair practices are in operation.

WALLS AND SCREENS FOR TRADITIONAL SPACES

A courtyard is an outdoor space that is contained by walls. This provides a sense of security and enclosure and is a crucial element of a traditional design, providing both privacy and an intimate ambience. It also serves as the atmospheric backdrop to the stage set of your garden, giving it a unique character.

Above: *This old flint and red brick wall is complemented by the apricot climbing rose.*

A Choice of Old or New

An old brick wall will immediately confer a sense of presence. City houses from the 18th and 19th centuries frequently feature such walls and they are also found in developments formed from large country estates. If your home is situated adjacent to an early industrial or institutional building, you might be lucky enough to have a high flank wall forming part of your boundary. If you have any existing walls, you have an ideal starting point for your courtyard design. If the condition of the brickwork is poor, it would be worth paying to have the joints repointed.

Many old walls have had patching-up repairs, often carried out with non-matching bricks. While it is a shame to paint brickwork, it may be a cleaner solution, using a pale tone that will help to reflect light.

Above: *A niche in this stone wall is supported by small stone pilasters.*

If they don't exist, consider building new walls. While not cheap, brick is traditional and would be the best option if it matches the house style. Reclaimed brick can usually be found for this purpose, and new,

handmade bricks are also available. Alternatively, walls can be built from cement blockwork, cheaper to buy and easier to construct. However, this is not pretty and the blockwork needs to be cement rendered, which can be pre-tinted or painted. This gives you a clean, bright background.

Plants for Walls

Climbing plants are an essential component of a traditional walled garden, transforming a blank façade into a lively and voluptuous tableau of flowers and foliage. A built wall gives the perfect support for fully grown specimens, which can be heavy and vulnerable to the effects of winds and storms. Climbers need a strong supporting structure, and walls are far more appropriate for this than fences, which are liable to movement.

Climbing plants cling by different means. Some, such as Virginia creeper (*Parthenocissus quinquefolia*) and common ivy (*Hedera helix*), need no extra help as they attach themselves by means of suckers or adventitious roots. Others need a helping hand: passion flowers attach themselves with tendrils, while clematis twine their leaf stems around supports. Trellis works for a lightweight clematis (see page 19 for erecting trellis panels and opposite for planting clematis), but most need something stronger. You can fix a series of robust steel wires, spaced horizontally 30–40cm (12–18in)

Left: *A red brick screen wall divides up the garden to create a courtyard space, with an elegant arched doorway inviting passage.*

Right: *Climbing clematis have an addictive scrambling habit. They like to have cool roots and their heads in the sun.*

apart, to the wall using bolts and tensioning devices (see page 18). Virtually invisible, this can hold up the heaviest of climbing species.

Climbers are always trying to reach impossible heights and mix with their neighbours, so in a restrained set-up you might need to formalize the display. Some species lend themselves to 'vertical pruning' by training the stems over wire forms fixed to the wall. Simple geometric shapes are easiest, but will need to be trimmed in spring and autumn. Evergreen climbers are a rarity, but the star jasmine (*Trachelospermum jasminoides*), with its dark foliage and perfumed white flowers, is perfect for a formal scheme. On a high wall with plenty of space, *Vitis coignetiae* can be trained in a similar way. This ambitious vine drops its huge leaves in winter, but not before unleashing glorious autumn tints of fiery vermilion.

PLANTING CLEMATIS AGAINST TRELLIS

In a traditional courtyard, classic flowering climbers such as clematis and roses help to set the scene, especially when they are combined with trellis. The summer- and autumn-flowering *Clematis viticella* shown here is ideal for small courtyards because in early spring you need to cut them back to about 30cm (12in) from ground level.

1 Select the position for the trellis and drill holes for the battens. Use plastic wall plugs and the appropriate size of screws. Screw the battens to the wall and fix your stained or painted trellis to the battens using galvanized nails or screws.

2 Fork over the planting area, removing any perennial weeds and working in organic matter such as home-made garden compost (soil mix). This ensures that the ground has sufficient moisture-holding capacity to support the plant.

3 Water the plant before removing from its pot. Dig a hole 30cm (1ft) away from the wall and twice the width and depth of the pot. Mix in a scattering of bonemeal, using latex gloves. Bury 10cm (4in) of the stem to encourage shooting. Backfill and water.

4 Climbers often come tightly fastened to a single cane and it helps to undo and separate the individual stems and fix them on to the trellis, bringing them close to the horizontal to stimulate flower and side shoot production. Use climber ties or soft twine.

Above: *This elaborate design shows a curved feature alcove covered with treillage, which tricks the eye into a false perspective.*

Left: *A combination of square and diamond mesh trellis panels, fixed in a timber framework, creates a garden backdrop, discreetly obscuring the terrace behind.*

Classical Treillage

French-style trellis, or treillage, is a traditional material, which creates an instant classical effect to decorate the blank walls of enclosed courtyards. It evokes a *trompe l'oeil* illusion by arranging a series of two-dimensional panels along the wall. Combinations of curved shapes and tall rectangles trick the eye into seeing three-dimensional walls and archways, thus increasing the impression of space and dimension. Climbing plants that would obscure the effect are not used here but mirrors might be introduced to increase the illusion.

Shaped treillage is available in many qualities and can be purchased ready-made, or you can commission a design. The panels are made up of narrow timber slats interwoven in diamond and square patterns, resulting in a silhouette of shapes that stand out against the supporting wall. The effect is best achieved by painting the treillage a colour that contrasts with a plain background. Period colours generally work best, offering an elegant solution when creating a restrained courtyard design.

The device is a brilliant way to clothe the walls of a courtyard. The rhythm of movement it provides is an especially successful technique to open up other potentially claustrophobic environments, such as a narrow entrance way, or to diminish the pace of a long wall.

By including panels of mirror in the design, the illusion of space can be further enhanced. This works particularly well when the mirrored panels are incorporated into arched sections of treillage. In the same way as mirrors in an interior, the reflected background appears to become a secondary area into which to pass, thus doubling the impression of size. The additional bonus is that reflected light will enhance what is often, by default, a shady area.

Trellis Screens

The enclosure theme can be developed by means of trellis screens to divide up the courtyard space into 'rooms', which add dimension to the garden and serve as secret places. This device is an effective and sophisticated way to create the surrounding boundaries for a roof garden space. The screens can conceal a quiet seating spot, hide a surprise feature such as a fountain, or simply disguise a service area. The individual screening panels might be formed from a criss-cross of fine diagonal slats that result in a high level of privacy while still admitting light. Curved archways, clothed in climbers, can be used to provide access to individual areas and to open up specific spaces, while long planting boxes incorporated between the screens will add interest to the design. This is an effective way of planting in a roof garden with solid floors.

Ready-made trellis panels enable you to make up your specific design, and include shaped profiles offering curved tops, arches, and panels with openings to allow a view through to what lies beyond. Differing formats of weaving the slats include diagonal lines and diamond patterns in a range of spacings and sizes. With such a wide range of options available it is possible to create a variety of courtyard effects. However, when budgets are tight, trellis at its simplest can be purchased ready to take away in rectangular panels of various sizes from garden centres and home-improvement stores.

Fencing Panels

It may be necessary to create or replace a boundary enclosure. The cheapest and most easily installed option is to use ready-made timber fencing panels, fixed a little above ground level to wooden posts set in concrete footings. Use solid portions where you need to provide privacy, then relieve the monotony by interspersing trellis screens over which you can train attractive climbing plants. Basic trellis offers an economic way to increase the height of an existing boundary wall or fence, its lightweight construction making it easy to fix by means of timber battens and bolts.

In most locations the maximum height restriction between gardens is 1.8m (6ft). You can fix narrow trellis panels to the top of the solid sections to give a higher screening effect without normally contravening building regulations, but check with your local authority. Discuss your proposals with neighbours before starting any boundary work.

Hedges

Topiary-like evergreen hedges have a role as a stabilizing element of green architecture and can be good partition substitutes in the formal, traditional garden – and these are much less expensive than stone or brick. Low-hedging materials include the upright form of rosemary, compact lavenders, *Santolina* (cotton lavender) and *Euonymus*. To achieve a crisp-edged effect use dwarf and ordinary box, golden or plain yew. These varieties cut surprisingly well as a low but wide block of a hedge. Or for a speedy, economical option try *Lonicera nitida*, the small-leaved evergreen honeysuckle with an ideal growth for hedging.

Below: *This arched trellis feature decorates the painted brick wall, making an excellent framing device for the tall, planted vase.*

Below: *A low hedge is used here to define the perimeters of a courtyard space that has more extensive grounds beyond.*

PLANTS AND CONTAINERS FOR TRADITIONAL SPACES

The design and material of containers for planting will exert a strong influence on your garden, and will help to reinforce the traditional theme. Equally important is to combine containers with complementary planting. It is a question of shape and proportion, and the intrinsic characteristics of pot and plant.

Above: *A collection of annuals, with a central cordyline, growing in a container.*

Classical Shapes

Italianate-style terracotta pots make a handsome contribution to a classical garden design. Their generous proportions and warm colour introduce a timeless stateliness and an image of shady terraced gardens under an azure sky. The 'lemon pot' style, with a wide mouth, narrowing gently to the base, is a perfect container for clipped box topiary, complementing the form of a round ball shape or a taller pyramid. Its restrained, dark green foliage would make a year-round evergreen sculptural statement. A vase-shaped container, supported on a stem, lends itself to floral displays, such as deep blue agapanthus to suggest a Tuscan heritage, or seasonally changing colour, such as hyacinths, for spring or cascades of deepest red, ivy-leaf geraniums for an elegant summer display.

Traditional Materials

Terracotta is a natural and practical material for planting containers because, being porous, it enables the soil to dry out evenly all over its surface. This results in slow evaporation, which, in turn, facilitates a good balance of water and air in the soil mix. If your region suffers regularly from winter temperatures below 0°C (32°F), you should choose

Left: *This classical stone vase and plinth are balanced perfectly by the soft planting of trailing helichrysum.*

Below: *Blue hyacinths and muscari set off the colour and form of this terracotta vase.*

only frost-proof pots. These will have been kiln fired at a minimum temperature of 1,000°C (1,832°F).

Handmade terracotta pots stand out dramatically from machine-made ones. If money is no object, then select magnificent examples from Impruneta near Florence, in Italy, fine enough to be passed down the generations as family treasures. However, there are also excellent-quality frost-proof pots made in the UK, and convincing replicas of more expensive pots made in China.

Replica Containers

Reproductions of classical stone urns are an alternative choice, especially if your local building materials are of stone. They can be found in different tones through whitish/grey and soft beige/yellow to complement the garden surroundings, while a buff pink can work well with red brick. These containers are formed in moulds

Above: *Red zonal geraniums partner a rope-edged, terracotta pot in a wall niche.*

Above: *Terracotta is ideal for plant pots, staying relatively cool in hot weather.*

and made from reconstituted stone – ground-up stone offcuts blended with cement to hold the shape. These are robust and handsome, especially when combined with raised detailing. The bright, new finish can be induced to weather down to a patina by applying a

proprietary aging product or by brushing them with natural (plain) yogurt. Because their characteristics echo traditional styles, evergreen topiary planting subjects, such as box, bay and holly, are suitably bold in form and structure to reflect the bulk of the container.

PLANTING A BAY TREE

The sweetly aromatic foliage of the bay tree has been a feature of formal Mediterranean gardens since antiquity. These are somewhat tender, and planting them in pots allows you to move them to a more sheltered spot over winter. Pot on specimens as they grow and at the same time begin training to a simple geometric shape such as a ball or cone. Or train with a single stem to create a standard or lollipop.

1 Choose a large pot with an inside diameter of at least 38cm (15in), except for small specimens that are to be grown on. Select clay or ceramic pots that won't blow over and add pieces of broken clay pots or pour in large-size gravel to cover drainage holes.

2 Part-fill with a loam-based compost (soil mix). Soak the bay tree in its container in a bucket of water, then knock the plant out. If wiry roots are tightly wound around the root ball, gently tease out a few. Test the plant for size and position.

3 Add or remove soil as necessary so that the top of the root-ball (roots) and soil level will be 2.5–5cm (1–2in) below the pot rim. Firm the compost around the roots, as evergreen trees like bay offer a great deal of wind resistance. Water thoroughly.

4 Add pot feet to keep the pot off the ground and maintain good drainage. Trim to shape with secateurs (pruners), avoiding cutting leaves in half as this causes brown edges. Shape between late spring and late summer to avoid new shoots becoming frosted.

Above: *A spiky* Agave americana *adds extra texture to this interesting low wall.*

Left: *A sequence of classical faux-lead containers, reinforced by tall, clipped* Ligustrum jonandrum, *border this canal.*

Planting to Fit

The built elements of a courtyard form a clean, unchanging backdrop for the planting scheme. Together they should create a harmonious balance, with the hard materials playing a strong supporting role to set off the energy of the plants. A plant's personality is expressed through its habit, shape, texture and leaf form. With many thousands of plants from which to choose, identify their individual characters and select those that fit into the planting theme.

Evergreens are the solid citizens, slow growing and important for the creation of a framework. They play a valuable role in the traditional style when clipped into tight shapes, and work well when arranged in formal lines or groups. Large boxwood balls and pyramids are especially handsome, while bay looks impressive grown as a standard on a tall, bare stem. Holly also lends itself to this treatment, looking more curvaceously chunky and appealing than its looser bush form.

Choosing Traditional Pots

Many traditional containers, such as those made of stone and terracotta, are very heavy. However, if you don't intend to move them once they are in place then there is no reason to deliberately avoid them – indeed their very weight gives substance and focus. Also featuring among the planter heavyweights is cast lead. They are usually replicas of Elizabethan or Regency pieces, and these finely detailed designs with their classical elegance belie their massive loading. But unless you cannot live without a dramatic lead cistern filled with ravishing black Queen of Night tulips, perhaps you would do best to restrain your selection to smaller rectangular forms.

In most circumstances, good-quality faux-lead reproductions made from glass fibre and resin are perfectly acceptable. These are quite convincing and are particularly useful where weight loading is an issue, such as on a roof terrace or balcony.

The best square-shaped planters for a traditional scheme are based on those conceived for the citrus and palm trees at Versailles, outside Paris, that make their annual transition from the huge orangery to the immense terraces. Taking the name of the palace, the 'Versailles tub' has become a perennial favourite. Normally made of timber, they are sometimes banded with steel, as the originals were designed to be taken apart. They are available in sizes able to accommodate a small tree.

Spiky leafed individuals, such as yuccas and dracaenas, are the outgoing party-lovers of the world, making strong contrast statements, and they look especially good in a bold container. Small-leaved, mound-forming reclusives, such as *Hebe pinguifolia*, with its tiny glaucous leaves, are good for cushioning bed edges, while feathery cotton lavender (*Santolina chamaecyparissus*) can be arranged into architectural groups of clipped grey-green spheres.

A clothing of energetic climbers is an essential backdrop. *Clematis armandii* and *Trachelospermum* *jasminoides* offer an evergreen screen with scented white flowers in spring and summer, respectively. Perennials are the showmen, bursting from the earth in spring to create a wealth of forms and textures. For style and elegance, nothing beats the hosta's veined foliage, combining sumptuous tones of grey, sulphur and lime.

CLIPPING A SPIRAL

Unlike symmetrical shapes, spirals brim with energy and movement. These classic topiary shapes look impressive and upmarket, and are relatively simple to create. Use the training technique below, but keep in mind the eventual size required. Either start with a bigger cone or add to the initial number of coils over time, merging lower coils and reshaping. When it is complete, avoid standing the spiral hard up against a wall, where one side could be heavily shaded, and turn it regularly. To make this easier, fix castors or stand the pot on a wheeled plinth.

1 Start with a cone with a single central stem that has been clipped several times to create dense interior growth. Tie string or raffia to the top of the plant, or start at the base, and wind it around as shown.

2 Using a pair of secateurs (pruning shears) or small hand shears, cut the initial groove. Go gently at first, working from the top of the plant down. Carefully cut any larger branches with secateurs. Keep standing back to survey progress.

3 Deepen the groove and create a coil with a rounded profile, rather like a snail shell. Stand the plant out of strong sun and wind, water regularly and feed with dilute liquid fertilizer. Clip in late spring and late summer to maintain its shape.

STRUCTURES AND FURNITURE FOR TRADITIONAL SPACES

To make the most of the available space, the vertical dimension in a courtyard must be utilized. Pergolas, arbours and gazebos, all traditional garden elements, provide decorative, three-dimensional forms that introduce focal points and ways to create separate areas. Timber or metal garden furniture provides the finishing touch.

Above: *A flowering yellow laburnum climbing over a pergola structure.*

Pergolas

A pergola is a freestanding structure formed from vertical wooden posts or stone pillars, which support rails that cross over the top to carry climbing plants. A versatile device, it has been used in gardens for centuries. The Romans liked to create shaded paths with overhead cover, while early illustrated manuscripts show latticed structures being used to support grapevines in medieval courtyards.

In a traditional garden, you might use a rose arch to frame the entrance to a long, romantic walkway displaying trailing wisteria. A pergola can also be adapted to become an arbour to make a cosy dining or seating place along a wall. In this

Above: *This bold but simple gazebo makes a compelling focal point, framing a paved court and magnificent planting.*

case, support posts are required only along the outside edge, while the rails are extended and fixed securely to the supporting wall by means of metal brackets. The flexibility of this type of construction means that it can be incorporated into any size of courtyard.

Pergolas can be constructed entirely from timber, which suits a 19th-century or Arts and Crafts style. The supporting posts should be made from bold, heavy sections, oak being a suitable choice. The cross rails can be somewhat lighter, but still sturdy (see construction method on page 133). Simple, economic wooden structures can be bought off the shelf, and posts might be clothed with trellis panels to disguise them. A pale, period-effect, painted or stained finish instantly upgrades an off-the-peg pergola.

Gazebos and Obelisks

The gazebo is a kind of garden folly that makes a fabulous focal point and a glorious dining area. Romantic styles work well for a traditional plot, especially when constructed from forged metal or, for an even lighter effect, delicate 19th-century-style wirework. Perfumed rambling roses, jasmine and honeysuckle would all make perfect planting subjects to enhance enhance warm summer days.

When a gazebo is made more weatherproof, protected with timber side panels and a solid roof finished with tiles, slates or metal such as copper or zinc, it has a wider range of uses.

Above: *A delightfully romantic, tiled roof folly makes the perfect, shady trysting spot.*

Where space is tight, or to add to the vertical texture of a larger courtyard space, you can use obelisks to introduce height. Place singly to create focal points or arrange in formal groupings – to set the corners of a parterre for example, or in rows. A pair of classically proportioned timber obelisks would handsomely frame an entrance door or mark the start of a formal pathway. Placed in a timber Versailles planter, an obelisk would make a fitting, stand-alone feature, best planted with an evergreen, such as the star jasmine (*Trachelospermum jasminoides*) or one of the smaller-leaved ivies. For a romantic garden theme, a more delicate steel or wirework obelisk would marry well with a large-flowered clematis or a pillar rose.

Right: *These tall, timber obelisks provide an excellent vehicle for climbing* Mina lobata *and completely alter the scale and presence of the parterre.*

BUILDING A TRELLIS ARBOUR

Decorative trellis panels, including shaped pieces, are available in a wide range of sizes. With some basic practical skills, you should be able to fit these to a framework of posts to create your own traditional garden arbour. You can also incorporate solid timber to form a seat, or you can place a bench under the canopy. Cover the arbour with climbers, such as honeysuckle and jasmine, to scent the air and provide leafy seclusion.

1 Trim the wooden posts to 2m (6ft), not forgetting to add the depth of the metal 'shoe' at the top of the spike that holds them in the ground. Check that you have all the trellis components, including the 2m x 90cm (6 x 3ft) back panel.

2 Set the posts for the back panel 2m (6ft) apart and use a club hammer to drive in the spiked metal post supports. With a No 8 drill bit, drill holes for the galvanized screws at intervals down each side of the trellis, then screw the panel into position.

3 Repeat this method to fix first the side panels – each 2m x 60cm (6 x 2ft) – then the narrow front panels and, as a decorative addition above, the shaped trellis section. Finally fit the 2m x 60cm (6 x 2ft) roof panel.

4 Paint the arbour with an exterior-quality wood stain. On ground too hard or stony to drive in post fixing spikes, use longer posts and dig holes to accommodate post bases and quick-setting, ready-mix concrete.

Above: *The climbers on this gazebo are supported with a central tree-trunk pillar and a metal-framed circular structure.*

Above: *Reclaimed cast-iron columns provide a strong and elegant support for this timber-roofed pergola.*

Appropriate Materials

Courtyards with a neoclassical theme demand elegantly proportioned columns to support the overhead structure. It is worth searching reclamation yards for suitable timber and stone beams that can be adapted to suit your purpose. Alternatively, use reproductions in reconstituted stone, sturdy timber uprights, or brick columns, if this fits with the style of the surrounding architecture. With the help of a builder or carpenter, a substantial design incorporating steel or timber for top rails can easily be created. This style requires planting of appropriate grandeur, and wisteria, with its pendant racemes or frothy rambler roses, seems best able to rise to the occasion.

Where the appearance of visual lightness is required, forged steel is an excellent material. Its combination of inherent physical strength and total flexibility allows it to be formed into fine and complex designs such as a period-style gazebo or rose bower. A wide range of structures can be purchased direct, or a blacksmith could create a composition dovetailed to your design.

Climbing plants can become exceedingly heavy, and the physical exposure of vertical structures makes them susceptible to wind pressure and the extra weight of snow. The main considerations when building pergolas, arbours or gazebos, therefore, is that they should be well constructed from stout materials, and that the vertical supports should be bedded firmly into the ground with concrete foundations.

Right: *This colonnaded arbour with cream pillars supporting a wooden frame looks toward a stunning sea view.*

Timber Furniture

The most traditional and robust designs of furniture tend to be made from timber. Seating forms are generous and shapes vary from rectangular and solid towards the more curvaceous lines of the rolled-arm bench, known as 'Lutyens-style', and lounging steamer chairs.

Most are made from exotic hardwoods, of which teak is the most beautiful and luxurious. These woods are weatherproof and need little upkeep, however, do ensure that your products are sourced sustainably. Oak is a handsome alternative, but should be properly seasoned to prevent it leaching tannin, which can stain paving. The best timbers can be left untreated, and over time they acquire a wonderful, silvery patina. If you prefer a more finished look, use a quality yacht varnish or give the wood an annual application of purpose-made oil. If you prefer a painted look, to make a focal point or to complement another feature, choose softwood, which does not contain resins that can resist the finish.

Right: Filigree, cast-aluminium furniture mimics the Victorian style, but is lighter in weight than the original cast-iron versions.

Above: This untreated teak bench takes on a silvery patina, setting off perfectly the red and orange dahlias and nasturtiums.

Metal Furniture

Lightweight wirework chairs and tables make a charming addition to a metal gazebo, reflecting the delicate tracery of the design, or would integrate subtly into a secluded corner. A Regency-style forged-steel bench makes a

Above: Curvaceous, American Adirondack-style seats from the early 20th century are becoming a new garden design classic.

handsome, understated feature, while chairs of a similar style can be combined with a metal dining or occasional table. Check that metal furniture is rust proofed before leaving it outside in all weathers. All metal can be painted, helping to keep it in good repair.

ORNAMENT FOR TRADITIONAL SPACES

Traditional statuary and ornament should be chosen to suggest a period style and to harmonize with surrounding architecture and materials. Placed in a key position, a classical statue creates a focal point, and can be lit at night for further emphasis. Decorative finials can also be used to embellish pillars and balustrades.

Above: *This stone ball finial gives the finishing touch to a carved stone balustrade.*

Sculptural Options

Introducing figurative form may seem to be the most natural direction to take in a garden setting, and animal and human forms have a familiarity in a traditional garden. Certainly, reproductions of classical figures are an understandably popular choice and allow you to emulate the glories of earlier centuries in your courtyard design. To make a strong, single statement, a Greek goddess, or perhaps philosopher, set against a hedge of dark, clipped topiary would add an appropriate air of calm and order. You can also integrate animals very well – a reclining lion gazing down from a terrace could look very handsome, while a jousting unicorn or tusked wild boar could add a more

fantastical touch to a formal pool. Mythical sea creatures and leonine masks work extremely well as spouts for wall fountains.

By contrast, geometrically architectural pieces are pure and unemotional. Obelisks provide punctuation points to mark an entrance or pathway, while you can use columns, crumbling or otherwise, to form circles and lines, or set them singly among a group of plants. Smaller pieces, known as finials, shaped as balls, acorns and pineapples, make excellent finishing touches for gateposts. Make your own by scattering bits of reclaimed or salvaged stonework on the ground, like the remains of an ancient ruin.

Tall, classical vases, often standing on plinths, play an important role as ornament and are useful vehicles by

which to introduce seasonal bedding. Generally, the planting space is small, so they are best when dressed with elegant flowers, such as tulips and trailing geraniums, with sophisticated colours of pure white and deepest wine red to suit. Wider, freestanding urns are best balanced by clipped box or other topiary plants.

Style and Materials

Hand-carved stone sculpture would be a fabulous and luxurious addition to a traditional garden, as would cast bronze, which is perennially popular for use outside. Antiques are costly, however, but all types of reproductions are widely available, using fibreglass and bronze substitutes. These do vary enormously in quality and finish, so do some research before ordering.

The style of the piece will dictate the material, but reconstituted stone is a popular choice. Its new appearance can be easily 'distressed' by the application of a proprietary treatment, or see the paint treatment opposite. Alternatively, if placed in a damp and shady spot, it will not take long for algae and moss to appear. Most designs can be found in this material.

As an alternative to the cool, pale colour of stone, choose the warmer tones of terracotta. Urns and vases should be made from frost-resistant materials. Cast-iron reproductions are an inexpensive choice, with lead as the luxurious option. Quality, handmade terracotta is handsome, while stone dust and cement mixes offer attractive-looking alternatives.

Above: *A classical figure, moulded from reconstituted stone, resin and concrete.*

Above: *This cast-iron vase has had a wash of white paint to relieve the intentional rust.*

HOW TO AGE NEW STONEWARE

Carved stone ornaments are expensive and reconstituted stone pieces are not cheap. For a more economical option, look for concrete ornaments that have been moulded from originals. These ornaments will eventually weather and age and become colonized with algae, but, if you want an instant transformation, follow the technique below and achieve the same effect in just a couple of hours.

1 Use a solution of PVA glue, diluted according to the manufacturer's instructions, to seal the concrete surface, including the inside. Repeat as necessary, and allow it to dry. This will prevent moisture from penetrating the concrete and lifting the paint layers.

2 Paint the ornament with a base coat of white emulsion, then, once it is dry, follow with a roughly applied coat of pale grey. This can be mixed by adding a touch of black artist's acrylic paint. The vase now has the appearance of newly carved stone.

3 Use a piece of dampened natural sponge to stipple on darker areas of grey and charcoal acrylic paint, working it into the cracks and crevices to accentuate the relief design and emphasize shadows. The vase is beginning to look more weathered.

4 If possible, find a photograph of mosses and algae colonizing stone to give you a colour and texture reference to work from. Mix up a palette of artist's acrylics in greens and yellows to mimic the plants and apply the colours randomly with the sponge.

5 Once you have achieved a natural-looking covering, with some darker green areas under the bowl and around the base and lighter yellowish greens on any prominent features, such as the fruits and swags here, brush on random patches of bright ochre to mimic lichen colonies.

6 Allow the paint to dry between each coat, then weatherproof the mock-aged patina by sealing it with a couple of coats of clear, matt exterior varnish. Set the vase on top of a plinth or wall column, cementing the base for added safety.

WATER FEATURES FOR TRADITIONAL SPACES

Water introduces a unique dimension of reflection and sound and features often have an architectural contribution. A built feature with formal lines and structure is the most appropriate for a traditional scheme. A water feature in this style will be defined by its ornamental impact, and by the nature of the water flow.

Above: *The sight and sound of a splashing fountain brings life and light to the garden.*

Using Pools

An above-ground pool makes a strong architectural statement and a striking focal point. It can be constructed from low walls, around 50–60cm (20–24in) high, using brick or natural stone. You can also use economical concrete blocks faced up in stone slips or rendered in stucco. A wider seating ledge, perhaps of smooth, dark slate instead of a simple coping, would encourage people to sit and enjoy the feature close up. A round shape is usually thought to be the most attractive, but a rectangular form is easier to build – important if you are doing it yourself.

A water feature at ground level can be a garden highlight, especially if it is set within an area of paving. Where space allows, two or more pools can be linked by a narrow channel, or rill, bordered on each side by a flagstone path. This creates a directional effect, leading the eye towards a garden feature, such as a statue or vase.

MAKING A CONCRETE POOL

Concrete pools are suitable in places where soil conditions are too unstable for sunken pools with flexible liners. They are also good for raised pools, which need strong sides to withstand water pressure.

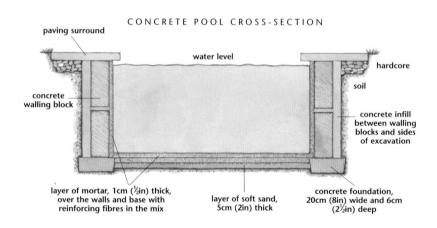

CONCRETE POOL CROSS-SECTION

- paving surround
- water level
- hardcore
- concrete walling block
- soil
- concrete infill between walling blocks and sides of excavation
- layer of mortar, 1cm (½in) thick, over the walls and base with reinforcing fibres in the mix
- layer of soft sand, 5cm (2in) thick
- concrete foundation, 20cm (8in) wide and 6cm (2½in) deep

1 Mark out the outline of the pool with string and canes. Dig out the area to a depth of 75cm (30in). If you are keeping the soil, do not mix topsoil and subsoil.
2 Dig a 20cm- (8in-) wide trench to a depth of 6cm (2½in) around the inside of the base. Add the concrete and level the top. Check with a spirit level. Leave to dry.
3 Dig out about 6cm (2½in) soil from the base. Spread and rake, removing stones, then level and firm a 5cm (2in) layer of soft sand below the top of the foundation.

4 Skim the sand with a 1cm (½in) layer of fibre-reinforced mortar with a plasterer's trowel, overlapping the concrete foundations by 5cm (2in).
5 After 24 hours, mortar concrete walling blocks on to the foundations and check the levels. Once set, fill in the gap between the soil wall and the walling blocks with a stiff concrete mix. Fill in the inside of the blocks if they have cavities.
6 Allow a further 48 hours for the whole structure to set thoroughly. Dampen the

whole surface of the internal structure before covering with a 1cm (½in) layer of fibre-reinforced mortar. To give added strength, make a rounded cornice edge where the walls meet each other and the base.
7 Replace the top 10cm (4in) of soil with hardcore. Mortar the paving edge on to the pool walls and the hardcore base. Place the paving surround so that it overlaps the inside wall by 2.5–5cm (1–2in).
8 Allow the internal walls to dry, then paint with a black waterproof sealant.

Fountains

Ornamental fountains in traditional gardens animate the more formal static elements of structure and planting. You can direct a fountain water jet through a sculptural ornament secured to the base of the pool, or it can spray directly from below the water's surface.

Installing Water Features

Water animates a space and in a smaller area will provide a central focus. A functional water feature involves watertight construction, electrics, as well as pumps and filters.

To stay clean, water needs to recirculate, and using a fountain powered by a submersible pump is a practical method to achieve this.

A rill would have to be excavated, lined and waterproofed, but the depth of water can be shallow. For the best results, a very dark lining imparts a sombre tone to the water and maximizes reflectivity. A separate water aeration and filtering pump would be needed.

You can create a wall fountain using a water-filled trough, fed by a spout in the wall above. Use an old

Above: *The black liner of this raised pool is a sober backdrop against the stone facings.*

Above: *The pump mechanism for this fountain unit is hidden behind the wall.*

stone or reproduction trough and combine the spout with a figurative mask with the mouth as the spout. The electrics and recirculating pump mechanism can be concealed behind the wall, or a small immersion pump disguised below the water's surface.

An underwater luminaire will provide the finishing touch for a night-time display.

Safety notes: *Take precautions to prevent children having access to ponds and other water features. Use a fence to deter toddlers from ponds and pools.*

Wherever electricity and water are used together, use an electrician to carry out the work.

Above: *A tiny feature can make a big impact; the pump is disguised below a shelf of cobbles in this self-contained unit.*

Above: *Built from stone slabs, this above-ground pool includes a seating ledge to enjoy the fountain at close hand.*

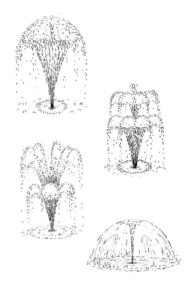

Above: *Submersible pumps come with a range of attachments to produce most of the more common small fountain shapes.*

LIGHTING FOR TRADITIONAL SPACES

The lighting in a traditional courtyard is subtle. Low-level path lighting and period-style wall lights enable the garden to be enjoyed at night with a degree of safety, and spot lights may also be used to create one or two dramatic statements, enlivening views from inside the house at night as well as outdoors.

Above: *Solar garden lights are ideal for lining a walkway or garden path.*

Wall Lights

Whatever period in history you take as your inspiration, when selecting wall lamps it is important to choose models that are in proportion with the space and to pick a style that blends with existing garden furniture, containers and ornamental features. Remember these lights will be very much on show and will add to the overall design theme of the garden.

There are scores of different models for wall lights but for period settings, Victorian-style coach lamps in black, white or weathered metallic finishes are popular and mimic the wrought-iron and cast-iron designs of old. Some of these designs are solid and chunky and work best against a backdrop of stone or rendered walls and within simply dressed, more functional spaces. For this type of setting and in more rustic locations also consider brass bulkhead lights.

Creating a Co-ordinated Look

You can often buy matching lamp-posts to go with wall lights, as well as lamps to fit on the top of gateposts. Ask to see supplier catalogues for the full range.

A softer look comes in the form of Art Nouveau inspired lights with a simple ball-shaped globe supported by an ornate arm or scrolled support. Italianate or Venetian-style wall lanterns are also available, sometimes in an attractive verdigris finish. These may be modelled on original lanterns and will certainly add to the charm of the courtyard.

Path and Step Lighting

There are two options for lighting pathways. One is to choose period-style lanterns on short posts to use in a line along path edges and seating areas. Another much less conspicuous approach is to use small white floor lights that fit in flush with paving. The black or brushed-steel surround is hardly noticeable. Alternatively, use modern black spots along the edge of paths and angle the lamp to shine down and across the stone, brickwork or gravel. Plants will hide the wires and fittings. Concentrate lighting particularly where there are steps and changes in level or direction. On a still summer's evening, you can use nightlights or small candles up either side of a flight of steps or along the top of a retaining wall to highlight the symmetry and formality of your courtyard.

Above: *The curling metal embellishments on this lantern add to its romantic appeal.*

Outdoor Dining

Oil or candle lanterns radiate the warm glow of a natural flame and create the nostalgic feeling of a time before electric lights. Outdoor candelabras are an inspiring sight when lit at night and they can also provide interesting decorative detail during the day. Choose from suspended candelabras that are supported on a chain used for raising and lowering, table candelabras and floor candelabras.

Traditional oil lamps, including brass lanterns, give out a soft glow and are an effective lighting option for night-time get-togethers. Never leave naked flames unattended.

Highlighting Elements

By day the garden is a constantly changing scene of sunshine and shadow and the form and texture

Above: *This functional lamp set against brickwork fits a Victorian courtyard theme.*

of sculptural elements becomes prominent only when shadows are sharply defined. But as the night draws in you have the opportunity to be much more theatrical, maximizing the contours of carved stonework, sculpture and even topiary using carefully positioned mini spots, either mains-voltage or solar-powered.

Always experiment first before setting the lights into their final positions. A powerful torch is a useful aid. You can light from either side, from the front and at points in between or try backlighting for carved screens. Wall masks and classical busts can look dramatic when the lights is directed just below the chin. In darkness, you can select just a few pieces for lighting and if these elements were ones largely hidden during the daytime, you could achieve a completely different feel when the lighting comes on at night. Subtly highlight raised beds, formal clipped hedges or pillars using uplighters, spots or mini floodlights.

Lighting Water Features

A simple idea for a summer party is to set night-lights at regular intervals around the edge of a raised or sunken pool. Still water can also look magical when lit from below using specialist lamps. But rather than simply lighting up the whole pool, it can be more impressive if you simply spotlight a water cascade from below or shine light up on to a water sculpture. Some fountain arrangements have integral lighting. As with any outdoor water feature, always employ a qualified electrician to ensure that the system is safely installed.

Right: *The framework of this traditional pergola is softly illuminated by several hidden spotlights.*

Above: *This limestone-lined canal flanked by pleached lime draws the eye to the Venetian-style well head at the end. As the light fades, the carved stonework becomes an even more dramatic focal point, lit by underwater spots set between the stepping-stones. These act as camouflage for the lights during the day.*

CASE STUDY: FORMAL TERRACE

This tiny courtyard forms the entrance to a private house. It is enclosed by high screen walls and dense, evergreen foliage, with a solid door with an impressive classical portico to the neighbouring street adding a theatrical touch of grandeur. Familiar themes hold the look together, with repeating spheres of clipped topiary in different sizes.

Above: *Perfectly clipped balls of box* (Buxus sempervirens) *give continuity of form.*

The overwhelmingly striking feature of this terrace is the mass of oversized planting that makes a bold, sculptural statement in its own right. The planting is composed entirely of evergreen subjects, which provide structure and interest throughout the year. Tall screens of mature, dark-green ivy surmount the walls, increasing the sense of privacy. A bare splash of a red rambling rose flashes through from the sunny side facing the street.

The garden otherwise tells a very clear colour story that helps to maximize the impression of space. It is comprised of painted white walls and fences, the painted gate and matching trellis panels piercing the ivy screens. A pale stone table with an amusing pair of rusty chairs with a cat motif form the centrepiece. A terracotta wall fountain (see installation method described on page 55) and small pots echo the material of the paving slabs, which are laid in a diagonal grid pattern to extend the sense of perspective with darker, contrasting edging that gives the paving a 'woven-carpet' feel.

The evergreen plants, including *Buxus*, *Ligustrum* and *Prunus lusitanica*, are clipped into curving shapes that are repeated throughout the garden. The sculptural hedges have a rounded profile and all the specimen topiaries are clipped into balls. Even though the planting is entirely of evergreen plants, the variety of different species provides contrasting leaf shape, texture and colour tone.

The garden plan for this formal terrace, shown overleaf, demonstrates clearly how the symmetrical layout is emphasized by paired plantings. Shade-tolerant ivy and camellia-clad walls create a leafy backdrop for the tiled central area. The green architecture includes large camellia (see planting method described on page 55), and Portuguese laurel standards and cloud-pruned specimens flanking the doorway.

Above: *This cat-embellished chair adds a sense of fun to the strictly formal setting.*

Right: *The terracotta tiles create an intimate sitting area in the garden, surrounded by a wall of dense, evergreen foliage that protects it from the street.*

CREATING A FORMAL TERRACE

Flooring:
- *Use just one or two hard landscaping materials throughout the scheme.*
- *Research classical patterns and incorporate them into the design.*
- *Contrasting dark and light tones helps to reinforce the layout.*
- *Use layout patterns to emphasize direction and changes of level.*

Plants and Containers:
- *Large clipped topiaries reinforce the classical theme and give a sculptural feel.*
- *Choose a core of evergreen planting to hold the structure and appearance right through the year.*
- *Maintain one shape as a clipping motif – round, square or pyramid – to preserve a consistent appearance.*

Structures and Furniture:
- *Keep to a single theme.*
- *Materials for focal points such as furniture or sculpture should fit within the main palette of colour or texture to maintain a consistent theme.*

- *Use bold statements, which help to give an impression of space.*
- *Disguise any awkward or ill-fitting features by painting them out in a scheme colour.*

Ornament and Water Features:
- *Use a neutral colour palette with a maximum of three co-ordinating elements.*
- *Use classical imagery throughout, from flowers to mythological creatures, to maintain the traditional look.*

FORMAL TERRACE GARDEN PLAN

wall fountain

10

street door

8

8

1

3

golden gravel

5

9

4

7

step

carved stone seat

1

7

6

6

7

6

4

2

6

2

3

brick surround

cobbles, leading to glass back door

Plant list

1 *Ilex crenata*
2 *Camellia* standard
3 *Buxus sempervirens*
4 *Polystichum* fern
5 *Camellia japonica* hedge, with *Hedera helix* and *Rosa* growing over
6 *Lonicera nitida*
7 *Hedera helix* (topiary)
8 *Prunus lusitanica*
9 *Buxus sempervirens* 'Suffruticosa'
10 *Hedera helix*

Below: Prunus lusitanica *is formed into two tall formal standards, and* Buxus sempervirens *is shaped into two low sculptural globes, giving the courtyard an impressive symmetry.*

Above: *Japonica camellias have a glossy green foliage and work well as an informal hedge, with a dramatic flower display in the colder part of the year.*

Left: *The formal, evergreen shapes of the* Buxus *give a clean-edged profile and a monumental presence.*

Above: *Ivy* (Hedera helix) *tumbles over the* Camellia japonica *hedge.*

Above: Lonicera nitida *'Baggesen's Gold' is a honeysuckle here used as sphere topiary.*

Above: Polystichum aculeatum, *or hard shield fern, thrives in light shade.*

INSTALLING A WALL FOUNTAIN

Wall fountains make the most of a small volume of water and are ideal for courtyard, basement and roof gardens where there isn't enough room for a stand-alone pool. This design uses a sunken, covered reservoir.

1 Select a traditional wall mask with a tubular metal waterspout already fitted.
2 Dig out the sunken reservoir and insert a rigid liner with a removable metal grill cover. These sets are commonly available from water garden specialists.
3 Thread the delivery pipe from the pump in the reservoir through and then angled up behind a double wall. Drill the holes using a masonry bit, switching to the hammer action on your drill.
4 Connect the pipe from the pump and the copper pipe in the mask to the pipe behind the wall with right-angle bends.

To do this, use a plumber's pipe bender or pipe spring.
5 Secure the mask and spill basin below to the wall with large fixing bolts. Drill the holes, using the appropriate masonry drill bit, and insert wall plugs before screwing in place.
6 Fill the reservoir with water and connect the pump to a waterproof socket approved by an electrician.
7 Test the flow rate, adjusting the tap on the pump until the desired effect is achieved. Replace the reservoir mesh and cover it with cobbles.

WALL FOUNTAIN CROSS-SECTION

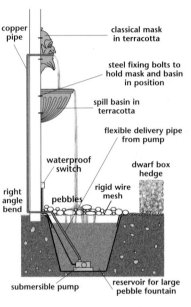

copper pipe

classical mask in terracotta

steel fixing bolts to hold mask and basin in position

spill basin in terracotta

flexible delivery pipe from pump

dwarf box hedge

waterproof switch

rigid wire mesh

right angle bend

pebbles

submersible pump

reservoir for large pebble fountain

PLANTING CAMELLIA

Camellias thrive in containers, particularly smaller, compact cultivars. Restrict growth by pruning after flowering. They are ericaceous, or lime-hating, plants, so use an ericaceous compost (soil mix). Regular watering is essential during the growing season. If you live in a hard-water area use rainwater collected in a water butt.

1 Use terracotta or stone containers for these heavy plants. Place crocks over the holes and begin filling with ericaceous compost (acid soil mix) with added loam. Mix some grit in to very large pots.

2 Soak the plant's root-ball (roots) before planting. Remove from the pot and check that the compost depth is correct. The final level should be about 2.5cm (1in) below the pot rim.

3 If the plant is pot bound, gently tease out some of the thickest roots with your fingers or a hand fork. Fill in around the root-ball, firm with your hands and add a support stake if needed.

4 Use a slow-release fertiliser for ericaceous (acid-loving) plants. Top dress with a layer of grit or gravel. Place the camellia in its final position, such as against a shady north-facing wall.

MEDITERRANEAN MOODS

The Mediterranean courtyard is a sensuous place. On summer evenings, protected from cold and wind by sheltering, climber-clad walls, the atmosphere is warm and heavy with exotic fragrance. Candle lanterns flicker enchantingly. This is the perfect place for unwinding after work or sharing a glass of wine with friends. If rain threatens, a chiminea-heated loggia provides a comfortable retreat.

During the day, the vibrant colour and texture of flower-filled pots and raised beds is a feast for the eye. Terracotta and ochre shades mingle with sky and cornflower blues of doors and shutters.

The taste of food magnifies when eaten alfresco under the dappled shade of a tree or vine-covered pergola and the scent of aromatic oils released from herbs and scented shrubs intensifies with the trapped heat and humidity. Close your eyes and soothe your senses by listening to the hum of bees on lavender and the sound of gently trickling water.

Left: *This sunlit corner features some of the typical elements of the Mediterranean style, including an old stone wall as a rustic backdrop and a jumble of pots with bright flowers.*

SUNSHINE GARDENS

This style of gardening appeals especially to gardeners who enjoy travelling to the sun. Bringing a flavour of the Mediterranean region back to our own gardens prolongs that pleasurable sense of carefree living. As well as including signature plants or hardier look-alikes that are readily available in the summer, you can also find an array of imported pots and planters and garden furniture.

Above: *A Marrakesh blue wall highlights the potted citrus and bougainvillea.*

Images from Abroad

Although there are similarities between the formal Italian Renaissance-style gardens with their geometric layout, clipped topiaries, aromatic herbs and ornate terracotta pots, the Mediterranean courtyard garden is much more relaxed. The lack of space and simple features results in a more homespun feel, with a jumble of pots and planters – some made from recycled containers – flowers and vegetables, herbs and fruits all vying for growing room. Practicality and productivity can be almost as important as aesthetics, and edible plants that are also attractive frequently substitute for ornamentals. As well as the family courtyard or outdoor room, alive with colourful and fragrant specimens, if space is available small vegetable plots are also lovingly tended. These provide everything from cucumbers,

Above: *A Greek-island style featuring a compacted clay floor and dusty terracotta.*

tomatoes, courgettes (zucchini), aubergines (eggplants), beans, potatoes and salads to apricots, peaches, pomegranates and citrus fruits. In a small courtyard you could still attractively incorporate these productive spaces by confining them in rendered raised beds and terracotta pots lined with plastic to conserve moisture.

Planting Choices

With relatively mild winters becoming more common, many gardeners in temperate northern regions can now grow borderline hardy plants outdoors year round without having to bring them under cover at any stage. And, particularly with the shelter that is afforded by courtyard walls and screens, you can try a very wide range of exotics. Heat that is absorbed by paving and brickwork during the day is steadily released into the surrounding air through the night, successfully keeping temperatures a degree or two higher and hopefully above freezing. If you have a frost-free greenhouse or conservatory you can overwinter many more tender plants and start seedlings, bulbs and tubers off earlier in the season to allow them time to mature, flower and fruit in the shorter growing season.

Expanding your planting repertoire by including plants that are commonly used in Mediterranean gardens creates a powerful visual trigger. Large-leaved specimens, such as cannas and hardy bananas, can be combined with succulents and cacti and

vibrantly coloured annuals and perennials to great effect, especially when used with terracotta pots, cane furniture and rendered walls. Even dropping in one or two quintessentially Mediterranean plants, such as a potted olive, lemon or bay tree, or planting a grape vine over a pergola suggests a sunnier location. Any of the more tender plants you use may then require some winter protection.

Preparing the Space

Throughout this chapter you will find inspiration for decorating and enlivening your Mediterranean courtyard. Before beginning, it is important to camouflage any parts of the existing surroundings that don't fit in. You could achieve this with paint or render, trellis panels, screens and climbers, pergolas and garden buildings.

Ornamental Detail

The typical rustic Mediterranean courtyard is furnished quite differently to the more opulent Riviera or Moorish style in terms of lamps, tables and chairs, pots and planters, water features, paving, walls and screens.

The following sections examine the different products and materials that you might use and how you can combine them to good effect.

Right: *Whitewashed walls studded with pots and planters, together with an array of houseplants clustered on the terrace, create an oasis effect.*

FLOORING FOR MEDITERRANEAN SPACES

With a legacy of classical Greek and Roman architecture and later Moorish influences, Mediterranean gardens have often featured beautifully crafted floors of mosaics, tiles, cobbles and setts. You can adapt tradition and add contemporary decorative flourishes utilizing the many different materials available today.

Above: Herbs and alpines nestle between rugged stepping stones and pebbles.

Simple Solutions

In small and unusually shaped courtyards, a plain flooring solution can help to throw the focus on to the plants and other decorative elements. Various grades of gravel, especially natural-looking pebble and shingle mixtures, work better than crushed stone, though rolled and compacted clay aggregate offers an excellent alternative. Choose warm-coloured materials, such as golden gravel or toffee-coloured flint, to create the illusion of a sunnier climate. To avoid weeds, cover the soil with landscape fabric first. Avoid fine-graded gravel, which tends to be kicked about.

Textural Choices

Try contrasting gravel with square or rectangular paving or exterior-quality ceramic tiles. Square and rectangular elements are best laid out so that the sides of adjacent pieces

Above: Reclaimed timber planks create a pathway across a loose surface of pebbles.

are parallel. For example, a widely spaced grid pattern could be used or a staggered line forming a relaxed path. You can be more informal with randomly shaped stone. Weathered reclaimed timbers may also be sunk in flush with the ground surface to create a wide meandering walkway or to mark a seating area.

Another option is to create a graded beach effect by working larger cobbles and pebbles into corners and against walls. Buy bags of pebbles in different sizes whose colours and textures combine well. Use the smaller grades at the front to blend in with the gravel and bring a few of the larger cobbles and rounded boulders forwards.

Concrete is frequently used to surface gardens in hot climates and it is an inexpensive alternative to paving if you want a smooth, solid surface. However, concrete alone looks too stark in a Mediterranean-

Above: Differently coloured gravel, pebbles and cobbles can be used to create informal patterns that flow into the borders.

style garden unless you lay it in smaller panels bordered by, for example, natural stone setts. You can soften the look of concrete by working shingle, pebbles and even quantities of cockleshells (available bagged) into the top layer. To create a weathered effect, brush away some of the cement with a stiff nylon hand brush dipped in a bucket of water before the mix sets to expose more of the pebbles.

A Cobbled Yard

For a more obvious pebble or cobble surface, lay mortar over compacted hardcore and press larger cobbles or pebbles into the surface before it hardens. Work in small sections at a time. Try to lay as flat a surface as possible,

Above: *Mosaic-patterned stepping stones add splashes of colour through a lawn of aromatic chamomile and thyme. The herbs' scent will be released with each step.*

Right: *Terracotta-tiled steps edged with contrasting blue-grey lead to an hexagonal dais decorated with an intricate pebble mosaic.*

otherwise the floor will be uncomfortable to walk on. Pebbles and cobbles often have a distinct shape, being slightly flattened for example, and you can create interesting effects by laying adjacent sections of cobbles either flat or edge on. Contain concrete and pebble floors and pathways with tanalized gravel boards held in place with stout wooden pegs, or use a line of bricks, pavers or setts, or strips of marble if they are available, to create a firm boundary. You could use these same materials to create patterns, such as a brick diamond-shaped grid infilled with stones.

Laying Paving

A wide range of paving is suitable for the floor of your Mediterranean-inspired courtyard, from natural stone to smooth or riven concrete pavers. Look for lighter colours of sandstone, including types with pink and yellow shading, honey-coloured limestone or subtly shaded equivalents in reconstituted paving. A rectilinear paving design, using four or five different shapes and sizes, will suit larger, more formal courtyard settings. Include a proportion of much larger stone pieces to avoid the design becoming too 'busy', and consider working bricks or cobble panels into the design to soften the appearance.

In more rustic surroundings, small areas of paving could be laid using large, randomly shaped and somewhat rugged looking stone pieces set together 'crazy paving' style, perhaps leaving planting holes for aromatic herbs, such as thyme, oregano and Corsican mint. When trodden on, these creeping plants release a scent characteristic of the Mediterranean countryside. Avoid plain, dark coloured slate and other types of sombre grey stone, especially in shady areas, and instead look for pieces marbled with red and orange veins to add warmth.

Above: *Bold agave and rounded pebbles contrast with simple paving slabs.*

Choosing Tiles

Glazed ceramic or plain terracotta tiles have long been used to create floors in courtyards and gardens across the Mediterranean region. In cooler, wetter climates, take care to select tiles that are frostproof and that provide a reasonable grip in damp weather – a perfectly smooth surface can be lethally slippery when wet or frosty. Unless very well compacted, ground can shift fractionally, so ensure that tiles are thick enough to withstand the stress of being walked on when the foundation is slightly uneven. A smooth, even concrete slab makes an ideal base.

Ceramic tiles have an advantage over other paving types in being easier to sweep and wash over when dirty. This makes them ideal for walkways and outdoor cooking and dining areas. You can often match the tiling of a kitchen or conservatory with that of the courtyard to create a visual link.

Ceramic tiles also come in a wide range of colours. Browns and terracotta shades suit the Mediterranean style perfectly. Use other colours, such as ultramarine blue or lemon yellow sparingly and for dramatic effect. Nowadays,

Above: *Sliced roofing tiles and stone chips create intricate patterns.*

Above: *Mini brick setts add extra texture to this curved edging.*

manufacturers tend to make mostly plain frostproof tiles and it is harder to track down patterns. You might, for example, wish to use a traditional Moorish design to create a border around a square of plain tiles for a Spanish-style courtyard. Complete Moroccan/Moorish tile panels are available from Internet stores, but if you visit reclamation yards you can often pick up Victorian tiles with suitable designs. In small, square or rectangular courtyards, or as a central focus for a larger site, combine tiles of different colours, shapes and sizes to create a Persian carpet effect, but ensure that the bulk of the 'carpet' is the same plain colour, perhaps rotated and laid on the diagonal for extra interest.

Mosaic Effects

As a focal point for your Mediterranean courtyard you might consider a Greco-Roman style mosaic using traditional tesserae – small squares of stone or ceramic tile. Complicated designs are a job for a mosaic artist, but simple designs combining tiles and

Left: *Areas surfaced solely with gravel can seem rather plain. To add texture and pattern, consider working in a design of quarry tiles or small square pavers, in warm shades of terracotta.*

pebbles, for example, can be easy and effective. An example of this might be creating a replacement centre to a pre-cut paving stone circle. Some manufacturers provide such panels ready-made, featuring birds, animals and insects, or sun or star motifs.

Mediterranean courtyards are sometimes laid using a plain paving material incorporating a repeating pattern of mosaic-like elements, such as a flower or star motif. These elements may combine differently coloured pieces of precision-cut stone, terracotta or ceramic tile or polished marble.

TILE SHARDS FOR MOSAIC

- *Use coloured, patterned pieces to create decorative borders, panels or wandering lines within tiles or paving.*
- *Fix tile shards to a smooth concrete base using exterior-quality waterproof tile adhesive and grout.*
- *Extend the flowing patterns of tile shards in floors up on to walls and on the sides of raised beds.*
- *Create mosaic designs, such as simple flowers and stylized birds, with coloured glazed shards combined with pebbles or shells.*
- *Use broken floor tiles to surface paths between raised vegetable beds, creating a free-draining surface.*

MAKING A PEBBLE FLOOR MOSAIC

A small number of mosaic panels, perhaps laid to replace plain pavers, will produce a wonderfully textured and eye-catching surface, helping to emphasize the Mediterranean style. Using pebbles in a mosaic feature, instead of tesserae or tile shards, makes the process much easier. A panel like this can be completed in under an hour. Try out the design on an identically sized area first, so that you know how many of each type and size of pebble you need.

1 Lift a paving slab to accommodate your mosaic, or leave a gap when laying paving. Over a solid base of compacted hardcore add a layer of builders' sand. Tamp down with a block of wood and check that the surface is level.

2 Add a ready-made bag of dry mortar mix. Wear gloves to protect your hands from the lime and work from a kneeling pad for comfort. Check that the finished level once the pebbles are in place will be flush with the rest of the paving.

3 Find the centre of the panel by marking the intersection of two diagonal lines. Now start placing your pebbles in position, starting with the blue metallic marble, then add white, black and grey rings of pebbles.

4 Continue to build the design in rings, setting the smaller pebbles on edge to create an interesting texture. Use a piece of sawn timber and a rubber mallet to check that the surface of the pebbles is at the same level as the surrounding paving.

5 Select larger corner and edge pebbles in browns and paler greys and arrange to bridge the gap between the main circular block and the surrounding paving. These will be the guidelines for filling in the rest of the design.

6 Fill the remaining spaces with more pebbles, choosing appropriate sizes to fit the gaps. Keep the design as tightly packed as possible. You may need to replace pebbles with ones that are a better fit as you near completion.

7 Check levels again with the piece of timber and mallet. Work in more dry mortar mix using a nylon hand brush to tamp the material down in between the pebbles. This mix will set solidly, forming a durable and weather-resistant surface.

8 Fill a hand sprayer with water and use it to moisten the dry mortar mix and to reveal the protruding pebbles. Clean off excess mortar with the spray and a damp cloth, but don't disturb the pebbles and scrape away too much of the mortar.

9 The moistened mortar mix will eventually set. Cover it with plastic sheeting if rain threatens or if the weather is hot and dry. Because the pebbles are laid flush with the paving, you can walk over them with ease.

WALLS FOR MEDITERRANEAN SPACES

Introducing a Mediterranean design style may not be compatible with the surrounding architecture. If your courtyard is enclosed by something other than plain, rendered walls, you can achieve the right style of backdrop by employing different camouflage techniques and decorative treatments.

Above: *This grey stone wall is enlivened by the blue door and pots with pelargoniums.*

Paint Effects

Thick, textured masonry paint camouflages uneven walls that may be made up of combinations of brickwork, building blocks or patches of rendering. This can be spray-painted for speed, using a proprietary spray kit for masonry paint, or painted with a roller. If the courtyard is surrounded by high walls, you only need to paint to just above the ground floor windows and doors. This helps to define the courtyard space.

Though houses in hot, sunny regions frequently use white, in cool, wet climates this quickly discolours and looks too cold and stark under grey skies. Consider white with a touch of pink, green, pearl grey or sky blue, or choose authentic colours, such as terracotta or an evocative Moorish blue. Adjacent walls could be painted in

different hues and you could confine a more strident shade to just one wall, almost like a huge outdoor canvas.

Above: *Dusty terracotta wall tints, looking like aged plaster, provide a mellow and relaxing backdrop to this Mediterranean-style courtyard.*

Rendered Walls

For a backdrop, hide brickwork or breeze (cinder) blocks using a coat of cement render. Block walls can be given character by incorporating scattered pieces of rough stonework, a carved neo-classical corbel or a terracotta wall mask, or by creating niches and alcoves for candles and oil lamps. Work the rendering so the features blend in.

Left: *For a more rustic, weathered look, consider using wood stains rather than paints for woodwork.*

Right: *Use colour to emphasize contrast between inner and outer walls.*

CREATING A DUSTY TERRACOTTA WALL

On a plain rendered wall you can mimic the appearance of weathered plaster and create a more aged and established-looking backdrop for your courtyard. This effect combines well with more rustic paving treatments, plain terracotta pots and elegant wirework furniture.

While the example here shows soft brown and orange shades, you can also try blending blues and greens with touches of copper and bronze for a verdigris effect. Alternatively, roughly apply a deep blue or maroon red over a paler base coat.

1 Ensure that the rendered wall is sound. Remove any flaking paint and clean off cobwebs and grime. If necessary, seal the surface with a solution of PVA glue and allow it to dry before applying a white base coat. Paint over with a light terracotta-coloured emulsion.

2 Mix some darker coloured terracotta into the paint already in the tray, such as artist's acrylic or paint from a paint tester pot. Dab it on lightly with a piece of natural sponge to give a mottled effect.

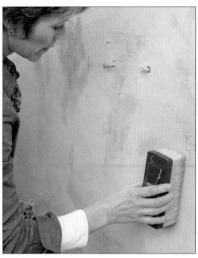

3 Work the darker colour or colours over a larger area of the wall, softening and spreading the emulsion in a circular motion using a wallpaper pasting brush, a decorating brush, or a sponge as shown here.

4 Apply white emulsion or artist's acrylic randomly using a small paintbrush. Roll the brush in contact with the wall, drag it downwards or just touch the wall with the tip of the bristles.

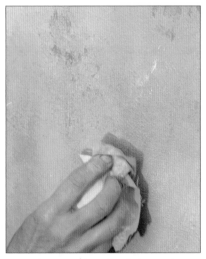

5 Continue to soften the darker and lighter shades using a rag or cloth to dab off excess or to add in colour. The white paint mimics salts that work their way to the surface. Once dry, weatherproof the wall using an exterior matt varnish. The different tones create texture, making the surface appear uneven and aged.

6 This backdrop is perfect for the mellow mood of a Mediterranean courtyard and makes a more suitable surface for displaying rustic ornaments, such as this ironwork candle lantern or a filigree Moorish screen.

Treillage for Flower-filled Walls

This style of decorative trelliswork, already mentioned in the Traditional Lines chapter (see page 36), can also be a feature in Mediterranean courtyards. The look is achieved using treillage panels carrying many small wall pots overflowing with flowers and foliage. Treillage panels can also break up the overly dominant impact of red- or buff-coloured brick walls and offer a stylish and relatively inexpensive makeover. Choose square or more ornate diamond trellis patterns, either with plain or curved tops to suit the mood. Fixing fence posts in between each panel creates the illusion that the trellis is freestanding and sets up a visual rhythm.

Screw the trellis to a framework of horizontal battens, as shown on page 19 (leave a gap behind the panels, allowing room for climbers and wall shrubs). Consider painting the trellis a pale or vibrant colour to contrast with the brickwork and to bring the focus forward and away from the wall. You can strengthen the effect further by painting the wall behind using a light-reflecting shade of masonry paint.

Above: *Once a wall fountain, this window-shaped niche, bordered with decorative tiles and overflowing with pink pot geraniums, creates a strong focal point.*

Above: *This blue diamond trellis provides a framework for numerous wall pots.*

Above: *Paint walls to complement the colour of climbers such as this bougainvillea.*

Above: *Grow heat-loving alpines and drought-tolerant succulents in dry stone walls.*

Right: *Choose geraniums and other drought-tolerant patio plants with brightly coloured blooms for wall-planting schemes.*

Living Camouflage

Fixed wooden trellis panels or a framework of horizontal and vertical galvanized wire stretched between vine eyes for support (see method on page 18), allow you to camouflage walls with foliage and flower. Lush, fast-growing climbers for a sunny courtyard include passion flower (*Passiflora caerulea*), flame-coloured Chilean glory vine (*Eccremocarpus scaber*) or the white- or purple-flowered potato vines (*Solanum*). The evergreen *Clematis armandii*, with almond-scented, late-spring blooms and glossy leaves, looks suitably exotic, and jasmine and honeysuckle conjure images of sultry nights. Honeysuckle thrives in shade and works well with the self-clinging climbing hydrangea (*Hydrangea anomala* subsp. *petiolaris*) and cream variegated Algerian ivy (*Hedera canariensis* 'Gloire de Marengo').

Wall shrubs also contribute to the courtyard scene, especially when clipped to shape and tied in to stop them encroaching. The evergreen, honey-scented *Viburnum tinus* 'Eve

Above: *Reed or bamboo panels create a backdrop for a productive area.*

Price' flowers all winter and into spring. Clip as a half cone. For variegated leaves and a neat, rounded habit grow *Pittosporum tenuifolium* 'Abbotsbury Gold' or 'Silver Princess' and, tolerant of cooler conditions, *Rhamnus alaternus* 'Argenteovariegata'.

Creating Boundaries

The cost of a new brick or stone boundary wall might be prohibitive, but you can make relatively inexpensive walls from concrete building, or breeze (cinder) blocks. To integrate them, render the surface and paint it. Consider adding an appropriate coping stone or tile. Use a pitched topping of reclaimed terracotta pantiles, or a flat slate or reproduction terracotta-effect paving slab. If possible, work in architectural details such as buttressing and narrow window slots for interest.

Standard wooden fencing, especially when it is a mix of different styles, needs camouflaging in a Mediterranean courtyard with a uniform material, such as bamboo or reed fencing. This is available in rolls ready to attach to the fencing support behind using a heavy-duty staple gun. To create divisions within the courtyard – for an intimate dining area, for example – use the same materials ready-made into panels or trellis. Lightweight screens should only need an 8cm (3in) post. Fix the post into a metal socket for ease of replacement or when dealing with a concrete floor. Alternatively, consider using troughs with trellis attached to the back so that you can combine plants and introduce vibrant colour and fragrance. You can move these screen troughs around with ease if you attach castors to the bases.

PLANTS AND CONTAINERS FOR MEDITERRANEAN SPACES

Without doubt, the two most important elements in creating a Mediterranean courtyard are the plants and the pots you put them in. Terracotta is a signature material of the region, and plant species linked with an almost frost-free climate, such as grapevine, citrus, palms and succulents, define the look.

Above: *This large Cretan jar makes a dramatic focal point.*

Mediterranean-style Pots

Terracotta in all its forms is ideal for the Mediterranean-style courtyard. Look for containers marked with a frost-proof guarantee, rather than those described as 'frost resistant'. Good-quality pots are made from different kinds of clay and are fired at a higher temperature. Avoid pots with any obvious cracks or flaking. Gently knock the container with your knuckles and listen for a bell-like ringing tone. If you hear a dull thud, there may be a hairline crack. To conserve moisture loss, for plants other than those requiring sharp drainage, such as succulents, line terracotta pots with thin plastic, keeping the drainage hole uncovered. Matching pot feet raise the container, creating a more elegant appearance and improving drainage.

Above: *Recycled containers can be used for planters, as this hand-painted cistern shows, filled with zonal pelargoniums, pinks and trailing nepeta.*

Above: *An amphora in a metal stand becomes a planter for a pink begonia.*

You may need to protect ornately decorated terracotta and pots that are not guaranteed as frostproof through winter; wrap them in situ with plastic bubble wrap, greenhouse insulation fleece or with hessian stuffed with straw. Otherwise, move the pots to a frost-free position.

Simple, traditionally shaped pots can be combined with ease and will fit in with most schemes. The pale, dusty white patina of some is particularly suggestive of hot, dry gardens, but the shape and surface design make some pots more suited to Mediterranean settings. Ribbed olive jars (*pithoi*) taper to a narrow opening and are often impractical for planting – although their large size works well to 'anchor' a collection of

smaller pots or you can also convert one into a water feature. Amphorae have rounded bases and handles and are usually displayed in a metal stand, although you can lay them on the ground and plant them with succulents seeming to pour out of their mouth. Both of these pot types work well in Greco-Roman, Moorish or Greek island-style settings. For a garden with influences from the Italian Renaissance or the Riviera, add a few more ornately decorated pots and planters, urns and vases. While in more rustic gardens, a

Above: *Plain terracotta pots and planters house a large cineraria (Senecio cineraria) in a signature pot and zonal pelargoniums.*

jumbled collection of cheaper containers, such as old olive oil cans, is often seen clustered together and painted in the same sky blue or peppermint as the doors and shutters.

Succulents and Cacti

While you may garden in cool temperate or maritime climes with plentiful rainfall, incorporating some drought-adapted plants will help to create the illusion of dry heat in your courtyard. Plants that can stay out all year include house leeks, or *Sempervivum,* and the similar looking *Jovibarba.* Both are called hen and chicks because of their creeping colonies, the parent plant being surrounded by the smaller offsets. Grow them in shallow pots filled with sharply draining compost (soil mix) or work them into paving and wall cracks and crevices.

Most creeping alpine sedum or stonecrop species and cultivars are also hardy and evergreen if they are given good drainage. Plants such as the dusty blue-white *Sedum* 'Cape Blanco' and the deep purple-red

Above: Sempervivum *(house leeks) make a fine collection for a ceramic trough.*

Sedum spurium 'Red Carpet' add to the colour palette. If you are looking to enhance your green credentials, any of these types of plant can also be used to create living roof coverings for sheds and other garden buildings.

PLANTING AN AGAVE

Succulents, such as this sculptural *Agave americana*, make wonderful pot specimens, but they need a special planting method to keep them healthy. Good drainage is critical. Plants can remain in their pots for several years as they don't mind being pot bound, but during the summer months they will benefit from regular watering and feeding.

In winter, drastically reduce watering and move the plant under cover, standing in a bright, frost-free place such as an unheated conservatory. Or if that's not possible, move to the shelter of overhanging evergreens or to the base of a sunny wall, where plants will be protected from frost and kept relatively dry.

1 The terracotta jar has a Spanish or Moorish feel but its narrow neck means that it will have to be broken when the agave needs to be extracted for repotting. Place a crock or a stone over the drainage hole to prevent the compost (soil mix) from blocking it.

2 Mix ordinary soil-based potting compost with a quantity of horticultural grit to ensure good drainage. Overly wet soil can cause the roots to rot and sharp drainage helps plants survive when winter temperatures fall.

3 Add some of the mixture to the pot and try the plant for size. The soil surface should sit a little below the pot rim to allow for watering. Work in more potting mix to fill gaps around the root-ball (roots). Firm the compost lightly. Water well. Stand the pot on 'feet' to ensure free drainage.

Other Succulent Options

A surprisingly diverse range of succulents survives year round within the sheltered environs of a townhouse or sunny walled courtyard, especially if pots are kept virtually dry through winter. Try the beautifully sculpted rosettes of *Echeveria* and *Hawarthia* as well as gasterias, crassulas and Aloe species and cultivars. The latter often have vibrant orange or salmon-pink flower spires.

Architectural succulents that make eye-catching pot specimens, but which will almost certainly need overwintering in a conservatory, are the century plant *Agave americana* (see potting sequence on page 69) and the almost black-leaved *Aeonium* 'Zwartkop'. Also consider the prickly pear cactus *Opuntia*, with its flattened, oval-shaped segments.

Floral Sights and Scents

The wild Mediterranean landscape gives off a pungent cocktail of aromatic oils and you can pick out the different scents from pine trees as well as carpeting herbs and shrubs, such as artemisia, thyme, oregano,

Above: *An impressive row of potted* Agave *tops this courtyard wall, adding a distinctly sub-tropical feel.*

sage, rosemary, lavender, Cistus (rock rose) and *Phlomis fruticosa* (Jerusalem sage). Use variegated and coloured-leaf herbs as a foil for flowering plants wherever possible and be sure to site lavender, rosemary and the tender wall shrub lemon verbena (*Aloysia triphylla*) close to doorways and sitting areas, where a cloud of fragrance will be released every time the foliage is brushed past. Similarly work in the fruity-scented chamomile, pungent thymes and Corsican mint into paving cracks.

As well as the evening-scented jasmine, honeysuckle and four o'clock plant, or marvel of Peru (*Mirabilis jalapa*), try using wisteria over archways and pergolas so that its fragrant blooms hang down just above head height. Climbing roses would also be in keeping.

A riot of colourful flowering plants grown in pots is typical of Mediterranean courtyards. Include classics such as pelargoniums and decorate patios with marguerite daisies, osteospermums, mop-head hydrangeas, lilies and flame-coloured gazania and arctotis. Australasian flowering shrubs are increasingly popular, ranging from *Callistemon* (bottle brush) to more unusual plants, such as *Metrosideros*

and *Grevillea*. With a conservatory you can more easily overwinter tender and borderline hardy shrubs and tuberous rooted plants such as the velvet purple *Tibouchina semidecandra*, fragrant angel's trumpets (*Brugmansia*) and Indian shot (*Canna*).

Above: *Herbs and sun-loving aromatic plants, such as lavender and Moroccan mint, add a touch of the wild Mediterranean.*

Above: *A large terracotta pot, lined with plastic, can house permanent plantings such as a vine or bay standard.*

TRAINING A GRAPEVINE

The vine shown growing in an Italianate terracotta pot on the opposite page (below right) has been trained in a version of the single-curtain system. Its support is the stout pier of the loggia and the horizontal branches run just under the roofline. When the vine fruits, bunches of grapes will hang down. Use a John Innes soil-based potting compost (soil mix) with added well-rotted manure as the plant will be in position for several years.

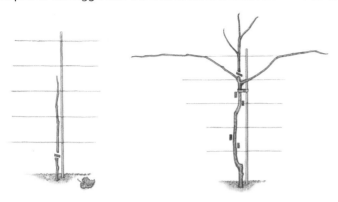 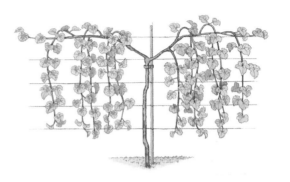

1 Start with a one-year-old vine planted in winter and cut through the leader about 15cm (6in) above the ground.
In summer, tie in the new leader as it develops. In the following winter, cut back the leader again, this time removing half of the previous year's growth. Tie in the leader as it develops and continue this process until you reach the desired height.

2 In the third year during mid-winter, remove all the laterals (side shoots) on the main stem except for the two positioned just below the wire support. Bend these out and tie them in to the horizontal wires. In the summer, side shoots on these two main laterals will develop and hang down, to form the characteristic hanging vine shape.

3 Allow the hanging shoots to develop every 30cm (12in). Pinch out the side shoots. Prune established plants in winter, cutting back all the hanging shoots to one or two upward-facing buds and allowing one shoot to develop on the previous year's spurs. Thin bunches of grapes for bigger fruits.

Sculptural Highlights

Palms, such as the hardy Chusan fan palm, *Trachycarpus fortunei*, and borderline hardy Mediterranean fan palm, *Chamaerops humilis,* add real drama with their large, exotic-looking leaves. Tree ferns produce a similar look in shady corners, especially when the 'trunk' is well developed.

For a leafy fountain effect, grow the cabbage palm *(Cordyline australis).* The plain-leaved version is remarkably hardy given good winter drainage and eventually forms a small tree. This familiar patio pot plant comes in purple shaded or variegated leaf forms, which can survive year to year given virtually frost-free conditions. A tougher choice for more exposed gardens is the New Zealand flax (*Phormium tenax*). This produces bold tufts of strap-shaped leaves and is not fussy about soil. There are scores of purple, yellow, copper pink and variegated forms, but these are not as tough as the species – although they do make spectacular potted specimens. The spear-shaped leaves of yuccas also catch the eye, especially bold-yellow variegated forms, such as *Yucca gloriosa* 'Variegata' and *Y. filamentosa* 'Bright Edge'.

Above: *Spiky* Cordyline australis *adds bold vertical accents to this 'hot' border.*

Above: *For living sculpture try the impressive flower spike of* Yucca gloriosa.

STRUCTURES AND FURNITURE FOR MEDITERRANEAN SPACES

The relaxed Mediterranean lifestyle revolves around sitting, eating and cooking alfresco, and structures such as pergolas and loggias are essential additions. Most courtyards are simply furnished. Add plain wooden seats and create a focus with a mosaic- or marble-topped table to help set the mood.

Above: *Create a casual style with mismatched furniture and fabrics.*

Left: *The eye-catching blue and terracotta walls of this pergola-shaded seating area, coupled with architectural plantings, creates a wonderful Mediterrancean ambience.*

Above: *This pergola, entwined with a well-established wisteria, provides welcome shade on a sunny Mediterranean terrace.*

Shade from the Sun

While not exclusive to the Mediterranean garden, pergolas fit beautifully with the style and give welcome shade in a sunny courtyard in which to sit and relax. Freestanding or attached to a wall, a timber pergola could be covered with inexpensive reed matting during the summer to give instant dappled shade. Remove it towards the end of the year to allow more light in, vital in cooler, cloudier regions. For the same reason, it is advisable to plant with deciduous climbers, such as grapevines, rambler roses, wisteria, potato vine and jasmine.

You can buy straightforward kits from garden centres and home-improvement stores but consider using reclaimed wood for rustic appeal. On existing concrete floors fix pergola posts by bolting on metal sockets (see method page 185). Avoid ornate trellis additions and make sure there is sufficient head height once climbers have grown, otherwise pergolas can feel claustrophobic. Starting with a 2.5m (8ft) clearance usually gives enough room for the foliage. Heavy uprights, including those made from natural stone or rendered blocks, and weighty cross beams give a feeling of robustness to the structure.

The Italian loggia – an open-fronted roofed area built against a wall – provides an all-weather spot from which to enjoy the garden. Covering the slanting roof with weathered terracotta pantiles and using uprights made from reclaimed oak or hardwood beams creates the illusion of age. Consider painting the interior wall white or a pale pastel shade to reflect the light and lay decorative tiles or perhaps cobbles on the floor.

Some courtyards are large enough to accommodate a small timber summerhouse, especially one designed for a corner position. Again, replacing a plain roofing felt covering with terracotta tiles helps the building look more authentic. Select a timber stain or exterior quality paint to evoke a Mediterranean mood, such as

cornflower blue, a good background shade for terracotta. Buildings such as this could house and camouflage a spa pool, where the more usual Nordic design log cabin would feel out of place.

An off-the-peg wooden shed might not look ideal in your Mediterranean courtyard, but storage space in small gardens is often a problem. You could build a concrete-block lean-to with rendered walls, a reclaimed wooden door and a roof planted with succulents. Also build storage compartments into low, rendered walls, using hinged wooden seats for access.

Outdoor Dining

In Mediterranean gardens it is quite common to find a simple charcoal barbecue grate built against a wall, with an adjacent log store, and you could also fit a traditional whitewashed log-fired oven with chimney if space allows. A built-in wall cupboard might house

crockery and glasses, herbs and seasonings, and the low walls of raised beds could be converted to make a casual seating area.

A large, tiled dining table, made from substantial reclaimed timbers or a block of stone, could be left outside all year round. Selected with care, such a table could act as a sculptural focal point. In summer, surround the table with a mismatched collection of kitchen chairs, some with woven wicker seats, to help create the more informal look of a Greek taverna.

Left: *A simple serving and dining area close to the back door encourages alfresco cooking and eating.*

Where space is limited, choose a small, square or circular café-style table with foldaway chairs. Metal-framed tables with mosaic tops are perfect for an Italian- or Moorish-style. You can also find marble-topped tables with heavy cast-iron bases.

Wirework tables and chairs add a touch of elegance and give character to a period-style courtyard, one that perhaps harks back to Edwardian times. Weathered Lloyd Loom armchairs also work well surrounded by lush, potted foliage and flowers. Ornate, black, wrought ironwork is reminiscent of Venetian houses and dining suites with glass-topped tables are perfect for more sophisticated Mediterranean settings. Avoid standing ironwork on paving or you risk rust stains appearing.

Wood is warm to the touch, unlike metal, and whether you are perched on a Moroccan-carved stool sipping mint tea or stretched out on a vintage-style steamer chair you can appreciate its natural beauty. Wooden furniture varies in style from a rough-hewn bench made from driftwood to a classic hardwood table and chairs set, complete with colonial-style canvas sunshade. Tropical or temperate hardwood,

sourced from sustainable plantations, is very durable, but for a greener alternative look locally for furniture made from reclaimed materials. In Mediterranean regions you will often see household furniture, such as a farmhouse-style kitchen table, used outdoors and it is possible to find furniture like this second-hand.

Wicker or cane pieces are not weatherproof, but could be used in a summerhouse or loggia. If you like

Above: *The combination of mosaic tiling on the table surface and scrolled wrought iron work adds a flavour of Italy to this courtyard dining space.*

the informal look of wicker, painted or natural, consider wicker substitutes made from UV-stabilized acrylic. Cheaper designs are coated with colour and can start to show wear: more expensive models are coloured throughout.

Above: *This simple mosaic tabletop features a blue themed geometric design.*

Above: *A serene space, covered in dappled shade from the vine-covered pergola, has been created with a stone table and bench suite and a decorative tiled floor.*

HOW TO MAKE A MOSAIC TABLE-TOP

The combination of Mediterranean colours and the simple design of this mosaic table creates a striking piece of furniture. Made from 13mm- (½in-) thick marine or exterior-grade plywood, the table can be used outdoors in good weather, but you will need to bring it inside during sustained rainy periods and for the winter. As an alternative to this simple floral design you could create more abstract patterns without using a template. For example, you could sketch a series of waves going across a square or oblong table-top or simply build up a series of concentric rings, varying in width, using the different shades for contrast.

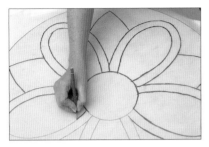

1 Mark out the table circumference using a piece of string tied to a drawing pin at the centre of the plywood and a pencil at the other. Cut out with a jigsaw. Trace your chosen design on to tracing paper, going over the lines thickly with a soft pencil.

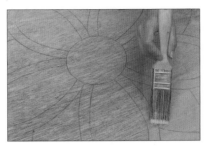

2 Turn the tracing paper on top of the plywood so that the pencil lines are facing down. Line up the template with the centre and rub over the lines with a pencil to transfer the pattern. Seal the board, including the rim, with diluted PVA glue.

3 Using tile nippers, and wearing goggles, cut the glass mosaic tiles into halves and thirds so that you have a variety of different widths. Make a small pile of each of the colours. Save some whole tiles to nibble into different sizes and shapes later.

4 Mix up waterproof tile adhesive and, using a flexible knife, spread it over one area of the design at a time, approximately 3mm (⅛in) thick. Select shards in four colours, pressing them into the adhesive. Leave a small gap between pieces.

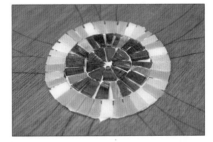

5 Prepare the next area for tiling, wiping off any adhesive spillages immediately. Fill in the area inside the ring with two colours of the mosaic pieces. In order to achieve a neat finish in the design, nibble the tiles into wedge shapes.

6 Following the same technique, begin to fill out the rounded petals. Outline the petals first with a rim of tile shards and then begin infilling. For this element of the design use the paler tiles. Nibble shards to fit the gaps neatly.

7 Begin filling in the pointed petals with darker contrasting tile shards. Fill the gaps in between the petals and table edge as well as the rim with the palest shades and leave it to dry for a day.

8 Wearing rubber gloves, mix up the grout in a bucket. Work the grout into all the gaps between the mosaic pieces using a tiler's spreader. Wipe over the table top and rim with a damp sponge to remove excess grout. Finally, polish with a soft, dry cloth.

9 When dry, turn the table-top over and spread the base with PVA glue. Allow it to dry. Mix up tile adhesive and spread it over the base evenly to seal it. Once dry, attach the table top to a metal table base frame using screws.

ORNAMENT AND WATER FEATURES FOR MEDITERRANEAN SPACES

In Mediterranean gardens, decoration and ornament are often provided by structural elements – mosaic floors, ironwork grilles and painted shutters, as well as smaller household pieces. Pots and planters, furniture or light fittings also play a decorative role and rills, raised pools and fountains create eye-catching flourishes.

Above: *A simple water carrier provides a pleasing poolside focus.*

Moorish Influence

There are numerous elements with subtle or overt references to the Moorish style: rendered walls painted to create a worn terracotta feel; a distinctive arched doorway or wall aperture; a carved wooden screen; or an ornate tile panel. Water features might include a formal rill, a carved marble or resin reproduction fountain or a mosaic pool. The latter can be decorated simply using mosaic sheets applied to a concrete base with waterproof tiling grout (waterproof as well as frost resistant). The individual square tiles, or tesserae, are held together by a mesh. You just need to work the grout into the gaps with a grouting tool and wipe the excess off.

Additional touches come in the choice of furniture, planters, fabrics and lighting. Consider a Moroccan hexagonal table made from intricately carved wood with matching stools; a large engraved brass water carrier or wall mounted tray; Moroccan metal lanterns and richly coloured cushions and throws.

Typical Decorative Features

Mediterranean gardens are full of pots and planters, and these provide numerous opportunities for decoration. Used sparingly, large pithoi and amphora, terracotta vases and jars act as simple focal points. Even broken pots look the part when their remains are colonized with encrusting succulents.

As well as painting walls to create a distressed look, you could stencil a design, such as the tile motif shown on page 85. Rubbing over parts of the painted areas with sandpaper creates an appropriately weathered effect.

You can also hang wall plaques to enhance your chosen style, including terracotta or metalwork sun emblems, which work well in simple and more rustic-looking whitewashed courtyards. Wrought-iron grilles aged by rusting can be purchased from garden centres. Set these in small window apertures knocked through the boundary walls or set them above a garden gate. Alternatively, fix a grille to a wall using a mirror behind to create the illusion of light streaming through. Finish by planting a colourful window box or wall planter beneath.

Neo-classical wall masks and terracotta friezes would suit an Italian-style courtyard and you could also set a small statue, bust or oil lamp in a wall niche or on a carved stone corbel cemented on to the wall.

Above: *A wall niche raises the profile of smaller decorative objects.*

Above: *Look out for salvaged ironwork pieces that can be integrated.*

Above: *Quirky mosaic wall art feels perfectly at home in a relaxed courtyard.*

CREATING AN OVERFLOWING URN

Self-contained water features, such as this bubbling urn, are ideal for small gardens where there is insufficient space for a pool. They are child-friendly and because the pump is low voltage, running off a transformer, they are safe to install. A project such as this could be completed in just a few hours.

1 Select a suitably styled terracotta pot that fits in with your courtyard. Apply several coats of diluted PVA sealant inside and out. This will frost-proof the urn and also allow the water to flow over the sides more evenly.

2 The urn has been sited in a raised bed. Raising a feature above ground level makes it more prominent. If the courtyard has a concrete base, you may have to build up around the feature rather than digging down. Dig out most of the soil.

3 Remove sharp stones, line the hole with pond or carpet underlay and cover with an off-cut of butyl rubber pond liner. Fold a piece of underlay or liner to cushion the pile of bricks that will support the urn. Cement these together.

4 Ensure that the bricks are level using a small spirit level and cover the hole with galvanized mesh. Overlap the edges to provide maximum support. Using wire cutters, snip a hole in the mesh to accommodate the submersible pump.

5 Put the pump into the cistern, feeding the wire up through the mesh at the back of the bed. Plug the pump into a transformer situated in a waterproof housing or inside a building. Check all connections with a qualified electrician.

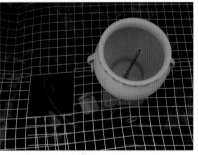

6 Drill a drainage hole in the urn to accommodate a 10mm (½in) water-tank coupler. Or, fix a rigid 10mm (½in) copper delivery tube in the urn, cutting it level with the rim of the pot. Seal the junction with the flexible pipe.

7 You can dismantle a water-tank coupler without breaking the watertight seal. Place the urn on the brick plinth, feeding the flexible tube through the slot in the top and down through the gaps to hold it in place. Connect it to the pump outlet.

8 Fill the reservoir and use the pump outlet adjuster to moderate the flow through the copper pipe. Turn down the jet so that it bubbles slightly above the water's surface. Cover the mesh with landscape membrane to filter out debris. Camouflage with cobbles.

LIGHTING FOR MEDITERRANEAN SPACES

It can be a relaxing ritual in the sheltered confines of a courtyard to light all the tea lights and candles as day turns to night. The flickering light of candle lanterns and oil lamps creates the authentic ambience of a Mediterranean-style courtyard. For convenience and safety, think about suitable electric lights.

Above: *White fairy lights shine through a coloured glass fish.*

Left: *Verdigris-coloured coach lamps provide general lighting for the terrace while pendant uplighters illuminate the climbers.*

Lighting Ideas

Your choice of light depends on what you are trying to create: a shady oasis, like that found in the centre of a traditional Marrakech home; a simple Greek island-style courtyard or the sophisticated elegance of the terrace of an Italian villa.

To add a chic feel to a courtyard with plain rendered walls and simple floor tiles, try placing shallow, jewel-coloured glass tea-light holders in wall niches and on ledges or around the rim of a raised pool. Similar coloured-glass jar candle lanterns with simple wire handles allow you to hang lights from a pergola or tree branches. And for a starlit effect, weave tiny white fairy lights through climbers and wall shrubs covering the walls. Often the simplest ideas are the most contemporary in effect. Try chunky beeswax or church candles in unadorned terracotta pots. Hold them in place or at the right height with sand, fine gravel or coloured glass chippings and set among the plants or space them evenly along the base of a wall.

Intricately cut brass or silvery coloured metal lanterns are a signature of North Africa. When lit, they throw shadow patterns on to the walls, creating a magical ambience. If you are using traditional-style carved wooden or ironwork furniture, mosaic-topped tables and Moorish tiling details, these will be the perfect finishing touch. You can also buy ceramic lanterns with a similar cutwork design. Simple metallic brass and copper oil and gel lamps suit this style of courtyard, especially ones set in wrought-iron tripod stands or those designed to be hung from chains.

For a creative effect, backlight a decorative ironwork screen or illuminate a wooden treillage panel, hiding the lamp with a foreground of lush foliage plants. Architectural specimens, including palms, phormiums and tree ferns, will throw dramatic shadows on the walls when lit from below or from the side.

Above: *Coloured glass lanterns cast a gentle light and add to the Mediterranean theme.*

SAFETY NOTE

Don't leave naked flames unattended and ensure that lamps and lanterns are positioned safely. They can become hot and should be moved with care.

Wall Lights

The Venetians left an architectural legacy throughout the Mediterranean region, and elegant, black wrought-iron wall lamps with scrolling detail would suit a traditional Italian style courtyard adorned with terracotta pots, clipped bay topiary and potted olive trees. Most are designed for electric lighting, but some wall-mounted candle lanterns reminiscent of the period are also available. Rusting ironwork or weathered copper verdigris effects create an atmosphere of faded elegance and would work with more rustic features and older style properties. Going back to classical times, torch-style ironwork lamps add a touch of theatre, perfect for an outdoor dining room, and there are some surprisingly effective electric versions available. Ironwork candle sconces and candelabras are a luxurious indulgence and they can often be found in designs to match wall lights.

Highlighting Sculpture

Inconspicuous black or brushed-metal minispot uplighters are invaluable for throwing light on to sculptures, pots and water features and should be set into the ground or paving to make them even less

obtrusive. Used with restraint, they can subtly transform the look of the garden at night and make the most of design touches that might fade into the background during the day, especially in shady corners.

Uplighting from the side emphasizes the three-dimensional form of a sculpture to best effect. But a classical bust or wall mask might be more dramatic lit directly from below.

Above: *A net of low energy LEDs mimics light coming through a Moorish fretwork screen.*

Below left: *These curved ironwork lamps echo the Venetian style that is found throughout the Mediterranean.*

Below: *A traditional Moroccan lantern such as this adds the finishing touch to a Moorish courtyard.*

CASE STUDY: TUSCAN HIDEAWAY

With a predominance of terracotta and sepia tones and a design of rustic simplicity, this courtyard brings to mind an old country farmhouse surrounded by olive groves, vineyards and fields of lavender. The walls of the house ensure that half the garden is in shade during the hottest part of the day and in summer the tiled pool surrounded by potted ferns becomes a cooling focus.

Above *The bright foliage of* Houttuynia cordata *smells of Seville oranges.*

Above: *The steps into the courtyard are decorated with clay pots and bright blooms.*

The roughly rendered walls and raised beds of this courtyard have been made from inexpensive breeze (cinder) blocks. The boundary walls are topped with reclaimed clay roof tiles, but plain curved pantiles would give a more informal look. The warm apricot colour wash makes an ideal backdrop for the verdigris-effect table and chair and the blue tiled pool. The same tile motif has been stencilled on to the wall and distressed to create the illusion of age.

Another simple technique is the floor treatment. The mellow gravel, laid on top of well-consolidated hardcore, picks up on the wall colours and makes a satisfying crunching sound underfoot. Exterior-quality floor tiles are laid in a simple grid pattern within the gravel to create textural interest.

Other understated decorative elements include the amphora and box and cotton lavender topiaries in weathered terracotta pots. Architectural planting accents add to the Mediterranean atmosphere and include young olive trees (*Olea europaea*), a variegated yucca, Canary Island date palm (*Phoenix canariensis*), New Zealand phoenix palm (*Phoenix sylvestris*), New Zealand flax (*Phormium tenax*) and a hardy fig. Frost is rare in such city courtyards and gaps in the raised beds have been filled with conservatory plants.

The garden plan overleaf portrays an intimate garden room designed as a relaxing space. It can be accessed from the upper floor by an external stairway and on ground level through French doors, behind the pool, which can be left open in warm weather. The tiled pool, with Moorish colours and patterns, provides a tranquil focus for the garden. No serious gardening is required here, but spare plants, watering cans, weatherproof garden equipment and compost (soil mix) can be hidden behind the screening wall.

Right: *Low walls, capped with old terracotta tiles, form a textural screen around this Mediterranean courtyard.*

CREATING A TUSCAN HIDEAWAY

Flooring:
• *Use beach shingle or flint chippings with contrasting areas of quarry tiles or rough stone slabs.*
• *Consider sandstone paving with inserts of terracotta/clay setts or simple pebble mosaics.*

Walls:
• *Render brick or breeze (cinder) block walls and raised beds and apply a dusty terracotta paint effect.*
• *Cap boundary walls with terracotta pantiles or rugged stone slabs.*

Pots and Containers:
• *Choose plain terracotta pots such as traditional Cretan pots and amphora.*
• *Fix pots to the wall using wire.*

Planting:
• *Select evergreen foundation plants such as slender Italian cypress, sweet bay, yucca, phormium, hardy palms, olive trees and simple topiary forms.*
• *Use drought-tolerant succulents and geraniums in pots.*
• *In the shade, use box,* Fatsia japonica *and ferns.*

• *Raised beds around the walls provide warm, well-drained conditions for herbs, salads and Mediterranean climbers.*

Structures and Furniture:
• *Use simple wood and metal folding furniture for a more rustic feel.*
• *Try mosaic table-tops, painted and distressed wooden furniture, old wirework or wicker chairs.*

Water Features
• *A small raised pool or wall fountain provides cooling relief in summer.*

TUSCAN HIDEAWAY GARDEN PLAN

storage space
for pots and
young plants

wall planter

verdigris
wall mask

wall of house

gravel

steps

site of
wall stencil
(see page 83
and opposite)

Greek-style
amphora

Plant list

1 *Rodgersia aesculifolia*
2 *Osmunda regalis*
3 *Houttuynia* 'Chameleon'
4 *Dryopteris cristata*
5 *Phormium tenax*
6 *Osmanthus x burkwoodii*
7 *Buxus sempervirens* 'Suffruticosa'
8 *Buxus sempervirens*
9 *Leucothoe fontenesiana* 'Rainbow'
10 *Phoenix canariensis*
11 *Olea europaea*
12 *Yucca gloriosa* 'Variegata'
13 *Ficus* 'Brown Turkey'
14 *Colocasia* 'Black Magic'
15 *Thymus* 'Pink Chintz'
16 *Carissa macrophylla*
17 *Santolina chamaecyparissus*
18 *Dryopteris erythrosora*
19 *Pelargonium*

Above: *The soft mellow finish of the low walls provides a subtle background for the planting of smooth, spherical topiary as well as spiky yuccas and phormiums.*

Above *Common box (*Buxus sempervirens*) is closely clipped into a rounded shape.*

Above: *Wild thyme* (Thymus *'Pink Chintz')* *is situated at the base of the olive tree bed.*

Above: *The Royal Fern* (Osmunda regalis) *softens the edges of the pool.*

Above: *Cotton lavender works in a pot, or as ground cover.*

CREATING A RAISED POOL

Installing a pool with raised sides gives prominence to the pool, and allows you to perch on the edge. The one shown here is freestanding but you could build it against a wall and combine it with a waterspout.

1 Mark out the pool. Level and compact the area and dig out a square-shaped trench for the wall footings (30cm/ 12in deep). Add compacted hardcore topped with 20cm (8in) of concrete and level off.
2 Build up the walls of the pool using breeze (cinder) blocks cemented with mortar. Check with a spirit level that the sides are level and perpendicular.
3 Once the walls are done, fill the base with 5cm (2in) of soft sand and tamp down.

4 Use a piece of black butyl rubber pond liner to make a waterproof inner, folding it at the corners and generously overlapping the blocks. Once the water is added the liner will adjust its position.
5 Roughly render the walls of the pool, or apply frostproof tiles using waterproof, exterior-quality tile grout. Keep the flexible liner in place and form a seat by cementing on overlapping coping stones or tiles.

MEDITERRANEAN POOL CROSS-SECTION

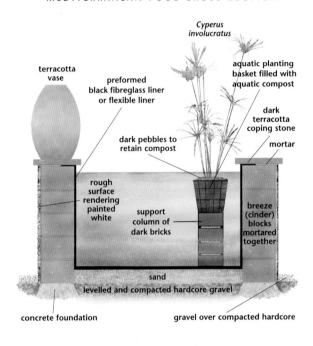

Cyperus involucratus

terracotta vase

preformed black fibreglass liner or flexible liner

aquatic planting basket filled with aquatic compost

dark terracotta coping stone

mortar

dark pebbles to retain compost

rough surface rendering painted white

support column of dark bricks

breeze (cinder) blocks mortared together

sand

levelled and compacted hardcore gravel

concrete foundation

gravel over compacted hardcore

CREATING A WALL STENCIL

Wall tiles were often used to add colour and texture to Moorish courtyard gardens, but it can be difficult to acquire authentic tiles. This technique enables you to recreate the effect purely in paint. A tile design from a magazine was simplified and enlarged and traditional paint colours were softened and distressed to create an aged effect.

1 Transfer a design to oiled manilla stencil card and cut out the sections to be coloured with a craft knife. Include a fine margin to define the tile shape.

2 Fix the stencil to the wall. Use three shades of artist's acrylic paint or stencil paint to stipple the paint on and build up darker shading on the petals.

3 Arrange the tiles to create a random pattern. Line up the stencils so that the same gap is used between each. Remove the stencil.

4 When dry, go over selected tile motifs with fine-grade sandpaper to create an aged effect. Seal using exterior-quality, colourless matt varnish.

OUTDOOR ROOMS

Tailoring an exterior space to work as a personal living space is a halfway house between inside and outside. Treated in this way the courtyard garden is no longer a separate space, but becomes an extension of the home, flowing from it and taking its theme and style from that of the furniture and decoration indoors. It is a place to relax and to entertain, and a green oasis for refuge and escape.

This room can be for pottering or playing, dining or debating. It can display a collection of artworks or be a habitat for wildlife. The theatrical potential of an outdoor room comes to the fore after sundown, when lighting can create an air of mystery and romance. How pleasant on a balmy evening to sit with friends around a candlelit supper table knowing that you can curl up later in a swing-seat under the stars, soothed by the sound of music or water in the background. Eating outside, surrounded by the calm and fragrance of foliage and flowers, is a marvellously simple way to enjoy your garden.

Left: *A bold timber pergola serves to create this intimate dining terrace, defining the space and providing a sense of enclosure without blocking the view to the garden beyond. Wooden furniture reinforces this strong but simple theme.*

OPEN-AIR LIVING

A successfully converted outdoor room will give you extra living space and a new extension to your home. This style of courtyard is not so much a visual statement as a way of maximizing living space. Furniture, cooking areas, beds and spas can all have their place, with the planting providing green furnishings and decoration and the hard landscaping new walls and floors.

Above: *Cushioned faux-cane armchairs entice the visitor to an intimate corner.*

Creating a Refuge

On the one hand, in a densely built urban environment, your space may well be defined by boundary walls, which provide a special sense of intimacy and refuge. On the other, an upper level terrace or balcony can give an exciting opportunity to extend your home, perhaps with an open vista of river or landscape. Without the benefit of either – a built enclosure or marvellous views – a simple screen of luxuriant foliage, perhaps in the form of a bamboo hedge or climber-covered screen, can create a personal corner in which to escape with a book.

Surrounding walls provide an excellent opportunity to set a special background theme. The restricted nature of the area allows you to indulge in bold colour statements that would otherwise be overwhelming in a larger garden

Above: *This lightweight aluminium and cane chair provides a shady spot for snoozing.*

space. Walls provide an excellent background from which to display a collection of sculpture or other artefacts. The exotic foliage forms of palm trees and ferns are strikingly thrown into relief against a colour-tinted wall, with lighting available to develop the effect at night.

The garden room becomes a real-life stage set that you can dress in the evening with candles and electric luminaires. Trees become shadowy forms and white flowers gleam eerily, while under-lit water develops a magnified depth and the noise of a fountain takes on a new vibrancy.

Function and Style

The theatrical possibilities provided by an outdoor room give you ample scope to create a special theme for a party or event. Formal, or romantic, let your guests explore the moonlit terrace studded with tiny uplighters set among tall vases of perfumed lilies and play soft music through a sound system of speakers set into the ground. A tented canopy furnished with huge cushions makes an exotic place to relax, especially when it is filled with pots of heavily scented flowers, such as jasmine and gardenia.

If by night the courtyard is all soft lighting and shadows, by day it is brought into focus by clear light and solid form. Colour and texture are now the key, with bright climbers adorning the walls and flowers spilling from containers. Early breakfast takes on a new dimension

when accompanied by birdsong, while later on a vine-covered pergola can shade a simple lunch.

Furniture plays an important role in the outdoor room, both in function and style, and it should reinforce your overall decorating theme. If your taste is for the contemporary, with sleek Italian seating and similarly gleaming kitchen, then your courtyard garden should reflect this. Clean-lined furniture will suitably echo your high-tech interior. Dining outside is a prime function, so lightweight aluminium dining chairs are practical – especially when upholstered in attractively understated nylon mesh fabric, making a perfect modern combination with a slate-topped table. Alternatively, generous cane armchairs and loungers are ideal for relaxing.

Hard-landscaping materials play an important role in creating the structure and should also reinforce the design style. Pale, smooth, sawn limestone combines with deep-toned slate for paving and steps, or fountains and pools. An understated planting scheme, based on foliage form, would complement this well. Slender, swaying grasses, New Zealand flax with its narrow blade-like foliage, interspersed with mauve clusters of *Verbena bonariensis* all contribute to a sense of light airiness.

Right: *Narrow timber slats create side screens and a canopy as an enclosure for this elegantly coordinated, modern roof terrace.*

FLOORING FOR OUTDOOR ROOMS

Galvanizing the overall 'look' of a space depends enormously on the flooring. This is the controlling factor in delineating space and also for creating colour, texture and mood. Although at first it may seem that the inside and outside are really separate spaces, in fact it is possible to make a truly fluid transition between the two.

Above: *A dramatic flooring feature made from curved sections of exotic hardwood.*

Choosing Materials

There are many materials suitable for exterior paving – wooden decking, natural stone, brick, fabricated slabs or gravel. Suitability for purpose should always be of paramount importance. Weight may be a consideration, especially with a roof terrace or balcony. Ease of access and portability are also important when building materials have to be taken through the house.

Wooden Floors

The first consideration when selecting flooring material is how to continue the textural theme of your interior. Wooden floors, currently a popular choice for interiors, can easily be made to float naturally through to the exterior, extending that warm ambience that works so well with a naturalistic planting scheme. The transition does require the use of an appropriate timber, one that will withstand the extremes of weather conditions, including rain, sun and frost.

Hardwoods are extremely durable and beautiful, requiring minimum maintenance. Tropical timbers, such as teak and iroko, are at the high end of quality and price, the former having a smooth, long-grained texture. In the case of all hardwoods check the supplies come from sustainable sources. Oak is an excellent choice, although it must be well seasoned to remove tannins that can stain surrounding materials. Hardwoods may be sealed with a varnish, giving them a deeper tone, or left to age to a sober, silvery grey.

Softwoods are well priced, but less durable. They must be pressure treated with a preservative, but even then have a tendency to distort and twist away from fixings.

There are economic, practical alternatives to hardwoods: Western red cedar and (to a lesser degree) Southern yellow pine have a natural durability, due to their rot-resisting resins, as well as an innate structural strength.

Timber becomes very slippery in regions of high rainfall so should be brushed and jet washed regularly to remove algae. Ribbed surface finishes are available to reduce the problem.

Wooden decking has increased in popularity, but it has too often been chosen as a cheap shortcut. This has been to the detriment of many spaces that would have been better served by traditional hard landscaping. Decking does fulfil certain requirements supremely well: it is useful when building raised areas to introduce changes of level and for transitions between different types of materials; and it makes an excellent pathway alongside water and through areas of natural planting.

Above: *A raised timber dining plinth gives focus and interest to a small terrace.*

Above: *A steep descent of steps with sawn timber is enclosed by retaining walls.*

Above: *Decking panels provide an easy way to cover up an unsightly solid floor.*

MAKING SIMPLE DECKING

You can find all the elements for creating a simple deck at larger DIY stores, including pre-cut, interlocking joists. Use pressure-treated timber supports and raise them off the ground to prevent rot. The simplest decks require minimal cutting. Consider the length of decking planks and avoid designs with multiple angles or curves.

1 Consolidate the area, and position concrete blocks or beams to support bearers. Set these on concrete foundations (on soft ground) ensuring they are level.

2 Treat cut ends with preservative. Use landscape membrane to prevent weeds as shown. Drill and screw the framework together at 40cm (16in) intervals.

3 Lay the decking boards across the joists. Secure with galvanized nails. Leave a gap of 6mm ($^1/_4$in) between boards for drainage and to allow wood to swell.

DECKING PATTERNS

Decking boards can be laid in a wide variety of patterns, (a) being the most simple. Prefabricated deck squares (b) are easy to lay (see also picture opposite). Designs on the diagonal are dynamic and include the chevron pattern (c) which is one of the more contemporary in effect, (d) a simpler version that can effectively 'point' like an arrow to a focal point, and (e), still stylish but within the capabilities of most enthusiastic amateurs. Design (f) is static and creates a calm atmosphere. If you want more texture, try the simple-to-lay interlocking design (g) or, for real flair, the diagonally cut version (h). Use recessed deck lights to emphasize deck patterns.

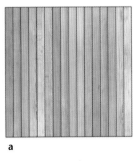

a

b

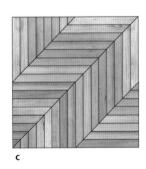

c

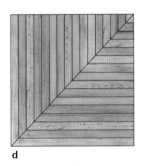

d

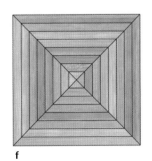

e

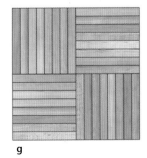

f

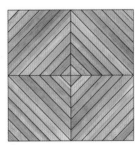

g

h

Left: *A soft and sinuous design is achieved with curvaceously cut, pale stone paving. Loops of darker stone provide relief detail.*

plain tiling can also be broken up using edging and details in a contrasting yet sympathetic material. Marble slips would be ideal for this as they are normally too fragile to be used outside as a walking surface. Tiles are available in a kaleidoscope of beautiful colours, making them ideal for intricate mosaic features. These make excellent focal points to enliven a neutral surface area or they can be used as border details to edge or highlight a path.

Natural stone is a popular choice for interior floor surfaces, especially in kitchens where its tactile qualities add to the creative environment. Pale limestone produces a restrained elegance, and this can be continued through to a terrace, reinforcing the cool and understated style. Slate, which, depending on its source, can be found in subtle, mossy tones and sober greys, provides a similarly restrained effect. Both have a contemporary, minimalist appearance when saw-cut and smoothly finished.

Linking Spaces

Kitchen and service areas are often the transition point to the garden and so provide a good place from which to develop your decorating scheme and extend into the outdoor room. For practical reasons, outdoor flooring materials may have to be adjusted, but the colour and texture can be carried through to make the passage appear seamless.

Tiling and Paving

A popular floor finish for kitchens, tiles are available in both ceramic and terracotta versions. However, it is essential that exterior flooring is weatherproof and, most importantly in the case of tiles, frost resistant. Natural terracotta works well indoors but tends to be porous and ceramic tiles are usually quite thin. High-fired exterior ceramic tiles can echo a Mediterranean or rustic look, and they have the advantage that out of doors they will not absorb water. Therefore, they will be less susceptible to damage caused by

freezing and subsequent thawing. Outdoor floor tiles must also be slip resistant, so always check this with the supplier before ordering.

Tiling over a large area can look hard and somewhat monotonous, so it is a good idea to create an interesting tile pattern. Areas of

Above: *A raised timber plinth creates a gentle transition from this garden bath house.*

Above: *Informal stone slabs surrounded by aromatic herbs makes an intriguing footway.*

Paving slabs manufactured from concrete are available in a wide variety of shapes, colours and textures, some echoing classical *trompe l'oeil* flooring designs. These can work well with traditional buildings and are considerably cheaper than natural materials.

Brick Floors

A popular construction material for centuries, brick is becoming more widely used as a facing material. With this style of building, brick pavers would make a sympathetic contribution to a flooring design. Pavers are versatile, and being small in size they can be laid in a variety of patterns (see also page 122). Brick can be used as an accent detail to add interest to a large expanse of stone paving and is invaluable in creating steps and low walls. Old, reclaimed wall bricks can have a warm texture, but they are completely unsuitable for use in paving. To avoid the risk of frost damage, it is important to use highly fired engineering bricks with low water porosity.

Above: *Old red bricks in a basketwork design lend a soft foundation to this terrace.*

Other Options

When a solid flooring material is out of the question, loose-laid gravel or stones may be the best option. The effect is informal and reminiscent of Mediterranean terraces, making an easy relationship with perennial planting and a cottage-style effect. Here it is entirely appropriate to use old bricks to create an edging detail for the planting beds.

Gravel is readily available, inexpensive and simple to lay. It can be found in various grades from tiny sharp fragments to large, smooth, rounded pebbles and cobbles that can be employed in beach-style features. Colours vary from white and grey to warm ochre and buff, enabling it to be used in a wide range of contexts.

To lay gravel, start with a simple foundation of compacted hardcore followed by a layer of medium-grade gravel mixed with a little dry cement. Water this in to achieve a weed-resistant barrier and then finish off with a thicker layer of finishing gravel. You can also use

CREATING A FOUNDATION

A secure foundation is required before laying any type of floor slab or tile. A level concrete base laid over a well-compacted stone and gravel layer will prevent subsequent movement that can cause tiles to crack. Otherwise the weight and volume of materials required may be outside the weight-bearing ability of the construction.

weed-suppressant mat directly under gravel (see page 20), or under the hardcore itself.

A series of single paving slabs create an informal Japanese-style path that is easy to traverse and sympathetic in appearance. Lay slabs individually on the second layer of medium-grade gravel and infill with the finishing material. Over a small area, fine gravel can be used instead of jointing to infill between slabs loose laid over sand. This non-permanent technique provides flexibility and has a softer appearance.

WALLS AND SCREENS FOR OUTDOOR ROOMS

From trellis to painted walls and fenced boundaries to fabric screens, the partitions in your courtyard will define its style. For an outdoor room with an interior style, these choices are especially pertinent. You have the flexibility to use colours and textures and plants in the same way as you might for a room in your home.

Above: *Wooden slatted screens divide up the roof garden to create separate zones.*

Using Trellis

Trellis provides a quick and ready-made screening device for the outdoor room. A useful technique for any courtyard, it can create a decorative backdrop, a private area, or hide an unwanted view (see also using trellis for a classic backdrop on page 36 and for a flower-filled Mediterranean screen on page 66).

To customize it to the outdoor room, you can vary its appearance by tinting it in exterior-quality paint. Choose from colours such as restrained greys and putty tones, or for a more vibrant effect, brilliant blues set off foliage and flowers to perfection.

You can fix trellis panels directly to a plain wall or fence to create an interesting relief design (see method on page 19). Alternatively, use the panels to create freestanding screens supported on timber posts (see opposite). In this situation, they make a perfect vehicle for twining plants, such as honeysuckle and jasmine, both of which give a long display of highly perfumed flowers. Augment these plants with combinations of climbing roses and clematis to take the season through from early summer to autumn.

Where there is no natural planting medium, a long trough can be furnished with a trellis screen. Troughs can be found in materials such as painted or natural wood, lightweight resin or modern zinc, all perfect for roof terraces where weight needs to be kept to a minimum. Troughs with attached screen panels can be fitted with castors to create movable room dividers.

Above: *Diamond-pattern mesh panels are fixed to a very solid timber framework, making a semi-opaque screen wall filled with a collection of terracotta pots.*

Creating Partitions

Newly constructed walls open up new structural opportunities. In the example on the left, a freestanding screen wall provides a complete separation from the garden, and gives a clean background against which to set the furniture. The wall is tied in with scaffolding poles, an inexpensive device that serves as structural support, leaving open sides for the view and a roof structure to support the sliding fabric sun canopy. Both the closed and open walls are fitted with long planting boxes and larger planters have been built at ground level.

Left: *A self-contained outdoor room constructed with scaffolding poles and a solid screen wall.*

ERECTING A TRELLIS SCREEN

Trellis is a versatile screening material that works well in a number of different settings. In outdoor rooms, free-standing panels can create a sense of privacy and seclusion around dining or seating areas. Since the panels let in light they are superior to solid walls or fencing when creating room-like divides in small areas. You can also add extra 'windows' using specially shaped panels available from upmarket trellis and treillage suppliers. These framed apertures can be square, arched or circular to suit different design themes.

1 Dig a hole 60cm (2ft) deep and around 23cm (9in) across to accommodate the first fence post together with a quantity of quick-set ready-mixed concrete. If you have several post holes to dig, it is worth hiring a special post hole digging tool to excavate the soil.

2 Position the post so that it is perfectly upright. Use a spirit level on two sides to check this and adjust its angle accordingly. If you are working on your own, loosely nail pieces of wood to keep the post in place. Check the post is perpendicular after attaching the wooden struts.

3 Preferably with someone holding the post, pour in the gravel, sand and cement mix (you can buy this pre-packaged for setting fence posts). Ram the mixture into the hole so that it is well packed around the post. Wait until the posts are solid before removing the supports.

4 Using the panel as a guide, dig the second posthole. As an alternative to digging postholes, and if the ground is not too stony, consider using spiked metal sockets that you drive into the ground using a special tool.

5 Once the concrete has set, hammer in a number of galvanized nails at an angle to attach the trellis panel firmly to the post. Use bricks to raise the panel off the ground and hold it at the correct height while you work.

6 Continue to build up the screen to the required size. Paint the trellis panels with an exterior-quality wood preservative or a decorative paint or stain. Protect any adjacent paving with plastic sheeting or newspapers.

Walls of Colour

A walled courtyard offers innumerable decorative possibilities, but there is always the risk of it running riot in such a restricted area. A plain cement-rendered wall cries out for a colour treatment, the tone of which will completely alter the mood of your space. Think of Marrakech and Yves St Laurent's famous Majorelle gardens, the intense blue of which is impossible to forget, and the towering, shocking-pink walls favoured by Mexican architects. These intense colours enable you to create a tropical paradise by providing a background bold enough to display the powerful forms of exotic foliage and flowers.

Strong earth tones, reminiscent of southern desert landscapes, will move the mood towards Santa Fe, with its classic Adobe architecture. Walls of ochre and burnt umber, while still dramatic in effect, offer a warm, relaxing atmosphere. These tones provide a strong visual support to arrangements of bold plant forms, including yucca and the phoenix palm, suggestive of hot, dry climates.

Walls do not have to make a major colour statement in themselves; they can rely instead on texture and relief

Above: *A bold shade of blue on the walls of the Majorelle Gardens in Marrakech.*

for effect. A neutral background of greys and creams makes for a subtle decoration suited to both classical and contemporary environments. Colour can be introduced by painting the wall with masonry paint, which you will need to reapply periodically. Alternatively, the cement mix can be tinted with a pigment, which produces a permanent, low-maintenance solution.

Additional Details

A plain, solid wall can create an overwhelming visual statement, and can benefit from some form of design additions and decorative detail to break it up. Wall plaques made from stone or terracotta, for example, make interesting relief details, while niches to display a figurative bust or statue can be carved into the structure. Freestanding plinths and columns make elegant platforms for sculptures or specimen plants, or a group in varying heights might make supports for an interesting arrangement for jardinières.

Left: *Hot planting with squares of coloured Perspex creates a counterpoint to the red wall.*

Above: *An open-air fireplace creates a cosy ambiance for late summer evenings.*

Openings in the structure itself will reduce its mass and provide peepholes through to the space beyond. Where privacy is not an issue, a fixed, glazed opening will admit light, provide a view and a weather barrier. Alternatively, wooden shutters would frame and focus the opening, and allow you to close it off for seclusion and protection.

Fencing Options

If you do not have a ready-made walled courtyard, you will have to enclose the boundary with fencing. Basic off-the-peg woven fencing panels are an inexpensive solution, but are neither uplifting nor durable. You can create your own designs, choosing from a range of screening options that are available by the roll. These include split bamboo and woven heather mixes that can be fixed to timber posts. Set these in concrete foundations or use special metal post-holding spikes designed for the purpose that can be used for a speedy solution where ground conditions permit. Ready-made panels made from reeds bordered by wooden frames provide an elegant, yet informal wall, while

Right: Screens of floaty, lightweight fabric introduce an exotic atmosphere to this rustic timber gazebo.

woven willow is excellent for a country-style backdrop. You can make your own cool, Japanese-inspired screens by using string to tie bamboo poles into combinations of diagonals and verticals (see method on page 153). For a contemporary fence or screen, use narrow timber slats set in horizontal or vertical parallels. These can be made less solid by leaving small gaps between the slats, or set them in a double layer to provide complete privacy.

Fabric Panels and Screens

To make the most of the precious summertime, temporary screening devices can transform your outdoor room into an intimate entertaining space. Panels of fabric provide an easy way to create such effects. Fix them vertically on a wooden or metal framework, using cable or strong cord laced through eyelets, to provide an intimate enclosure. To create shade and privacy from above, fix sections of fabric horizontally on wires across a pergola. They can be drawn back concertina-fashion along wires strung between the cross members.

Fabric is lightweight, easy to install and can be opened and closed to accommodate different requirements. Suitable materials include traditional canvas and some of the many new high-tech synthetics that repel moisture and are easy to clean and maintain. These are suitable for relatively rigid installations as long as they are able to withstand breezy conditions. The fabric will act as a sail, however, placing extra strain on the

supporting framework. Where a softer effect is required, consider curtains of floaty muslin.

Vertically fixed Roman blinds, drawn up into flat folds when open, are a versatile screening device. Classical striped ticking is a good fabric choice and might suggest a shady courtyard in southern France. The blinds can be easily attached to the crossbeam of a pergola fixed to the house wall, or construct a temporary freestanding framework just for the summer made from rustic timbers. These will need to be fixed firmly to withstand wind and weather.

Where it is not possible to create a structure, an off-the-peg dining gazebo might suit the purpose. These tented structures are supplied with curtains, which can be drawn against sun or light showers, and they can be fitted with light strings for tying back. Easily assembled, they can be folded up and stored.

Left: A wall constructed from slices of tree trunk supported within a steel framework.

Far left: These rigid fencing screens are made from reeds fixed in a timber frame.

PLANTS AND CONTAINERS FOR OUTDOOR ROOMS

The style of the outdoor room will dictate the containers and planting. A highly focussed garden space linking directly with the house, it needs a sense of co-ordination and will be most successful if the outdoor theme reflects the texture and ambiance of the interior, producing a comfortable visual transition between the two areas.

Above: *Hanging baskets create long-lasting confections of flowers and foliage.*

Left: *A Victorian-style conservatory leads on to a terrace. Period-style wirework and cast-iron containers complement the planting.*

Classic Approaches

A traditional theme gives the scope to introduce some rococo styling, with elaborate pedestal vases and urns made from cast iron and lead, or moulded from terracotta. These pieces are frequently decorated with a confection of cherubs and ribboned swags, or embossed relief fruit and flowers. They tend to be weighty, so can present problems for roof gardens and areas with reduced access. In such cases, use good quality replicas moulded from resin and glass-reinforced plastic (GRP).

Turn-of-the-century-style wirework offers another lightweight solution to support plants. The delicate interwoven system of fine wires translates well into elegant plant stands and étagères, its openwork structure suited to display a collection of pots. They can also be lined with sphagnum moss and plastic to disguise and contain the soil for direct planting.

For a romantic planting style use traditional containers filled with colourful flowers that can be changed throughout the year. Seasonal bedding plants create big splashes of instant colour in an outdoor room. Tender geraniums (*Pelargoniums*), love full sun and are the best container plants for giving endless summer colour with minimal watering and maintenance. Bushy zonal types in blowsy pinks and vibrant reds make a great display in large containers, while elegant trailing ivy-leaf varieties with sophisticated deep magenta blooms, show off their graceful, trailing habit in tall urns and vases. Petunias love the sun too, and their blue, pink or purple blooms combine well with the trailing silvery foliage of *Helichrysum*. For those frequent shady spots, gleaming Busy Lizzie, (*Impatiens*) cannot be surpassed for a continuous show of brilliant colour.

Modern Options

A contemporary outdoor room calls for a bolder, more structured approach. Clean-shaped planters with no superfluous ornamentation make sculptural statements that are especially effective when placed in oversized pairs or lined up in sequential, identical groups. Tall and relatively narrow forms make a huge impact and can be found in either soft round or robust, square-sectioned shapes. These combine most effectively with architectural shrubs, especially evergreens such as box, clipped in low shapes. These can be round or cubed, to counterbalance the container height and emphasize the sculptural effect. This creates a cool and understated European look, especially when the planters are made in the new, black, taupe or cream coloured terracotta.

Spiky or exotic plants also work well in a modern setting, offering a contrasting energetic style. Large architectural specimens, such as agave and yucca, fit the bill perfectly, as do palms and banana. However, these plants tend to be wide and sometimes top heavy so they need appropriately broad containers with enough physical weight and volume to sustain such vigorous giants.

Flowers are not out of place in a modern setting, but in order to complement the formal architecture, they should be applied in a structured way. Plant bold, simple flowers in blocks or groups, keeping to a single co-ordinated colour tone or shape. Canna lilies offer bold, exotic form with striking foliage and vibrant blooms in shades of orange, yellow and red. More discreetly, the tall, slender green stems of agapanthus are surmounted by clusters of blue or white bell-shaped blooms and are divinely cool and elegant.

Flowers for Colour

Pelargoniums, also known as geraniums, love full sun and are the best container plants for endless vibrant colour, minimal watering and low maintenance. Bushy forms in blowsy pinks and reds give a brilliant display in large containers. Elegant, ivy-leafed forms, available in sophisticated deep reds and magentas, show off their graceful, trailing habit in tall vases and urns. For overflowing, continental-style window boxes, choose bright red or pink balcony forms. Some, such as *P. crispum*, suit a topiary treatment.

Endless attractive combinations can also be made with petunias, in lovely shades of pale to deepest blue. For shady spots, scarlet, orange and pink busy Lizzy (*Impatiens*), give an iridescent show. For a country look, mix bright-yellow marigolds (*Tagetes*) and orange nasturtiums (*Tropaeolum majus*), with blue *Felicia* or *Brachyscome*.

Above: *A massed display of pots with mono-planting makes a stunning wall feature. Geranium is really the only choice for this treatment because of its low water requirements.*

PLANTING A WALL BASKET

A bare wall can seem an inhospitable place for growing flowers, but a large manger-style basket or a hayrack, up to twice the size of the container illustrated, has enough space for a substantial amount of compost (soil mix) and a good variety of plants, including smaller evergreen shrubs and spring bulbs. Group several baskets together for additional impact. These are useful where there are no borders for growing climbers and wall shrubs in the ground. Long trailing plants, including Surfinia petunias for summer and ivies for winter, cover bare wall effectively.

1 Using handfuls of sphagnum moss (collected from a sustainable source), begin to line the basket to produce a 'nest' capable of holding the plants and compost (soil mix). Alternatively, line the back section with polythene.

2 Put a little compost into the bottom of the basket to support the plants' root-balls (roots). Make holes in the moss and feed the plants through from the front so that the neck of each one lies within the basket, surrounded by a moss collar.

3 Continue to build up the front of the basket. Then add some larger basket plants in the top, such as the variegated fuchsia and ivy-leaved geranium shown here. Fill in the gaps with more compost and water well.

Left: *A pale grey palette makes this tiny space feel larger. The subtle silver/ grey and white planting maintains the cool, airy feel.*

Sensory Planting

Warm, summer evenings suggest lazy salads and barbecues, so think about including containers of aromatic herbs to add flavour and colour to your dishes. Rosemary and thyme flavour roast meats, while pungent fennel seeds and stalks add a special touch to fish. Don't forget parsley, coriander, marjoram and tarragon.

Still, evening warmth releases flower perfumes, bringing a sense of night-time romance to your courtyard. Especially effective are annual white tobacco plants (*Nicotiana affinis*) and night-scented stocks (*Matthiola incana*) that pervade the evening air with their musky scent. The glossy-leaved, evergreen shrubs Japanese mock orange (*Pittosporum tobira*) and Mexican orange blossom (*Choisya ternata*) reward year after year with their sweet, citrus-like scent. Lilies (*Lilium*) have a glamour to match

Right: *Blue plumbago makes a perfect foil for the intense, ultra-sky-blue wall.*

Far right: *The heavy, drooping ooms of the datura (Brugmansia) cre es interior theatre.*

their perfume, while lavish, but poisonous, datura (*Brugmansia*) waits until dusk before releasing its fragrance, attracting night-time pollinators to its huge dangling bells. Pots of equally tender gardenia and stephanotis will enrich your table setting with their evocative scents.

Planting for Height

Climbing plants enhance the vertical dimension of your boundary walls, arbours and pergolas, and some can

have the added bonus of fragrance. Common jasmine (*Jasminum officinale*) and the valuable star jasmine (*Trachelospermum jasminoides*), one of the few flowering evergreen climbers, have a rich, oriental-style perfume. For a more European touch, sweetly scented roses, such as 'Alberic Barbier' and 'Madame Alfred Carriere', give out an evocative, old-fashioned fragrance. All of these flowers are white, so they will glow at night in any reflected light, while infusing the air with their fragrance, which is especially intense in the evening.

Climbers with coloured flowers make their impact in daylight. *Passiflora* 'Amethyst', the purple passion flower, is a must for a sheltered spot, while also loving a sunny wall, the classic blue *P. caerulea* will finish with showy orange fruits in late summer. To fill in spaces, clematis will integrate with other climbers, mingling especially well with climbing roses to increase the length of the flowering season. They can stand alone, trained on

tripods to make local features, or be allowed to cover an area of trellis. Unbeatable scramblers for hot climates are showy bougainvilleas in irrepressible shades of orange, red and purple, the power of which can be beautifully offset by soft, powdery blue plumbago.

Integrating Containers

In the outdoor room, containers fulfil some important functions, enabling you to introduce focal points and to alter and emphasize the planting design according to seasonal requirements. The pots themselves make a huge architectural contribution to the design, so choose with care to ensure that you are sending out the right message in terms of material, colour and shape. Generally, the most successful way to arrange containers is to select those that match in either material or shape.

Below: *Three tall square shaped containers planted with tightly clipped box make a strong sculptural statement.*

In this way, you can build up groups of containers to make strong visual statements.

You may already have a collection of interior plants, in which case you could repeat either the form or colour of their pots in the garden design. Oriental stoneware pots exist both in sensuously curvaceous forms and tall, straight-sided designs that can complement the inside/outside function excellently. Such examples can be found in earthy, wood-fired finishes that would work well within a restrained contemporary design. They also exist in a subtle range of dreamy glazes, ranging from celadon green through to deep blues and purples. Such glazes can introduce smouldering elements of colour to your outdoor room. These are usually frost resistant, which means the same containers can be used indoors and out, giving a consistent element.

Ceramic and terracotta are more porous than stoneware and the clay body has an effect on the depth of the glaze that can be achieved. These pots can often be found in brilliantly coloured glazes, including yellows, reds, greens and blues, which contribute well to a design with a hotter theme. However, be aware that these glazes are often fragile and vulnerable to water penetration, and this will lead to frost damage in cold climates. Always check that pots are suitable for outdoor use before making a purchase, or be sure to empty them of soil in winter and preferably store them somewhere dry and frost-free.

Above: *Soak up the atmosphere of an open-air barbecue on a summer's evening.*

STRUCTURES AND FURNITURE FOR OUTDOOR ROOMS

Structures and furniture for outdoor living include pergolas and awnings to create shade, and luxurious seating areas in which to relax and entertain. You might like a modern streamlined barbecue to prepare food, or perhaps a rustic style with a fire pit. Other ideas for an enviable outdoor space are a plunge pool, jacuzzi or shower.

Constructions in Wood

Wood is a material that gives permanence and stability to the outdoor room and timber is easy to source and work. So use traditional wooden garden structures, such as pergolas, shelving and seating, and also create or commission new structures in wood to give your outdoor space the permanent character of a room. Bold sections make ideal posts, with strength and the ability to blend with different roof structures and styles. Narrow wooden slats provide an elegant, lightweight canopy that can be angled like a pitched roof. Another option is yacht wires strung through the beams to support a temporary fabric awning for shade and style.

An Overhanging Roof

A solid, overhanging roof gives you a veranda suitable for all-weather use. The roof structure might be clad in tiles or slates, providing excellent shade, something that is crucial in hotter climates. In more temperate regions, where sunlight is at more of a premium, transparency is desirable. In this case, the roof can be broken up with sections of glass or Perspex while still providing protection from bad weather.

Barbecues and Dining

The pergola can be interpreted in a freestanding form to create a special feature area for a barbecue and dining space. You might think of enclosing two sides with walls to increase the intimacy and provide shelter. The walls would provide a support and chimney for the barbecue and make it possible to include a preparation area. The barbecue, combined with an open fire and comfy sofas, will tempt you outside even in the cooler evenings.

This design would be suitable to accommodate a proper outdoor kitchen, complete with power and plumbing for preparation, refrigerator and cooking. Having it all to hand in this way adds an extra dimension to your daily life. If your culinary ambitions extend to it, try using an outdoor pizza or bread oven. The pergola shelter can be used in all seasons, if the weather is not too severe.

Above: *Tiny spaces need vertical thinking. A planted wall, a water feature, hidden cupboards and bike storage leave room for a sheltered canopy and a cantilevered bench.*

Above: *A screen wall and canopy provide stylish protection for an outdoor kitchen.*

Heat and flame are compelling elements, and a fire pit makes a wonderful focal point for a social gathering at night. This simple and innovative concept is basically just a hole in the ground where you can burn logs or coal. It could be used for warmth or be readily adapted for cooking for small or large numbers. A fire pit might be built into an area of terracing that has been designed with low-level seating and an informal dining space. This is an excellent project for a keen home-improvement enthusiast, as it is simple to construct using brick or rendered cement blocks. Stand-alone fire grates that come in a very wide range of stylish designs are now readily available as alternatives.

All-purpose Furniture

An outdoor dining room needs practical furniture. The decision about style depends on your taste and preferences, but what the furniture is made out of and how it is made are crucial if it is to withstand the rigours of sun, rain and varying temperatures.

A generous-sized table is a must and it needs to feel solid and stable. The refectory-style provides a good-looking timber option, using bench seating that echoes the table's uncomplicated lines. Benches are easy and informal, adapting to suit the number of guests. The simple, clean, everyday look can easily be livened up with coordinating fabrics for the seat cushions and table cover.

Contemporary outdoor furniture designs often combine wood and metal to create elegant and streamlined tables and chairs that are streets away in style from clumsy, conventional shapes. These provide a manageable, lighter-weight option that blends well in either a modern or a more traditional setting.

Above: *Screen walls with closable shutters and a timber-slatted roof admit light but ensure protection from damp and breezes.*

Modern-day furniture needs to be adaptable to cope with a faster lifestyle. Large parties and unexpected guests demand tables that are adaptable in size. Many designs are supplied with sections you can slot in to extend the length, but two square tables may suit you better. These can be set around the garden for small groups and then brought together as required to accommodate larger numbers. To really enjoy a long relaxed meal, the dining chair should be comfortable. Cushions are a must, though some seats are made of soft, synthetic fabrics that do the same job. It helps if chairs are light enough to move around easily, and for winter storage you might consider designs that can be folded or stacked.

Comfortable, weather-resistant outdoor furniture is now widely available. New plastics technology has produced fibres that can be woven into basket chairs with all the charm of wicker but with zippy, modern styling. These seem to have been created with just the outdoor sitting room in mind. Comfy sofas team up with generous armchairs and low-slung tables designed for after-dinner conversation. When you want to snuggle up with a book and escape, choose a sinuous day bed or, even more eye-catching, a huge, circular lounging pad enclosed beneath a curvaceous woven cover. Natural colours, such as sand, coffee and cream, create a sophisticated look that works beautifully within the indoor/outdoor space.

Soft Furnishings

With space always at a premium, it is good to have a few enormous floor cushions that can be stacked away when not needed. They are available

covered in brilliantly coloured weather-resistant fabrics, some plain and some screen printed in super-sized flower and foliage designs. Matching deckchairs and a parasol will complete a tropical garden set. To complete the integration of interior and exterior, try a colour theme using other soft furnishings.

Above: *Resin fibre imitating cane is shaped into inviting, organically styled chairs that make a crisp, sculptural statement.*

Below left: *Floor cushions and a low granite table create a stylish spot to eat sushi.*

Below: *Cushions and a mattress transform a low oriental table into a superb sun bed.*

A pavilion would make an excellent setting for passing a lazy afternoon. Many designs are available, often from wrought iron, which will look attractive and create a focal point all year around.

Below: *A hot tub is simple to install, with decking giving cover for the feed pipes.*

Left: *An outdoor shower in an available corner of a tiny roof terrace will freshen you up on a hot day.*

In summer, furnish the pavilion with a fitted canopy and curtains to screen out the sun. Pile floor cushions, Eastern style, over the ground and you have an instant Bedouin tent.

Courtyard Bathing

Outdoor bathing is now an attainable luxury. At its simplest, a small plunge pool gives you the chance to cool off on a hot day. It can be built as an 'above-ground' feature if you intend to conceal it within a stepped deck arrangement, and so will not need expensive excavation. If you prefer warmth, a Jacuzzi or hot tub could be incorporated into a courtyard. A long, narrow lap pool is a real luxury for keen swimmers and it makes an elegant feature. Advanced pool technology makes real exercise possible, even in a restricted space – powerful jets set into one wall push water out with such force that you swim against a real current.

A quiet, shady place provides respite from the sun when it's time to cool off. A built structure is not always the most desirable option, especially when a feeling of space

Above: *Simplicity and contemporary sculptural form – this sleek sun bed is the perfect place to relax.*

and movement is wanted. Yachting sails combine naturally with water and air, and this marine technology has been adopted for the land. The latest shade canopies incorporate the sail principle, stretching hi-tech textiles into elegant, almost bird-like forms that seem to float between their tensioned supports. These make a beautiful design statement in an outdoor space. They can be sited beside a pool to shelter a seating area, arranged to form a link between the interior and exterior space or to create a niche for bathing.

An outdoor shower is an invigorating way to start or end the day. Find a corner close to the house in which to set up a small showering area. Make a screen wall to hide the plumbing and fix up one or more showerheads. Provide a soakaway for the used water with a slatted plinth to cover it. Towels and soaps can be stored informally in baskets placed on a long, low bench seat. If possible, site the shower where you have direct access to it from the bathroom or your bedroom for an even more luxurious bath-time treat.

ORNAMENT FOR OUTDOOR ROOMS

The outdoor room provides an ideal setting through which to exhibit ornamental and architectural features, providing both a garden stage and backdrop. However, as the space is likely to be used for a range of different purposes, the level and type of display and decoration should be adaptable in order to cope with these varying demands.

Above: *Animal sculptures like this wire-mesh chicken bring fun to a courtyard.*

Above: *The organic form of these tall bar stools with curving metal legs shows modern furniture as a sculptural statement.*

Style Continuity

In a defined space like an outdoor room, it is important to maintain a clear impression of its style. Space is at a premium so it is preferable to keep ornamentation to a minimum, perhaps using it as part of overall decoration rather than adding too many set pieces. Work in a small palette of colours to reduce an impression of clutter, and focus your approach towards the texture of materials. Picking up and repeating some of the design elements of the interior will help the sense of continuity between inside and out. Pale background colours such as soft greys and creams give an added impression of space, permitting ornamental elements to be shown off clearly.

Useful and Ornamental

Furnishings offer decorative possibilities in their own right – they are also likely to take up a significant amount of space. Care in the selection of furnishings will ensure that they play an integral role in the overall design concept.

Chairs, especially in modern designs, offer plenty of ornamental potential. New plastics and moulding processes permit sculptural forms that introduce their own decorative statement. The tall bar stools shown to the left demonstrate some of the possibilities. With their organic form, the metal legs seem to have grown just like stems, with the seat appearing like an opening flower bud or a bursting seed pod.

Garden planters, too, can make decorative statements. The traditional Mediterranean olive jar in curvaceous 'Ali Baba' shapes can be found in giant sizes that really make a visual splash. Made from terracotta, their soft colour and texture evoke a sun-filled climate and will add a touch of southern warmth to the garden.

Sculptural Form

Using sculpture in the landscape is a technique that allows the display of contemporary artworks, commercially produced objects or interesting 'found' objects. The use of such objects continues the interior décor theme.

Contemporary sculptures, often abstract in form, can be curvaceous, inspired by a human or animal shape. Alternatively, strictly angular and geometric shapes might fit more appropriately into a cool, architectural concept.

The physical presence of practical features often assumes a defining ornamental role. For example, the shape of a shade can add to the overall visual value of the space. A screen wall will physically anchor the canopy, but also visually, by use of the same colour paint. The large organic ornament on the opposite page could be overpowering, but it is coordinated by the colour finish.

Wall Decorations

Exterior walls can be enlivened by the inclusion of decorative objects, and don't use up valuable floor space. Salvaged household items can also be given a makeover and found a new life on a wall or screen. An ornamental door, an old gate or iron

Above: *A group of identical earthenware oil jars makes a strong sculptural statement.*

Above: *In this dramatic space, tall timber pillars and a triptych of narrow wall prints lead the way to a sphere and sculptural roof.*

railings can be transformed by a coat of paint and make an effective *trompe l'oeil* effect. More conventionally, use carved or moulded plaques, which make excellent details and are easy to fix on the surface, or can be incorporated into openings in the wall's structure.

Grouping Similar Pieces

Collections of similar items work well where space allows. A group of old wirework jardinières would add interest to a traditional terrace. Striking pots and vases make a big impact when arranged as a highlight feature.

Right: *A redundant Victorian fireplace sees a new role as part of a planting design to decorate a boundary wall.*

WATER FEATURES FOR OUTDOOR ROOMS

The possibilities for water features are many, dividing between the natural or formal (in style) and the functional or decorative (in purpose). For an outdoor room, formality and functionality make a good combination, so opt for water sources for bathing and cooking, or features that accentuate the architecture.

Above: *Enliven a tiny formal pool with a quirky fountain such as this.*

Water to Delight the Senses

The presence of water adds life to an outdoor room, encouraging wildlife visitors, such as birds, butterflies and frogs. Water, which sparkles in sunlight and reflects shadows and shapes, can be organized in a diversity of forms, from an energetic gurgling fall to a still, shallow reflective pool in which birds can splash and bathe.

A formal water feature, due to its organized structure and appearance, is more likely to complement the outdoor room. A modestly sized pool with enough space to allow people to move around it makes an eye-catching centrepiece for a formal garden. It can be constructed above ground by means of a retaining wall of rendered blockwork, brick or stone. Alternatively, it can be dug out and finished with an edging at ground level. Either type of construction requires a waterproof lining and a means of filtering the water to keep it clean and aerated.

A round pool is a classic design feature, and seems to work well in the above-ground format. It is always pleasant to gaze into water and this style allows the addition of a broad seating ledge to replace the coping. A ground-level pool has the advantage of being viewed from above. It can be set into a wooden deck or incorporated into a paved terrace or courtyard floor. Irregular shapes can be integrated into an

existing architectural structure to enhance the features of a background wall. Alternatively, a rectangular form, bounded by benches, provides a peaceful retreat.

The effect of still, dark water is calming and tranquil, aspects you can accentuate by introducing water lilies. A narrow canal of shallow water can bring a different dimension to the garden room and an interesting way to divide space. You may even be able to incorporate a path of stepping-stones in a rectangular pool to help dissect the space.

Moving Water

An integral fountain creates movement and sound and a sense of life and energy in either a raised or ground-level pool. Various visual effects are possible depending on the pump and water outlet. A single, central spray, for example, will give the classical romantic style of fine, cascading droplets. More modern jets can be arranged singly or in groups to gurgle high or low to break the surface tension.

A cascade effect can be readily incorporated into a rectangular pool by means of an integrated fountain wall of water. It can take the form of a free-standing screen, or it can be built into an existing supporting wall. The pump can be set so that water emerges in a rush from a mouth or chute, or it can trickle gently over a wide ledge. A selection of ready-made fountains in stainless steel are a simple solution to introduce some elements of gleam and sparkle.

Right: *This glazed timber bathing cabin is the ultimate private space, overlooking a series of formal pools in a jungle of planting.*

Right: *An above-ground plunge pool can be easily incorporated into a timber deck.*

Tailor the aural qualities of water to your requirements. Many water features produce a variety of sounds, some soothing, others energetic. When selecting effects for a small garden space, consider their proximity to your neighbours – they may not appreciate the noise escaping into their space. On the other hand, the sound of a gentle cascade or fast-moving waterfall breaking over stones can be used effectively to disguise urban noise.

Water Containers

Any watertight, frostproof container is suitable for creating a small water feature and is ideal for areas of raised deck or on roof terraces, where a more traditional pond may be impractical. There are many options, from grey steel bowls in geometric shapes to wide shallow stone or concrete bowls. Wooden barrels, available from most garden centres, are good water containers and come ready-treated against rot. Alternatively, free-standing stone fonts or troughs, large terracotta bowls or curvaceous urns make instant gardens for miniature water lilies. Large bowls or pots, which can be bought with a pre-drilled drainage hole, can incorporate a small fountain, whereby the pump sits on a level spot at the bottom with its plastic-coated wire passing through the hole, which is then sealed with silicon. Most small pumps are designed to run off mains electricity. Plants added to the water in barrels or bowls are best kept in baskets to control their growth and for easier maintenance, and it is best to use rain water in any small planted water feature. Avoid placing container water gardens in a hot spot.

Safety note: *Children should be supervised at all times when near water. Protective fences can deter toddlers, but if children use your courtyard space, the safest measure is to avoid water features.*

Above: *A cascade of water falls from a concrete spout into the pebbled pool below.*

Above: *The constant trickle of water provides movement and gentle sound.*

Above: *This steel water container can house aquatic and moisture-loving plants.*

LIGHTING FOR OUTDOOR ROOMS

Outdoor lighting for the courtyard has to be decorative and practical. Avoid the prison-yard effect produced by overlighting, as this will destroy any sense of intimacy. The lighting you choose for your outdoor room will depend on its function. A contemporary jacuzzi and deck area needs a very different treatment compared with an elegant period-style dining space.

Above: *Simple lights with paper shades are perfect for special celebrations.*

Basic Lighting

Once you have sorted out basic safety lighting for steps and other changes in level (see page 199), and have adequate illumination around any cooking areas, you can begin to light your outdoor space more creatively. Courtyards used as outdoor rooms have much the same lighting considerations as indoor rooms.

For a start, remove any wall-mounted, downward-facing floodlights, as these have more to do with security than creating a relaxing ambiance. In addition, avoid generating unnecessary light pollution by installing too many lights – this is likely to alienate neighbours as well as obliterate any view of the stars. Keep additional lighting at a relatively low level, mimicking indoor lamps set on occasional tables, or use contemporary wall lights to throw the beam upwards. Even modern outdoor fairy lights can make a useful contribution.

Above: *Interior backlighting provides a distinctive atmosphere at this stylish home, adding shadows and glinting reflections around the deep black pool.*

Spa Lighting

Consider fitting white or coloured optical-fibre lighting around a hot tub set into a deck area. Each light strand in a large bundle is accommodated in a hole drilled through the wood and so this is something that is far easier to do during the final stages of deck construction. Discrete neon-blue LED (light-emitting diode) spots can also be set into decking to produce random scatterings of light, to define the shape of the tub or be set out in rows to highlight and define steps.

The lighting for an outdoor bathroom needs to create a relaxing atmosphere. Spa baths often come with their own integral lighting and so the surrounding area can be softly lit – perhaps by candles or spherical ceramic oil lamps.

Try uplighting surrounding specimen plants or an interestingly shaped tree to create an oasis effect or throw the focus on to a sculpture or water feature that can be viewed from the hot tub.

Above: *Mini floods set into the paving softly illuminate the walls.*

Dining by Starlight

In colder climates, opportunities for alfresco dining are limited, so make the most of those precious warm, dry evenings. In a period setting, candlesticks and candelabras with a distressed, gothic finish add a grandiose touch. Wind some ivy trails around the uprights and set church candles in clear glass holders among low-level flower and foliage arrangements. If the table is underneath a pergola, consider winding LED fairy lights through the climbers (see method below) and hang coloured glass tea-light lanterns at varying heights. You can also weave LED fairy lights through the trellis screens surrounding a dining area to create a more intimate atmosphere.

Left: *Ornate glass lanterns, an array of tea lights and chunky church candles add a softly glowing touch of romance to this outdoor dining area.*

INSTALLING FAIRY LIGHTS

Modern outdoor LED fairy or string lights come in a range of colours and are more luminous and durable than those fitted with standard bulbs. Use them to add a bit of magic to an outdoor dining room at night. They can be easily and securely attached to structures such as trellis panels, but also try weaving them through climbers on a pergola, over a small specimen tree or topiary standard stem or, for a contemporary effect, up through the vertical culms of bamboo. Wind them more tightly to concentrate the intensity of the lights.

1 Wind the lights around the supports, maintaining an even, but unordered, coverage of LEDs. It is much easier to do this if you bunch the cable up and feed it out. Check distribution by temporarily plugging it in to an extension lead.

2 To keep the LEDs firmly in their correct positions, use plastic-coated wires or small black cable ties. If you are fixing lights to plant stems, use soft twine rather than wire, which will cut into the plant stems over time.

3 The transformer needs a waterproof housing if it is positioned outdoors. Use a qualified electrician if you need to install a new socket. Feed the thin cable through from outdoors and plug it into the transformer.

CASE STUDY: MOROCCAN NIGHTS

This colourful, exotic location combines different levels, strong architectural features and separate areas for dining and relaxing. The sumptuous detailing provides not only visual stimulation but also elegant comfort. It is the quintessential outdoor room, with the styling and purpose mirroring the architecture of an interior. But instead of an enclosed ceiling, here the sky takes its place.

Above: *Mounds of ethnic rugs and cushions bring colour to a bench.*

A vibrant Moroccan theme reverberates through this sensual courtyard, lushly planted with climbers, architectural palms and colourful, perfumed flowers. Castellated parapets and Arabian-style keyhole doorways define the high, enclosing walls. Rendered and painted a soft pink to match the pale terracotta paving, both are relieved by the blue and gold mosaic-tiled surface cladding and floor insets.

An intimate, plant-filled alcove enclosed by tall, tile-clad columns provides a private seating area set with a comfortable bench, while in a quiet viewing niche there is a metal table and chairs for relaxed dining and entertaining. The table is set with opulent blue and gold crockery, while the bench, invitingly covered with colourful rugs and velvet cushions, is the perfect place to pass a few idle hours or to relax with friends after an alfresco, candle-lit meal. The alcove also has a marble bowl balanced on a tiled plinth to provide a gentle splash of water. The reservoir holding the bowl is shallow and finished in ceramic glazed tiles.

Vertical interest is further provided by changes of level, with tiled steps leading down to a lower terrace. The main point of interest here is a dramatically long, formal pool. A tall, wrought-iron minaret, based on the minaret at the Hassan II mosque in Casablanca, Morocco, dominates this. Beneath, on a submerged plinth, sits an elegant amphora planted with an exotic *Agave americana* 'Variegata'. The pool's still water is ideal for growing the white water lily *Nymphaea* 'Gladstoniana'. The pool is crossed by two square stepping-stones, bringing the viewer closer to the water.

The garden plan for this Moroccan courtyard is shown overleaf, along with instructions for building a flight of steps and tiling step risers.

Right: *A keyhole opening gives access to the plant-filled inner courtyard, with its tall pillars clad in glazed deep blue and yellow tiles.*

Above: *High walls in soft terracotta provide a serene backdrop to the dining area.*

CREATING A MOROCCAN COURTYARD

Flooring:
• *Pave the floor with terracotta tiles, using decorative tiles as relief insets.*
• *Create changes of level with steps tiled in mosaics.*

Walls and Screens:
• *Render with cement stucco tinted in rich warm colours.*
• *Use tiling to add decorative relief to vertical elements.*
• *Folding perforated screens made from cedar or wrought iron introduce decorative vertical elements.*

Plants and Containers:
• *Use tall palm trees to introduce strong foliage form.*
• *Add architectural interest with curvy Ali Baba pots made from terracotta.*
• *Citrus trees, stephanotis and hibiscus add an exotic touch for summer time.*

Structures and Furniture:
• *Build high architectural blockwork walls for seclusion and intimacy.*
• *Add castellations or crenellations to provide a themed decoration.*
• *Use arched and curved shapes.*

• *Choose wrought-iron chairs and mosaic-topped tables.*

Ornament and Water Features:
• *Create key-hole wall niches for lanterns and other ornaments.*
• *Water features should have a pool with a central fountain.*
• *If you have room, add channels or rills.*

Lighting:
• *Introduce delicate spangles of light with lighting strings.*
• *Use filigree candle lanterns on tables.*

MOROCCAN NIGHTS GARDEN PLAN

wrought-iron minaret

rendered block wall

Moroccan-style pillars

Amphora jar

steps

tiled step risers

Long pool

Left: *An open niche reduces the impact of the high wall and provides a decorative opportunity with this potted agave.*

Below: *A small space can appear larger when changes in level are incorporated. Wide, gentle steps provide the perfect introduction to the long formal pool below.*

Plant list

1   *Chamaerops humilis*
2   *Phormium tenax* 'Purpureum Group'
3   *Achillea filipendulina* 'Cloth of Gold'
4   *Rosa* 'Irish Eyes'
5   *Griselinia littoralis*
6   *Helenium* 'Wyndley'
7   *Canna* 'Roitelet'
8   *Rosmarinus officinalis*
9   *Convolvulus cneorum*
10   *Phygelius* 'African Queen'
11   *Nymphaea* 'gladstoneana'
12   *Sisyrinchium californicum*
13   *Agave americana*
14   *Heuchera micrantha* var. *diversifolia* 'Palace Purple'

15   *Tagetes* Gem Series
16   *Artemisia* 'Boughton Silver'
17   *Hakonechloa macra* 'Aureola'
18   *Agave americana* 'Variegata'
19   *Fatsia japonica*
20   *Rosa* 'Snowball'
21   *Arundo donax*
22   *Onopordum acanthium*
23   *Cercis canadensis* 'Forest Pansy'
24   *Cytisus battandieri*

Above: *Luxurious cushions help to soften the effect of walls and tiling.*

Above: *Table settings are strongly co-ordinated with the overall theme.*

Above: *Orange and purple planting makes a good foil for the terracotta paintwork.*

BUILDING STEPS

Changes in level add interest to a small garden and a shallow flight of steps can be created fairly easily without the help of a professional builder. Plan the steps carefully and choose materials that will integrate naturally with their surroundings. Draw up a cross-section on squared paper first and then peg out the area for construction.

FLIGHT OF STEPS CROSS-SECTION

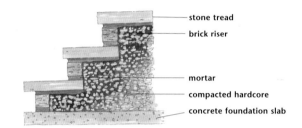

stone tread
brick riser
mortar
compacted hardcore
concrete foundation slab

1 Measure the overall height and width of the area where the steps will be located. This should be at least 1.5m (5ft). The height of each riser should be 10–15cm (4–6in) only and the depth of each tread 30–40cm (12–18in).
2 Excavate and lay a concrete foundation under the area of the steps, extending it slightly in front of the first riser. When the concrete is

dry, lay a course of bricks bedded in mortar to form the first riser.
3 Infill behind with hardcore and consolidate firmly by tamping it down with a wooden post.
4 Lay a mortar bed to the depth of the tread over the bricks and hardcore. Set the stone tread so that it projects over the riser by about 2.5cm (1in). Check

the level of the slabs with a spirit (carpenter's) level to ensure that there is a slope to provide a run-off for rainwater.
5 Spread a layer of mortar along the back of the tread and lay a course of bricks over the slab for the second riser.
6 Infill with hardcore, and lay the stone tread as before.

7 Continue building, checking the levels with a spirit level to ensure a slight slope for water run-off. Make sure that the top tread finishes level with the upper ground surface.
8 Glazed ceramic tiles to suit the scheme can be mortared to the riser of each step.

CREATING TILED STEP RISERS

Sophisticated detailing, such as these tiled risers, helps to blur the distinction between indoor and garden rooms, and

can link up with other features, colours and design themes – in this example, a Moorish motif of blue and gold.

1 Clean the steps with a brush. Arrange the tiles equidistantly along the step to calculate the spacing and then fix each one with quick-bonding, exterior-quality tile cement.

2 Mix up some mortar, adding sufficient water to create a stiff consistency. Using a small grouting trowel, push mortar into the gaps between, above and below the tiles.

3 Make the mortar smooth and level with the tiles except along the top; angle the mortar there back under the slab to minimize water retention and staining. Repeat along the bottom.

4 Use a damp cloth wrapped around your forefinger to carefully wipe off excess mortar. Then use a clean, dry cloth to buff the surface of the tiles, removing any smudges.

PRODUCTIVE SPACES

The challenge of creating a courtyard in which you can cultivate seasonal produce – fresh fruit, vegetables, herbs, edible flowers and blooms for cutting – is a question of harnessing space efficiently. Your growing area may be restricted to a small terrace, but with clever planning and the careful selection of produce to fit with your location, a courtyard or patio can overflow with fresh, home-grown delights.

All kinds of edibles can be grown in large pots, troughs and even hanging baskets, or in easy-to-construct raised beds. Practicality is essential in the kitchen garden, with flooring that allows all-weather access. As well as growing crops, incorporating more decorative planting in the form of herbs, flowers, shrubs and climbers draws in pollinating and beneficial insects (natural predators) as well as keeping the courtyard pretty.

Left: *Raised planting beds allow you to grow produce all the year round, even where there is no natural soil available. Create them with heavy timber planks and make an allowance for water to drain freely.*

HOME-GROWN PRODUCE

A country-style courtyard is the perfect setting for combining edible produce with colourful cut flowers for the house. What could be more satisfying than preparing a meal from home-grown vegetables and fruit, with freshly cut herbs to add zest and colour to both hot dishes and salads, with the added pleasure of arranging your own garden flowers for the table?

Above: Aubergines, squashes and beetroot vie for space with nasturtiums.

Design and Selection

Creating a flower-filled, countrified garden space calls for a natural approach to the design of the courtyard as well as to the selection of appropriate plants and materials. Aim for a relaxed, informal approach to its planting, with just enough 'edge' to lift the design into the realms of something special.

Divide the space up with paths surfaced in crunchy gravel and edge them with tumbling herbs. Extend the scope and dimensions of the available space by introducing vertical elements using vine-clad structures, such as arbours, screens and arches.

There is an opportunity to grow a wealth of traditional cottage garden plants, including hollyhocks and lupins, delphiniums and columbines, with roses underplanted with catmint for a soft, final touch. The planting can appear random and unplanned, mixing a riot of colours, textures and scents, or it can be organized into groups of toning colours and harmonizing shades.

To make the most of a restricted space, set vegetable plots within a framework of decorative planting. This not only maintains interest for the greater part of the year but also protects produce from pest damage by drawing in natural predators such as hoverflies and lacewings.

Climbing roses, honeysuckle and golden hop can all be trained on walls and fences or over arbours and screens. Colourful climbing squashes look impressive, too. Introduce a Mediterranean flavour to a sunny spot by combining tall-growing globe artichokes with underplantings of scented lavender, thyme and sage.

Apples can be trained along stakes and wires to make low screens and divisions. Dwarf plums and cherry trees will deliver fruit to make jams and pies, while in warmer areas you can train peaches and apricots against a south-facing wall.

Where space is at a premium, you will be amazed at just how much edible produce you can grow in pots and containers. Select the largest pot or container you can find to give enough space for good root growth and plenty of water and nutrients. Discarded industrial containers, such as oil drums, make excellent planters, but ensure that they are thoroughly cleaned before use.

Generously proportioned, purpose-built wooden planters and troughs can be placed along walls where they will benefit from the warmth and shelter. Alternatively, use them to create divisions in the garden. Raised beds make excellent planting areas where there is inadequate depth or quality of natural soil. Form the side walls from heavy timber planks or railway sleepers and fill with a mixture of existing soil and new compost (soil mix), incorporating lots of well-rotted farmyard or horse manure to make instant and easy-to-work beds.

Seed Varieties

The choice of flower and vegetable seeds to grow has never been wider, with many new and improved choices to make trial and selection a real seasonal treat. Old-fashioned vegetable varieties make it possible to grow food that you could never find in the shops. Striped tomatoes, pink carrots and black beans are among the tempting and colourful choices to include in your home-grown vegetable dishes. To make the most of a small space, use vegetables that are best picked fresh, such as runner (green) beans, salads, baby carrots or cherry tomatoes.

When it comes to fruit, there are many new, so-called 'patio' varieties, dwarf trees such as apples, apricots, peaches, pears and cherries that quickly become the real jewels of any small or container garden.

Above: Tomatoes grow well in pots against a sunny wall, but need regular attention.

Right: This courtyard combines vegetables, fruit and flowers for decoration. Cane wigwams, which will be clothed in colourful climbing beans, add vertical interest.

FLOORING FOR PRODUCTIVE SPACES

A vegetable garden should be practical, with easy access for planting, maintenance and harvesting. This is especially true for a small courtyard space. Floors should be functional, paths should be wide enough for a wheelbarrow to pass and beds should be easy to reach for frequent tending, watering and harvesting.

Above: Loose-laid paving slabs have an informal look, and provide a secure walkway.

Gravel and Chippings

Ideal in a productive courtyard, gravel is easy to lay, inexpensive and allows water to soak away naturally. Normally it is sold as washed pea gravel for use in making concrete. You can buy it in large sacks from builders' merchants or have it delivered in bulk. Its slightly yellowish-grey tone blends in with most architectural backgrounds, so it has a universal application.

Lay gravel directly on to well compacted hardcore or crusher run. Bear in mind, however, that gravel has a tendency to move underfoot, so retain it with some sort of edging material. A terracotta or stone edging tile fits the purpose, while timber planks work well, too.

Gravel is ideal for paths between raised beds, as the walls of the beds work to retain both soil and gravel. Avoid laying it more than about

Above: This gravel-surrounded plot benefits from a protective boundary of shrubs and trees to shelter the produce from cold winds.

5cm (2in) thick or pushing a wheelbarrow becomes hard work. You can also lay it over a weed-suppressant mat (see page 20). Another approach is to mix the gravel with a little dry cement, and water it in gently to set and compact in place.

Slate chippings provide an equally informal, though more stylish, flooring treatment. The larger texture and soft grey tones give a more contemporary look and blend especially well with an exotic- or Mediterranean-style planting. It makes an excellent complement to silvery leafed herbs, such as santolina and lavender, and to vegetables, such as globe artichokes, aubergines (eggplants), black beans and tomatoes.

An informal pathway through the gravel will make your footing more secure and ease the task of pushing heavy wheelbarrows and cultivators.

Stepping-stones do the job perfectly and fit well with this type of garden. Set them in place on the surface of the ground and lay the gravel to fill in around them. Old, heavy pieces of reclaimed timber work very well in this situation, too, especially if it matches the material used for the walls of the raised beds.

Disguised Concrete

Concrete sleepers that look remarkably like weathered wood are available from builders' merchants and larger home-improvement stores. They come in easy-to-handle lengths and, laid within gravel, add a distinctive tone to the vegetable plot. Prepare the ground thoroughly before laying, using well-compacted

Above: A gravel path works well in a productive garden such as this one.

hardcore topped with sand, as unevenness or soil shifting can cause cracks to appear. Use them to create entire pathways, hard-wearing steps, centrepiece designs and edgings.

Paving Slabs

One of the most practical and hard-wearing surface materials for the productive garden is paving slabs. Unlike gravel and slate, which become weedy if you spill soil on to them, stone or concrete slabs or quarry tiles are easy to keep clean with a hose or brush, as well as weed free. A foundation of blobs of cement laid on hardcore and sand provides a durable base for any kind of paving and results in a smooth, level surface that is easy to maintain.

It may be that a relaxed look is more desirable, so you might want to lay tiles and slabs directly on to

Right: Rectangular concrete blocks, created in timber moulds, set in a gravel pathway.

the earth. Level and compact the earth first and then apply a good layer of sand to receive the pavers, which are tapped down to bed them in. Over time, the paving may become slightly uneven, but this only adds to the charm.

Above: A gravel floor is a practical option, with zinc containers holding flowering pinks, scented geraniums, cabbages and thyme.

Below: Paving slabs bedded in a concrete base are secure and practical. Terracotta pots and kitchen herbs soften the look.

Above: *Reclaimed setts are laid without mortar to allow water to run away.*

Above: *Rustic cobblestones make it easy to brush and hose off debris.*

Above: *Flagstones offer an attractive and sturdy floor for a produce-filled garden box.*

The Kitchen Garden

The potager, or kitchen garden, is a working area of the garden, so a stableyard styling could fit well with a courtyard theme. There are several ways to achieve this look using paving blocks. These have a distinctive look, being much thicker and with a smaller surface area than other paving materials.

Cobblestones or Setts

A traditional form of paving for stableyards and mews passageways, cobblestones for this purpose were selected for their round shape and high-domed profile, which sheds water and makes it easy to hose them down and brush them off.

Cobbles are normally set into cement mortar, with gaps between them to allow for water run-off. They are smooth and gleam beautifully when wet, but can be uncomfortable to walk on.

It may be possible to source cobbles from building reclamation yards, but it is more common today to use new pieces of granite known as setts. These are square in shape with a flat, low-slip profile. They are extremely dense and durable, and are perfectly suitable for a hard-

working surface. It is normal to set them into a concrete base but you can also bed them into sand, enabling excess water to run away easily.

Good-value concrete flooring appears in many guises. Concrete setts are most realistic, while modular paving slabs, which are often used to make driveways, offer a variety of sizes, tones and textures suited to paving, steps and edgings.

Brickwork

Old brick paths can be seen in many Victorian and Edwardian walled kitchen gardens and if you're looking for a period feel for your productive courtyard, lay brick paths using one of the patterns below. Reclaimed frost-proof bricks are charming, but normal wall bricks tend to be soft and

suitable only for light traffic. For a durable flooring use strong, hardwearing engineering bricks, made from dense clay fired at high temperatures to withstand water penetration and frost damage. Choose colours such as deep plum and nearly black for a modern look.

The way you arrange brick pavers will affect the look of the garden. Use a simple pattern or stretcher bond, such as that found in brick walls, for hard-working areas, traditional cottage-garden-style plots and pathways. The herringbone bond has a more ornamental feel – but cutting triangles of brick to fill in gaps along the margins is complicated. The basketweave pattern is modular and therefore useful if you are paving around square or rectangular beds, and looks best over larger areas.

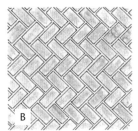
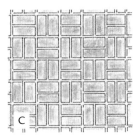

Above: *When laying brick pavers, you can use a simple pattern or stretcher bond (A), a herringbone bond (B) or a basketweave (C).*

Floor-level Planting

Hedging is a traditional way to edge beds for the kitchen garden and it combines well with brick paths – the scale of the brick sits comfortably with small edging plants.

For a more formal arrangement of vegetables and flowers, organize them into a parterre design. Create a framework of beds divided by paths edged with evergreens. Box is ideal; deep green and slow growing, it needs shaping only once or twice a year. Lavender and santolina have the added bonus of flowers and scent.

Take the idea a step further by creating a floor made up entirely of plants. Using the knot-garden format, make an intricate design using evergreen foliage set off by gravel. This centrepiece would be a perfect foil to exuberant vegetables and flowers and the potager would then always have an element of year-round interest.

Right: *In this parterre, the beds are edged with box. Red and green salad leaves form a geometric pattern beside yellow feverfew and orange marigolds.*

MAKING A PARTERRE

There are numerous pattern variations for knot gardens (with interweaving strands) and parterres (separate shapes and blocks). Even before the plants have knit together, the simple parterre shape illustrated appears sufficiently well defined to begin planting and sowing herbs and crops. Thorough ground preparation prior to planting the box edging, incorporating plentiful organic matter, promotes more rapid establishment.

1 Use a set square to check the right angles making up the outer square. Create diagonals and, at the centre, fix a peg with a length of string attached to mark out a circle.

2 This simple pattern, which you can mark out on the ground with sand or white marker paint, is planted at 15–20cm (6–8in) intervals with dwarf box.

3 Within two years the box plants will have knitted together to make a seamless hedge. Trim them in late spring and again in late summer using hand shears.

4 Depending on the scale of your potager and your requirements, you can either plant each segment with just a single type of plant in a grid pattern or subdivide each one.

WALLS FOR PRODUCTIVE SPACES

Enclosures play many important roles in the kitchen garden. Not only do they give shelter from cold or damaging winds, they provide a support for training fruit trees and climbers and help to maintain a microclimate for your plants. Any existing wall should be employed as part of your design and new partitions, such as fencing, hurdles or hedging, can be added to suit the produce.

Above: *A south-facing brick wall is an ideal location for climbing gourds.*

Walls for Training Fruit

Masonry walls, built from brick, stone or blockwork, have heat-retaining properties that give them the edge over other screening choices. They provide an ideal situation to train more tender fruit bearers, such as cherry, peach and apricot, and in colder climates pears will benefit, too.

Depending on the specimen, choose between espalier-style plants, where side branches are trained horizontally from a central vertical stem, and fan-trained examples, where several stems are produced from the base of the plant and fanned out equally all around (see also page 71 for training a grapevine).

These training systems need wall support. The most practical and least obtrusive is to have a series of wires fixed horizontally, enabling plants to be tied in place as they grow. Strong galvanized wire can be fixed to vine eyes and tightened using a tensioning device (see page 18 for training plants against walls). For extra support, thread the wire through a sequence of eyes set at intervals of no more than 1.8m (6ft).

Above: *The side wall of a timber hut provides a sheltered seating corner and a support for the vine-covered pergola.*

Below: *The roots of the golden hop spread over any available wall or partition.*

WHERE TO GROW FRUIT

• *On a south-facing wall – choose figs, peaches, apricots, grapes and pears. This site will be too hot for apples.*

• *On a west-facing wall – suitable for all fruits except those that require maximum sunshine and warmth. A good spot for cordon tomatoes, which like some shade from the midday sun.*

• *On an east-facing wall – this site only gets the morning sun, so tougher forms are needed here. Avoid anything where early blossom might get damaged by frost melting too rapidly in the morning sun. Grow fruit that won't flower early, such as raspberries.*

• *On a north-facing wall – this is the shadiest and coolest aspect, but options include the sour 'Morello' cherry, cooking apples and blackberries (although these won't be as sweet as they would be on a sunnier site).*

• *On trellis screens, archways and pergolas – anything with a strong climbing habit, such as squash, smaller fruited pumpkins and climbing courgettes, will benefit from getting light from two directions. Grapes and kiwis grow well on pergolas and arches. On trellis, try thornless blackberries and hybrid berries.*

Multi-stranded, stainless-steel yachting wire is another option. This is stronger than galvanized wire, but it, and its fixings, are more expensive. Climbers and wall-trained shrubs are heavy, especially when laden with fruit, so make sure all bolts and eyes are of adequate size and length to be fixed securely to a wall (see also page 71).

Building New Walls

For a traditional walled kitchen you might want to replace existing fences or low walls with higher enclosing walls – if planning regulations permit. This creates more shade but will provide a sheltered microclimate. A traditional period walled garden would have used brick. A breeze (cinder) block wall will be much cheaper and can be built by an experienced amateur, but will need a coat of cement render applying

to give a clean finish to the wall. An element of colour will add interest – a tinted white is clean and bright, or a warmer ochre or terracotta hue will help to hold the heat of the sun. The render can be tinted with pigments to provide a permanent colour finish, or painted over regularly with a

masonry product to keep it fresh. A brick theme could also be introduced by building brick piers or topping the breeze-block wall with engineering bricks.

Below: *The cordon method of training employs heavily pruned single stems, tied diagonally to horizontal wires.*

Below: *The espalier method of training fruit is productive, decorative and a good method to use on a high, warm wall. All fruit trees can be trained in this way, popular varieties being apple, pear and plum.*

Above: *A flourishing runner bean uses a metal handrail to support its climbing, leafy tendrils.*

Left: *Off-the-peg trellis panels make instant plant trainers. These have been attached to the wall and painted in a pale colour so they disappear into the background.*

Trellis Support for Climbing Crops

Wooden latticework trellis provides an alternative means of training climbers. These ready-made panels are useful for a range of lightweight annual climbers, such as beans, sugar snap peas and mangetouts (snow peas), hybrid berries and sweet peas. They can also be used for the more sprawling types of climber that can take up too much room horizontally, such as squash, baby pumpkins and climbing courgettes (zucchini), but not for training fruits and other permanent shrubs that need a long-term foundation. The panels are normally fixed directly to a wall or fence (see page 19). Use small pieces of wood as spacers to provide an air gap for the plants to twine.

Screens have a decorative role as well as a functional one, by dividing up the beds and providing a backdrop

Right: *A brick path, bordered with leeks, beetroots and marigolds, passes beneath a wooden pergola and trellis divisions entwined with runner bean plants.*

to other planting. Trellis panels can be employed as free-standing screens for climbing vegetables (see page 95 for the method). Used in this way, light and air can reach all round the plants. Trellis divides can be made using roofing laths and rustic poles,

so that the mesh can be made the size you like. Adaptable modular fencing screens are available in different styles – constructed with metal poles and combined with black climbing mesh they give an excellent foundation for climbers.

Wattle Hurdles

An alternative to trellis is the more rustic look of wattle hurdles, which suit the productive garden well. There has been a strong revival in country crafts over the past few years, and it is easy these days to source country-style wattle hurdles in a variety of sizes and styles.

The hurdles are rigid panels woven from willow, hazel or chestnut. These make attractive screens and dividers, as well as lending a sense of history. However, quality, and therefore durability, varies enormously, so if you want a product to last for a few years, you should not necessarily opt for the cheapest available.

Hurdles are not primarily used as climbing plant supports, but they are very efficient when employed as boundaries and windbreaks around a vegetable plot. The fine gaps in

the weaving allow air to be filtered through gently, thus avoiding the turbulence that can cause planting problems when solid barriers are used. It also cuts out wind chill and traps sunlight to create a more protected climate for your plants.

Above left: *A woven willow panel provides wind protection, creating a sheltered micro-climate for the young apple tree.*

Above right: *Rustic wattle hurdles make up a low screen fence to separate the potager from the rest of the garden.*

FIXING WATTLE HURDLES

Traditional hurdles can be made from split hazel, chestnut or woven willow wands (the latter are illustrated here). They form a natural-looking backdrop or screen where conventional fencing panels might appear visually jarring. As well as forming a delightful rustic backdrop for fruits and vegetables, you could also use them to screen off a composting area or to set off a border of cottage flowers and herbs. Fix the hurdles to stout wooden posts or, for a modern touch, use aluminium posts.

1 Measure the width of the hurdles and then set fence posts securely into the ground the right distance apart using a quick-drying concrete mix or spiked metal sockets. Then fix one end of the panel to the post by overlapping it and drilling through the hurdle into the post.

2 Use long galvanized screws to attach the hurdles to the posts using the predrilled holes. You can also erect lower hurdles using metal angle irons driven into the ground. Attach the hurdles to the angle irons by threading electrical cable ties through the holes in the metal.

3 Attach the other end of the panel to the support and continue in the same way to create the fence. Raise the hurdles off the ground to slow down rotting at the base. Hurdles can also be used as temporary garden dividers or boundaries while hedges are still growing.

PLANTS AND CONTAINERS FOR PRODUCTIVE SPACES

Your planting choices need to fit within the fixed perameters of your courtyard, as well as its aspect and light quality, if your fruit, vegetables and herbs are to flourish. An orderly planting style helps you to identify what is growing where, but a little unruliness with some mixed planting will soften the look.

Above: *These potted succulents create an attractive display outside the kitchen.*

Choosing Containers

Wooden barrels are ideal planters for vegetables that demand depth of soil. Potatoes, carrots, runner (green) beans and leeks can be grown in deep containers such as old rust-resistant galvanized dustbins or washtubs.

Other ideas for cottage-garden style containers are large, lined metal colanders used as hanging containers. Or, make an all-summer salad garden in old butlers' sinks or stone troughs. Use these to sow successions of colourful salad leaves, from tightly crisp green varieties, such as 'Little Gem' ('Bibb'), through to curvaceous cut-and-

come-again picking leaf forms, including 'Salad Bowl', purple 'Lollo Rosso' and red-tinged 'Sangria'.

Edible scented flowers and leaves add spice to salads and rice dishes and are ideal container plants. They give colour and interest to containers with less-attractive fare, such as aromatic herbs or vegetables. Choose mauve and yellow violas, orange and red nasturtiums, or peppery pinks.

Herb Options

If space is limited, use fresh herbs as edgings to border other plants, or sow them in pots. Choose herbs that you like to cook with and that make

Above: *Raised beds provide extra soil depth for greedy vegetables. These willow planters are filled with tomatoes, artichokes and herbs.*

good garnishes, and those that are expensive to buy or hard to get hold of, such as basil or coriander. Fill a big container with vitamin-packed parsley and another with chives, both of which can be used in large quantities in the kitchen. Choose thyme varieties for their pungent flavours, as well as purple and green sage, upright and creeping rosemary, and marjoram. Mint is rampant in open ground but is also happy to grow in containers.

MAKING A HANGING BASKET

A hanging basket, planted up with a combination of herbs, vegetables, fruits and edible flowers, is ideal where you have limited room for beds or floor-standing containers. Most herbs – including thyme, sage, basil, mint, oregano, parsley and chives – will grow happily in a basket. Other edibles include salad leaves, tumbler tomatoes, and cut-and-come-again vegetables, such as rainbow chard and baby spinach. Hanging baskets are, however, prone to drying out, so you need to water them regularly, at least daily.

1 Before planting, puncture the plastic liner up the sides. Add slow-release fertilizer to good-quality compost (soil mix) and fill two-thirds full.

2 Plant taller elements, such as the rainbow chard, in the centre and then add nasturtiums (*Tropaeolum majus*) to trail over the sides.

3 Plant alpine strawberries, or *fraises des bois*, so they cascade down the sides. Tumbler tomatoes or dwarf French beans are other options.

4 Fill with smaller plants, such as French marigolds. Top up the compost, water and stand in a shady, sheltered spot. Hang on a sheltered wall.

KEEPING A HANGING BASKET

• *If growing tomatoes, give the basket some some midday shade.*
• *Water regularly, deadhead and remove fading leaves to keep plants healthy and productive.*
• *Harvest a little at a time to give plants a chance to regrow.*
• *Feed with liquid tomato fertilizer from mid-summer.*
• *Keep small pots of replacement salads, annual herbs and edible flowers available. Remove the dead plants and add the new ones.*
• *Cut off the flowering stems of leaf vegetables and herbs grown for foliage, such as parsley and mint.*
• *In winter: take down the basket; cut perennial plants back to tidy them; pinch off dead leaves; and remove annuals. Stand the basket in the top of a large plant pot at the base of a sheltered wall. Replant, refresh the potting mix and add new varieties in the spring.*

Left: *You are unlikely to forget to water a hanging basket that is located just outside the kitchen door.*

PLANTING A STRAWBERRY URN

Strawberries are enjoyed for the colour they bring to the garden, as well as their sweet taste. The strawberry urn has small side pockets or openings that hold the small plants, and allow the plants to bear fruit using the full depth of the container. The container must have drainage holes in the bottom of the pot, critical in order to keep the roots from rotting. When the planting is finished, be sure to position the urn in full sun.

1 You will need to wet an urn made from terracotta, because otherwise the clay will wick the water out of the soil. Either place the urn in a tub of water for about an hour, or hose and wet the urn. You can get strawberry urns in plastic, but the terracotta ones are more attractive.

2 Put about 2.5cm (1in) of your soil in the bottom of the container and then cover this lightly with a layer of pea gravel or small rocks or broken crockery. This will help with drainage.

3 Continue to fill the urn with soil until you reach the lowest level of pockets. Insert one of the strawberry plants in each of the lower pockets, filling around them with soil and firming it gently. Make sure the crown of the plants is just above the soil level.

4 Water the lower level and each newly planted pocket. Fill the urn with soil until you reach the next level of pockets. Repeat the planting process. As you do this, place a 2.5cm (1in) PVC pipe drilled with holes down the centre of the pot so that each plant gets adequate moisture.

5 Stop adding soil when you get to 5cm (2in) below the rim of the pot. You can then add three to four plants in the very top of the container, and fill in with soil around them.

6 During the growing season, water the plant at each side opening, as well as the plants in the top layer. Keep the soil moist but not soggy. Every two weeks, apply a half-monthly amount of complete fertilizer. Special strawberry pots such as the one pictured are made with planting pockets.

Plants for your Productive Garden

To ensure an extended growing season, plant a good variety of perennial and annual flowers alongside your edible produce, such as cheerful winter pansies that will go on flowering through the low months. An abundance of climbers will also give vertical interest. Fill containers with brightly coloured flowers.

Insects and birds will flock to the pollen-laden blooms of mallows, rosemary, lavender and honeysuckle, and to the energy-giving seedheads of poppies and love-in-a-mist, helping propagation and pest control.

Companion Planting

Certain combinations of herbs and vegetables benefit from each other by encouraging healthy growth and diverting attention from unwanted pests. For example, tomatoes like to be planted alongside lemon balm and borage, which in turn encourages bees to aid in pollination. Parsley is good to tomatoes, carrots, asparagus and chives. Basil is the perfect table companion to tomatoes, and a few pots around the doorway will discourage flies and mosquitoes. Plant garlic near your fruit trees to repel pests.

Above: *Teeming with produce, this corner bed includes curly kale,* Hemerocallis *'Stella de Oro', strawberry, globe artichoke, French marigolds, Lollo Rosso lettuce, fennel, red cabbage, corn and borage.*

MAKING A STONE TROUGH

Solid stone troughs, such as old butlers' sinks, are difficult to source at a reasonable price, as well as being heavy to move about. Simulated ones, however, can be made with an artificial stone mixture or hypertufa.

Here, a glazed sink is coated to give it an authentic cottage-garden appeal. Once completed, the 'stone' trough could be used for planting herbs and salads, as well as other plant varieties.

1 Stand the sink on a narrower plinth so the coating does not stick to the support. If using a glazed sink, score the glazed surface with a tile-cutter to give the coating grip.

2 Coat the sink with industrial glue and leave it until it has gone tacky. Mix equal parts of sphagnum peat or peat substitute, sand or grit and cement, adding water slowly.

3 Wearing rubber gloves, apply the mixture, or hypertufa, working from the bottom up. The covering should be just thick enough to give a rough texture.

4 Cover the sink with plastic sheeting for up to a week until it is dry. Paint the hypertufa with liquid fertilizer to encourage the growth of mosses and make it look older.

STRUCTURES FOR PRODUCTIVE SPACES

Exploit the vertical dimension of your courtyard to utilize every available space. Boundaries offer instant backdrops for fruit trees and climbers, while arbours and arches, and temporary features such as willow wigwams, offer a multitude of edible and decorative possibilities, as well as offering extra privacy.

Above: *A hazel wigwam makes a support for abundantly fruiting cherry tomatoes.*

Left: *Apple trees trained over a pergola, protecting a patio seating area.*

Above: *A steel arch framework makes a good support for vines and climbing squashes, or for training pears.*

Structures for Training Produce

Edible produce trained over a timber arbour, or pergola, fixed along a house or boundary wall, creates a cloistered dining area with a special appeal. Trained with a grapevine, a pergola will provide shade in summer and cascades of luscious fruit for the table in autumn.

For a courtyard garden in a warmer climate, the Chinese gooseberry, *Actinidia chinensis*, twines vigorous, hairy stems to support show-off handsome, architectural foliage and a crop of juicy kiwi fruits.

A wrought-iron or timber gazebo is another good permanent structure for training fruit or vegetables. Make the gazebo from rustic poles topped with a hazel branch roof to shelter a twisted timber seat. Plant it up with unconventional soft fruits, such as thornless blackberry or tayberry, for a late summer crop for pies and jellies, or an ornamental vine with autumn colour, such as *Vitis* 'Brandt'.

Arches and Tunnels

A simple double arch made from steel or timber provides a framework for training a variety of climbing plants. This could make an excellent entrance point for a pathway or a dramatic framing device.

You could introduce a succession of arches linked with wires, to create a tunnel walk. Planting possibilities would then include yellow climbing squash, ornamental gourds or baby orange pumpkin, runner (green) beans, climbing nasturtiums or sweetpeas for cutting. Purple climbing French beans look and taste good, while the glamorous hyacinth bean, *Lablab purpureus*, is a true prima donna; its cerise flowers are followed by enormously long, gleaming, purple pods that are edible, and also make superb decoration. These, together with squash and small fruited pumpkin, require a very warm and sunny situation.

BUILDING A SIMPLE PERGOLA

You can buy pergola kits at larger home-improvement stores, garden centres and nurseries. The kits include all the fixings and brackets you need, as well as the timber pieces pre-cut for easy assembly. It is also possible to buy the various elements separately for modular constructions. In the sequence here, uncut timbers and fence posts have been used to make a cube-shaped pergola. This small structure would make an ideal spot for enjoying the fruits of your labours and by fixing trellis panels and overhead wires you could clothe the pergola with climbing fruits and vines. Thornless blackberries, for example, cover a large area in no time and combine pretty flowers with a succession of fruits. Try growing grapes or kiwi fruit overhead.

1 Excavate a 45–60cm (18–24in) deep hole using a trenching spade and post-hole tongues. Water the base, add dry, ready-mixed post-hole concrete. Ram the concrete to consolidate it and water in.

2 Start with 2.5–3m (9–10ft), 10cm (4in) uprights, so that the finished pergola allows head room of 2.3m (7ft 6in). Use a crosspiece and a spirit (carpenter's) level to check the post is perfectly level.

3 Check the right angles using a builder's set square and lay the long joists on the ground to calculate the distance and position required for the next post-hole to be dug.

4 Using a 5 x 10cm (2 x 4in) crosspiece with a spirit level between two adjacent posts, check that each of the four uprights are perpendicular and level. Rectify any errors now.

5 Lay the first crosspiece over two pillars and, allowing for a generous overhang, mark on the timber the width and position of the upright fence post to locate the notched fixing.

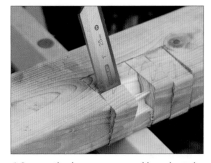

6 Secure the beam on a workbench and, using a saw, cut down into the notch to create four segments. Then use a sharp wood chisel to remove each segment, as shown here.

7 Lock the crosspiece in place at both ends and pre-drill holes through to the uprights. Fix the crossbeam with 70mm (2¾in) galvanized screws. Repeat this process for the parallel crossbeam.

8 Taking two more identical pieces of wood, measure the positions of the crossing beams and saw and chisel out notches as before. Fix this second set of beams securely in place.

9 Edge the base of the pergola with timber, securing it to the posts and, after removing the turf and laying a landscape membrane, surface the floor area with bark chippings or gravel.

Forged steel is the most suitable and enduring material from which to make a curved profile shape for such structures, although cheaper plastic-tube systems that can be adapted to many heights and lengths are also available.

It is possible to have a bespoke curved timber arch made to your specifications. Such an addition to the garden would certainly be very beautiful, but the cost would also be high. Wood is more usually found in square profile, using upright posts for support with a slatted roof. In a kitchen garden, the rustic pole concept is practical, cheap and very much in keeping with a country style. This would make a perfect foil for climbing runner (green) beans; to make a real impact, try pink-flowered 'Sunset', white 'Desiree' and 'Painted Lady' splashed with both red and white.

On a smaller scale, there are support staging structures on the market that provide effective growing frames. In combination with a standard growbag, such vertical frames will support heavier fruits and vegetables that like to grow vertically.

Above: *A staged support structure for tomatoes makes the most of a small space.*

Raised Beds

You can experience two main difficulties when creating a vegetable plot in an enclosed space: poor soil and insufficient light. Creating raised beds within retaining walls should, however, help to remedy both problems at once – first, by increasing soil depth and, second, by bringing the plants out into the light.

Retaining walls made of brick are good-looking, though fairly costly. Reduce the expense by using

Above: *A small wooden potting bench, with raised edges to retain loose soil.*

Left: *Raised beds provide additional soil depth and bring plants nearer to the light.*

concrete blocks, but you will then need to give them a decorative finish of some type to improve their distinctly utilitarian appearance.

Finishes include render and paint, or you could face them with terracotta tiles or clad them with woven wattle, depending on the style of their surroundings. However, for a simpler and more straightforward form of construction, you could make the walls of the raised beds from reclaimed railway sleepers (ties) or some other heavy timbers (see below).

Good soil drainage is vital for raised beds, so you will need to build on open ground that has been cleared of perennial weeds and dig it over to break up the soil. Don't forget to create drainage holes with pipes near the base of the walls to take away surplus water.

Raised beds must be filled with good-quality topsoil incorporating generous quantities of bulky organic matter, such as garden compost (soil mix), manure or composted bark. The success of your crops depends on this foundation.

Above: *Heavy, sawn timber planks make it easy to construct good-looking raised beds.*

MAKING A RAISED BED WITH SLEEPERS

In a small garden space you have to ensure that even the practical areas are attractive. Meeting both these requirements is this type of raised bed, ideal for growing vegetables and herbs. Railway sleepers (ties) are used to create a low retaining wall. Their weight and stability make construction easy, and only minimal foundations are required. Modern sleepers are usually tanalized, so line the inside with plastic to prevent soil contamination.

1 A chain saw or circular saw is the only practical way to cut sleepers. If you don't feel confident using a saw like this, ask the supplier to cut the sleepers to size for you.

2 To avoid wastage, make a bed that requires least cutting. Lay out the first course of sleepers in a recessed trench filled with hardcore and then start building up.

3 As you build up the layers, arrange the timbers so that the corner joins on adjacent layers don't correspond. Overlapping the timber like this gives extra stability.

4 Use corner brackets as shown in the four corners of at least the top layer of sleepers. This layer is the one most likely to be sat on, leant over and knocked.

5 Fill the bed with sieved (strained), weed-free topsoil mixed with well-rotted manure or compost (soil mix). If using tanalized timber, line the sides with heavy-duty plastic to avoid contamination.

RAISED BED CROSS-SECTION

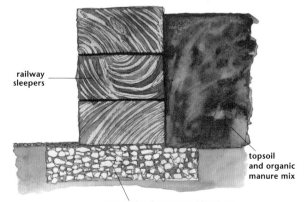

railway sleepers

topsoil and organic manure mix

ground level compacted hardcore

WORKADAY ORNAMENT FOR PRODUCTIVE SPACES

Using 'ornamental' features in a productive space is not the contradiction you may think. Utilitarian features often have a character that fits with their purpose – displayed antique tools, attractively age-worn implements and containers, and structures for feeding or sheltering animals.

Above: *Even a tiny residence like this can house a surprising number of white doves.*

Above: *Characterful tools such as these give enormous pleasure in their daily use.*

Above: *An old basket, here used for tending aromatic basil and tomato plants, creates an attractive picture.*

Utilitarian Features

Everyday gardening hand tools are the ornament of a productive garden. Spades, forks, rakes and hoes have a functional beauty in their own right, whether brightly shining stainless steel, exclusive horn-handled varieties or simply those you have collected over the years. Choose your tools carefully, checking their weight, balance and quality, and look after them, cleaning and oiling regularly.

Old garden and farmyard implements can be found in junk shops and fairs. Weathered zinc watering cans, buckets and milk churns are decorative and evocative. Return these tools to daily practical use. If they are too battered, turn leaky holes to advantage by transforming them into planting containers. A discarded domestic water tank makes an excellent rainwater butt; you might combine it with a cascading fountain feature, using old watering cans.

Pieces of rusted farm machinery can be given a new lease of life, used as a three-dimensional plant support for climbing beans, or as a stand-alone sculpture by a planting bed. Antique, long handled rakes, spades and forks can be fashioned into a distinctive, cross-bar garden gate or fixed on a wall to train annual climbers. Rusty chains, dangled from a wall or canopy, make excellent supports for scramblers and tendril climbers such as sweetpeas. The possibilities for reinventing discarded objects are limitless.

Above: *A redundant galvanized tank transforms to garden butt and fountain feature, conserving precious rainwater.*

Above: *Recycled tins sprayed in bright colours make ornamental herb planters.*

Above: *Old metal pots and buckets make useful planters.*

Above: *Provide a number of seed and nut feeders to attract a wide variety of birds.*

Welcoming Wild Creatures

Visiting wild creatures are a natural part of the potager. The garden life cycle needs earthworms, butterflies, greenfly and slugs to feed birds, aerate the ground and pollinate flowers. So choose plants that attract insects, and avoid pesticides and herbicides that could harm your garden visitors. Birds can be easily attracted with a range of treats including seed mixes, nuts, fat balls, suet cakes and fresh fruit. Maintain a regular feeding routine with tables, seed dispensers and nesting boxes in a quiet place where they are easy to see, which will encourage birds to return to your courtyard.

HOW TO AGE CONTAINERS

• *To age a terracotta pot, soak it and stand in a damp, shady place to build up a coating of green algae.*
• *To rust a galvanized bucket, follow the steps below, using rust-coloured acrylic paint in place of aqua-green.*

CREATING VERDIGRIS, RUST AND LEAD EFFECTS

The luminous, blue-green tones of weathered copper (verdigris) are simple to reproduce on metal and matt plastic containers. Here we have used a cheap, galvanized bucket. But any recycled metal container such as an old flower arranger's bucket, a recycled olive oil can or a large colander (where you will need to fit chains and line it with plastic), could be transformed, making a decorative rustic container for salads, herbs or strawberries.

1 Sand the surface of the bucket and then prime (paint) it with a metal primer. Allow to dry thoroughly for about two to three hours. Next, apply gold paint and allow that to dry as well for another two to three hours.

2 Paint with amber-coloured shellac and allow it to dry. Mix up some white artist's acrylic paint in aqua-green and add water to make a watery consistency. This will give the colour known as verdigris.

3 Sponge some of the aqua verdigris paint on and allow it to dry for one or two hours. Use a kitchen towel or rag to dab off excess before it is dry. Seal and protect the finish with a coat of matt polyurethane varnish.

4 To use the bucket as a planter, turn it upside down and make drainage holes with a 15cm (6in) nail. Part-fill with gravel before adding compost (soil mix). Plant a row of buckets with purple cabbage, lavender or chives.

WATER FOR PRODUCTIVE SPACES

Water is essential in the kitchen garden to irrigate your crops. You will need to decide on an effective and reliable watering system that suits you and sustains your plants. Watering by hand is convenient, but not always the best option. You can also save rainwater by storing it in a rainwater butt and recycle greywater from the house so that this resource is not wasted.

Above: *A seep hose has minute holes along one side of a plastic or rubber pipe.*

Watering Fruit and Vegetables

Productive crops are especially thirsty and irregular watering will reduce the crops of most vegetables – so you will need an effective and regular watering system. The beginning and the end of the day are the best times to water. Water your crops deeply, and allow the soil time to dry a little before watering again. Light watering can do more harm than no water at all. This is because it stimulates the plant roots to come to the surface, where they are damaged by sun exposure.

Overhead watering is effective if you work within these guidelines. However, the wet foliage that this creates can encourage diseases to settle. A controlled watering system reduces water wastage and supplies water to the base of the plants, just where they need it. A leaky-pipe, seep or soaker hose, is made of recycled rubber and is easy to install in a raised bed (see opposite) and allows water to slowly permeate the soil.

Another effective way to water a vegetable garden is to use a drip or trickle irrigation system, available as kits, connected to an automatic timer. This works well for vegetables that are spaced far apart and for container gardens sited on a deck or terrace. Small tubes are inserted into holes in the main hose line at intervals and water is distributed at low pressure wherever the tubes are placed.

Water Storage

Use a rainwater butt to collect roof water via a drainpipe. Plants prefer rainwater, so you will be doing your fruit trees and vegetables a real favour. The simplest above-ground container is a plastic tank with a spout and tap near the base. These are functional, but not terribly attractive to look at; you may prefer a resin replica of a tall oil jar or stone column if that suits the style of your garden space. Site the container in a shady spot to help preserve the quality of the water inside.

An industrial zinc water tank, even though it is completely utilitarian in appearance, could be made to look less jarring and appear to better integrate into its surroundings if it is partially obscured with plantings of ferns and other shade-loving specimens.

Wooden barrels that have been sealed to retain water can be used in a similar way. A complete barrel would be large enough to function as an irrigation tank in its own right, while a lower, half-barrel could be used to house a fountain feature.

Above: *When using a watering can, water your crops deeply and regularly.*

Above: *Large beer and wine casks make excellent water-storage butts.*

Above: *This water butt has a tap for easy access to the recycled water.*

IRRIGATING A RAISED BED

Watering vegetables, or other bed plants, overhead with a hose could make them more susceptible to disease, because foliage that stays moist too long can cause fungus. A practical and easy way to irrigate raised beds is to combine a soaker hose and a regular hose using a hose connector. This system will ensure that your raised bed plants get a good deep soaking where they need it, and that the foliage stays dry.

1 Mark on your wooden garden frame where the entry point of the irrigation hose should be. In one end of the raised bed, drill a hole that is just large enough to accommodate a standard size hose.

2 Calculate the lengths of garden hose required to cover the distance from each raised bed to the connector (see next step) and from the connector to the water source. Having purchased the hose, cut into shorter lengths to suit these calculations.

3 Use a two-way hose connector valve with built-in shut-offs. These valves connect one or more hoses to the spigot, or to each other. Having a shut-off valve in each connector arm means you can redirect the water flow. Using female hose couplings, attach two pieces of hose.

4 Insert the other ends of the short pieces of hose through the holes you drilled. Inside the raised bed, attach the short pieces of hose to whatever length of soaker hose you need. Outside the bed, attach another length of hose using a female hose coupling.

5 Arrange the soaker hoses in the raised bed in an S-shape to distribute the water. Arrange them at the base of the plants in the row so that water is distributed evenly over the plant roots. If you prefer not to see the soaker hoses, it is fine to bury them beneath the soil.

IRRIGATION TECHNIQUES

• *Use watering systems such as canvas soaker hoses, perforated plastic sprinkle hoses and drip-type irrigation that ensure water gets where it is most needed. These systems disperse water in a long, narrow pattern that is ideal for beds. Drip irrigation has the advantage of wasting less water.*

• *Water your beds regularly and frequently – effective drainage in a raised bed means that overwatering is minimized, but problems linked to underwatering are increased, especially in deep beds.*

• *Bear in mind that the amount and frequency of watering depends on the water-holding capacity of the soil, weather conditions and the preferences of your plants.*

CASE STUDY: EDIBLE BOUNTY

This unusual potager is set against a lush background of exotic tree ferns and Australian gum trees, which together provide protection from the wind and shade from the heat of the sun. A setting as dramatic as this demands an equally bold selection of complementary and exuberant vegetables and herbs to create a beautiful yet entirely practical garden space.

Above: *Raised planting beds are made here from sheets of exterior-grade plywood.*

The planting areas of this potager have been devised as a series of raised beds to provide the benefits of deep, good-quality soil. The extra soil depth helps to overcome the problems associated with cultivation in a generally dry environment.

Above: *This decorative chicken will never disturb the crop of alpine strawberries.*

The beds are manageably sized to simplify access and maintenance and their curved, organic shapes integrate well into the wild surroundings. The beds are imaginatively contained by sheets of painted exterior-grade plywood, riveted together and painted earth red. The pathways, generously wide to allow wheelbarrows to navigate easily, are covered with gravel spread over compacted earth and hardcore.

Bold, rustic timbers have been used to construct the sturdy, cabin-style shed. An essential, shady veranda, roofed with traditional corrugated iron and supported on tree-trunks, has been incorporated to one side. Outside, furniture has been fashioned from pieces of reclaimed driftwood. Rambling orange nasturtiums provide ground cover as well as a colourful foil to the bleached timbers, and the whole effect is one of barely tamed domesticity in a savage environment.

The exuberant winter planting introduces bold form as well as vitamins and includes varieties of cabbage, kale and broad (fava) beans. Climbing varieties are supported on suitably curvy, local tree branches.

An abundance of rampant herbs, including parsley, chives and thyme, bursts over the edges of the beds. A curled-up hosepipe hints at water delivered from a sheltered, above-ground tank that captures every drop of precious rainfall.

The garden plan for this potager, shown overleaf, portrays a cultivated space, a productive oasis within a wild landscape. Also included on page 143 are two practical features, one on creating a hot-pile compost bin and the other explaining how to lay tiles on gravel to give a practical floor on which to cultivate your produce.

Right: *Every inch of space is utilized here with the exuberant planting of pungent aromatics and heavily textured kale.*

CREATING A SUCCESSFUL POTAGER

Soil Preparation:
• *The soil must be deep and have good structure and texture.*
• *Incorporate plenty of bulky organic manure to improve light and sandy soils or heavy clay soils.*
• *Remove all perennial weeds before starting soil preparation.*
• *Cultivate the soil with a mechanical device or dig it over thoroughly to improve its structure.*
• *Remove stones and rake the surface to a fine tilth before seed sowing.*

Screens and Divisions:
• *Sunshine should be available for most of the day, but in extreme conditions, shade trees or other types of screening should be in place.*
• *Grow fruit and vegetables on walls and other vertical structures. Attach a trellis or wires for climbers such as runner (green) beans or gourds.*

Maintenance:
• *Protect bean and pea seeds and soft fruits from bird attack using netting.*

• *Provide a drip-style hose irrigation system that can be controlled by a timer.*
• *Allow for hand watering by hose at planting time and for specific areas.*
• *Water evenly to maintain growth, and thoroughly to encourage deep roots.*
• *Remove weeds regularly or use an organic weed-suppressant mat.*
• *Avoid treading and compacting moist soil when planting and weeding.*
• *Lay horticultural fleece over beds of seedlings to discourage insect pests and provide protection in cold weather.*

EDIBLE BOUNTY GARDEN PLAN

cottage-style flower garden

chicken shed

reclaimed wood for posts

open area for planting up and storage

large wooden hot-pile compost bins

pool

bench

veranda for hanging baskets and potted plants

pale gravel beach shingle

pathway of stepping stones set in gravel

Plant list

1   *Tropaeolum majus*
2   *Beta vulgaris*
3   *Daucus carota*
4   *Brassica rapa*
5   *Petroselinum crispum*
6   *Phaseolus vulgaris* var. nanus
7   *Ocimum sanctum*
8   *Solanum lycopersicum*
9   *Spinacia oleracea*
10 *Brassica oleracea 'Hispi'*
11 *Vicia faba*
12 *Brassica oleracea* var. capitata
13 *Beta vulgaris ssp cicla*
14 *Brassica rapa*
15 *Lactuca Sativa 'Lollo Rossa'*
16 *Allium schoenoprasum*
17 *Pisum sativum 'Dwarf Sweet Green'*

Below: *Vegetables and taller herbs are supported with sticks and brushwood from early on in their growth.*

Right: *A throne-like garden chair is positioned to look into the spiral-shaped vegetable plot.*

Above: *Legumes enrich the soil by converting nitrogen from the atmosphere.*

Above: *Swiss or ruby chard make the plot more decorative with their colourful stems.*

Above: *The large shed makes a rustic backdrop for this relaxed kitchen garden.*

MAKING A HOT-PILE COMPOST BIN

Every productive garden should have a compost heap where organic materials are recycled to create a highly nutritious soil conditioner. Use any vegetable matter that is disease free and will rot down.

1 Place the bin on the soil, water and add twiggy material.
2 Add alternating bands of drier 'brown' materials and fresher 'greens'. This introduces oxygen and prevents the pile from becoming wet and airless.
3 Every couple of layers add decomposing microbes with compost from another heap, or garden soil. Leaves of nettle or comfrey act as activators.
4 Cover the bin to conserve heat and moisture.

Nitrogen-rich 'greens' include grass cuttings, raw fruit and vegetables, seaweed and garden pond clearings, tea leaves, manure, non-seeding annual weeds and soft hedge clippings.
Carbon-rich 'browns' include coffee grounds, dry plant stems and twigs (preferably shredded), scrunched-up paper, egg shells, straw, hay and torn-up cardboard. Water the brown layers in the bin.

HOT-PILE COMPOST BIN CROSS-SECTION

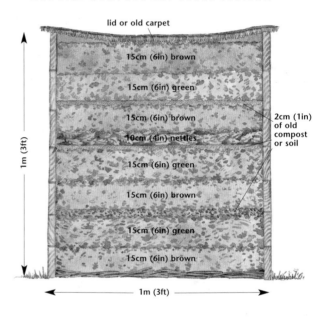

lid or old carpet

15cm (6in) brown

15cm (6in) green

15cm (6in) brown

10cm (4in) nettles

2cm (1in) of old compost or soil

15cm (6in) green

15cm (6in) brown

15cm (6in) green

15cm (6in) brown

1m (3ft)

1m (3ft)

SETTING PAVING SLABS IN GRAVEL

Gravel is a relatively low-cost alternative to paving, but in large areas it can feel monotonous. Add textural variety with paving slabs as shown below, or use real or concrete wood-effect sleepers. Another advantage in introducing paving slabs or sleepers into an area of gravel is that they provide a more secure passage for foot traffic.

1 Lay out the tiles or paving slabs. The ones used here are sandstone pavers with a riven surface, but you could use quarry tiles or concrete, stone-effect paving.

2 Ease away the gravel around a tile to mark where to dig. Remove the tile and excavate a square hole, just large enough to accommodate it, scooping out the hardcore.

3 Set the tile back in the hole and check it is at the same level as the gravel. Move the gravel back around the tile using a straight-edged piece of wood to level it out.

4 Quarry tiles or small slabs can relieve large uniform areas of gravel or slate. Set them closer together to form a grid to create a level sitting area.

CONTEMPLATIVE RETREATS

The pace of modern life leaves us with a need to find peace and tranquillity. This can be achieved in a courtyard or terrace with an inspiring and sympathetic planting, natural textures and the relaxed design of the contemplative retreat.

Some elements from this style are borrowed from the restrained aesthetics of oriental garden design, characterized by a pared-down, natural approach. An effective courtyard haven will provide spiritual nourishment as well as physical relaxation, giving you the space and surroundings in which to pause, be still and reflect. It will bring you close to nature, helping you to understand and appreciate the rhythm and cycles of the seasons, revealing new shoots, flowers, fruits and seeds. Nurturing the soil and its plants forms part of this healing process, helping to refresh your spirit and calm your mind.

Left: *Enclosure, texture, calm and longevity are brought together here. A tranquil glade of bamboo* Phyllostachis nigra, *with its slim black stems, lines the boundary screen, while the gnarled trunk of an ancient olive stands sentinel.*

OUTDOOR RHYTHMS

A contemplative courtyard should feel natural and understated, ordered but free-flowing. It should stimulate your senses, drawing you in mentally and physically, inviting the discovery of lush greenery with the life-giving moisture and oxygen it brings. It will provide a place to lose yourself among the sounds of breeze-rustled foliage, trickling water and birdsong.

Above: *Swathes of grasses and soft-flowering perennials create a soothing mood.*

Lush Greenery

A dense covering of plants will help to create a sense of privacy in the contemplative courtyard – and that sense of being away from other people's notice can be a rare and precious asset in a busy urban setting.

The appropriate choice of plants can create a living screen to enclose your space, principally achieved by building up layers of sculptural greenery. For example, try placing tall bamboos at the rear of your space to create an impenetrable barrier and then gradually reduce the height and bulk of the planting in front. In this way, you introduce a new dimension – the usual height and spread, but also the third dimension of depth.

Impressively architectural, tree ferns provide a dappled canopy of long, arching fronds, while clipped evergreen shrubs, such as *Ligustrum* sp. and tailored pines, will introduce bold outline and form.

To soften the near distance, plant swathes of delicate grasses to sway and rustle in the breeze, with a low underplanting of perennials, ferns and mosses at their base. By mixing sculptural evergreens with deciduous shrubs and perennials, you can form a miniature landscape that will reflect the changing seasons, from delicate spring bulbs and blossoms to fiery autumn tints and with the skeletal outline of bare branches in the winter.

Hard Landscaping and Structures

Provide your contemplative courtyard garden with layers of structure and textural interest through the elements of hard landscaping you introduce. A small space will be enlarged by even small changes of level. Ensure, however, that any such changes in level are not so subtle that they become trip hazards.

Link different levels with steps that are slow and shallow, meandering into sinuous paths to lead you gradually through the garden, allowing plenty of time for you to appreciate your surroundings. Crunchy gravel or layers of slate chippings look informal and introduce an interesting texture to contrast with the softer forms of the surrounding foliage.

Structures should blend sympathetically with the natural design approach. Create them from textural and sensuous raw materials, using natural wood and stone in a

Above: *A symbolic Zen garden suggesting mountains, forests, fields and seascape.*

form that is close to its raw, natural state. Timber sleepers (ties) and reclaimed driftwood combine well for steps and retaining walls, while blocks of natural stone, as well as being practical elements, can be introduced as sculptural forms in their own right.

Observation Points

So that you can appreciate your surroundings, provide comfortable seating at various points, especially to enjoy a special aspect of the outside space. A Zen-style viewing garden could make an interesting central feature. This could be designed in the classically cool style, with an area of raked gravel to be punctuated by a group of specially selected rocks and minimal, evergreen planting. A solid bamboo fence would provide a suitable, though austere, backdrop. Alternatively, a screen of living bamboo would offer a valuable green relief, without distracting from the main feature.

The Power of Water

Water in the garden will never fail to relax and invigorate both mind and body. A still, quiet pool provides a cool, clear space that will capture shadows, reflections and glints of sunlight. If you border it with willowy water plants, then birds and other wildlife will be attracted to drink and bathe.

Right: *Some uprights in this timber post screen are painted an ox-blood colour, complemented by the planting of silver-leafed helichrysum and bronze dracaena palms.*

FLOORING FOR A CONTEMPLATIVE RETREAT

Select natural, unprocessed materials for floors in this soothing, simple courtyard. Untreated timbers and rough-hewn stones are key materials to use as floors. Naturally textured and weathered surfaces help to give the impression that materials evolved from the site, and designing in flowing lines creates a calming atmosphere.

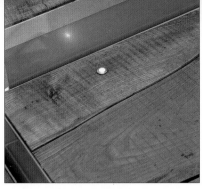

Above: *A coat of varnish brings out the grain of rough-sawn softwood.*

Gravel, Pebbles and Chippings

The loose nature and crunchy texture of gravel provides a low-key surface that suits an organic design. Gravel is a term that covers a range of stone aggregate in varying sizes. Most often it is applied to pea shingle, which is quarried from riverbeds. Shingle is inexpensive, readily available and excellent for paths and large background areas. Stone chippings are tiny pieces of marble, limestone or granite mostly used as a decorative mulch.

Beach pebbles make an elegant alternative for surfacing. Sea-washed smooth, their subtle colours vary in tone through cream, pink and grey to almost black. Sizes are graded from a few millimetres – ideal for paths – to generously proportioned

Above: *A pathway of recycled, green-coloured glass stones, edged with brick, picks up on the surrounding plant greenery.*

cobbles – an excellent complement to water features and plantations of grasses. Combine pebbles in different sizes to make an integrated design. To define a path of small-grade stones, line the edges with pebbles of a larger size to add texture and to hold back the planting on either side. Strew mounds of large cobbles to make sculptural 'beds' that contrast with simple screen planting beyond, and throw in an occasional giant stone for extra effect. Make a rocky beach surround for a natural pond, grading the sizes gradually down to the water's edge.

Slate chippings make a handsome alternative. Their form is reminiscent of scree and so produces more of a mountainside effect in contrast to

that of the beach, while its mossy colours of green and plum make it an excellent complement to naturalistic planting.

Fine, crushed slate makes a subtle decorative mulch, while chunky 40mm (1½in) pieces can be used for heavier duty areas, such as walkways. It is perhaps most successful when employed to create a dry river bed effect, mimicking a stream snaking down a slope. Although pebbles can be used instead, slate's darker tone is more reminiscent of water and is effective when wet, the hillside colours taking on an extra intensity.

Above: *Boulders, rocks and beach pebbles achieve a texturally interesting pathway.*

Above: Smooth, oblong limestone slabs create a cool-looking terrace around this fountain feature.

Solid Surfaces

Blocks of dark granite would be a classic choice, but other stones of character can be used, too. Thick slabs of slate would look especially handsome when wet, while an Indian sandstone containing fossil remains would demonstrate its primeval origins. Heavy rocks may also be used to suggest an imaginary path through foliage that is not intended for a physical passage.

Stone offers obvious natural connections with the earth, but wood is also an interesting material in the contemplative garden. Trees grow from the earth so timber will reconnect us by providing walkways. Blocks of heavy wood, used like stepping-stones, will have a powerful visual impact, introducing textural contrast to gravel paths.

Where slopes and changes of level are encountered, thick wooden planks can be used to retain the soil on the bank, and the surfaces covered with gravel to create shallow steps.

Gravel has a tendency to shift when walked on, so the timber will also serve to secure the aggregate to make walking easier. Sawn-up railway sleepers (ties) or reclaimed structural beams are ideal for the purpose, while large pieces of driftwood would add a sculptural quality. Sink them into the ground so they sit at just the finished height of the surrounding aggregate.

Above: Weathered timber planks create a secure, textural transition across pebbles.

Left: *Timber decks, fixed on foundations below, appear to float on the pond to create an intimate and calming viewing platform.*

upward dimension. The concept works well if it creates a passage across or alongside a pond or stretch of water, providing a haven for wildlife. Where it is not feasible to build a pond, the impression of bog garden can be just as visually effective. Plant an area with tall reeds and grasses, which will produce evocative rustling sounds and drooping seedheads and push the walkway through them.

In place of the boardwalk, you might prefer to install a timber viewing deck. This would be an ideal device on a hillside plot to take advantage of any vistas below. If you are thinking of making a pool, a deck provides a practical seating area, especially if it is cantilevered out over the water, enabling you to feel closer to nature and more part of the wildlife environment. Another idea involving wood is to build a low, raised bed from railroad sleepers (ties) (see also page 135).

Paths and Walkways

The main role of the path in a contemplative garden design is to create a slow, meandering journey, allowing time for reflection. It should not be possible to see the destination immediately, but little vistas should open up along the way. A Japanese-style path made of loose-laid stepping-stones would provide an excellent textural contrast to either a gravel or a grassy track, while also making a sympathetic and practical walkway. Choose bold slabs of stone in similar but irregular sizes with random edges and profiles for the most natural effect.

Boardwalks can introduce a fascinating element to this style of garden. The timber planks are very much in keeping, and by raising the pathway on stilts you create a new

Above: *Rocks and boulders can create the effect of a dried-up stream bed.*

Above: *Loose-laid stepping-stones bedded into grass create a more natural pathway solution than conventional paving in concrete.*

MAKING A PEBBLE BEACH FEATURE

Swirling patterns and textures created with natural materials can make pleasing features for the contemplative garden. This stylized, free-flowing design takes its inspiration from the wave-form ceramic plaque, but also symbolizes the opposing yet complementary forces of yin and yang. You could easily centre the design on a circular stepping-stone with Japanese or Chinese lettering, or on a shallow ceramic serving dish filled with water, which could double as a birdbath. Alternatively, work the pebbles around a tall, rough-hewn rock.

1 Decide precisely where the main elements are to go, including any pot groupings, the centrepiece and the large, water-worn boulders. Bed the centrepiece and boulders down into the gravel slightly to give them more of a natural, established appearance.

2 Pour a bag of cobbles, in muted browns and greys, into the gaps between the boulders. These don't need to be precisely arranged, as they will form the backdrop and unifying element of the feature. Part burying the boulders mimics the look of a natural beach.

3 Continue covering the ground with a sack of grey speckled granite cobbles. A few of these should also be placed on top of the cobbles to blend the transition. Alternatively, use the same muted brown and grey colours, but in a smaller pebble size, and mix as before.

4 Using shingle, fill the gaps between the larger stones and blend in the edges to link them with the original background of gravel. Note that it is illegal to collect gravel or pebbles from a beach without the permission of the landowner.

5 Finally create a dramatic swirling waveform that winds through the feature using sparkling white pebbles. This flourish tails off between the plants and pots. Thin the pebbles at the edges to create the suggestion of sea foam.

6 With split bamboo and brushwood screening at the rear making a uniform backdrop, and using oriental-style plants such as sedges and bamboo, this feature would fit into an oriental scheme or even a narrow side passage or balcony space.

WALLS AND SCREENS FOR A CONTEMPLATIVE RETREAT

A sense of enclosure is an important aspect of the contemplative courtyard. Walls and partitions can use a soft natural material, such as bamboo, or shiny and reflective surfaces can add an air of mystery. Less sympathetic partitions can be broken up with other devices, such as fabric screens and obscuring greenery.

Above: *The raffia panel, intended to mark a pathway, drifts atmospherically in the breeze.*

Above: *A plain wall with a liquid crystal panel is set off by a stand of tall bamboo, making a serene backdrop to this area.*

Bamboo Screening

Traditionally, Japanese screening is made from cut bamboo poles tied together with black string. Such screens can be purchased ready made, but quality ones can be expensive. This is a viable project to do yourself if you can find poles of a suitable diameter, around 3–5cm (1¼–2in). Arrange them in a diagonal diamond pattern and tie them together with identical knots using heavy-duty, tarred garden twine in place of the traditional black string.

Bamboo is relatively weather resistant, but keep it away from the ground or it will rot. For this reason, secure the panels to preserved timber posts concreted into the ground. This will give you an open screen to define an area or provide a backdrop.

Where a more solid screen is required you can create a framework of preserved timber slats on which to build your screen. You will need vertical posts set into the ground, with two horizontal rails set at around 15–20cm (6–8in) from the finished dimensions at the top and bottom, on which to fix vertically the bamboo poles. Pre-drill holes through the poles and fix them to the timber rails with brass screws or more economical stainless-steel-headed nails.

Ready-made bamboo screening is available by the roll, so simply fix the screening directly to your basic framework using wire ties or twine. This lighter-weight system is suitable for use as a wind shelter. It is made either from wooden posts (see method opposite) or fine bamboo stems held together with steel wire.

Lightweight raffia panels can make an airy, ephemeral statement. Suspend them from one side, letting them fly freely in the breeze – high up and horizontally to emphasize an area, or vertically to mark a pathway.

A screen wall of living bamboo gives an entirely different effect, combining green foliage with stems ranging from bright yellow and green to black. Bamboo can be invasive so if you are concerned, commercial root-retaining barriers are available by the roll.

Above: *Ready-made bamboo screening is fixed to supports, creating a lightweight screen.*

Above: *Cut stems of silver birch saplings create a delicate semi-open screen.*

Right: *Bamboo will suffer from wet and rot if pushed directly into the ground; these canes are fixed to a timber framework to create an elegant and durable fence.*

CREATING A BAMBOO FENCE

The design and construction of bamboo fences and screens in Japan is a highly specialized art, but if you prefer a more instant solution then buy ready-made screens, or follow these steps. The materials here are widely available and you can create an authentic look without having to purchase expensive imported goods.

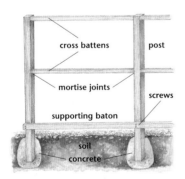

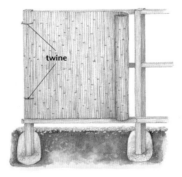

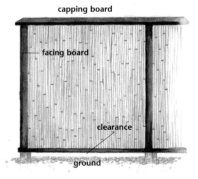

1 Set posts 1.5–2m (5–6½ft) apart. Dig holes up to 45–50cm (18–20in) deep by 20cm (8in) wide. Concrete the posts in place, screwing on the lower baton 4cm (1½in) off the ground. Chisel out mortises in the posts for the cross battens halfway up the posts and at the top of the posts. Screw the joints into the posts.

2 Support the roll of ready-made bamboo fencing material on the lower supporting batten, temporarily attaching one end of it to a post with some twine. Unroll the fencing material, attaching it to the cross battens with twine.

3 Hold the bamboo in place using facing boards screwed on to the posts. Cut the posts level with the bamboo. Lay capping boards over the post tops, both for their appearance and to stop rain getting into the end grain, and screw them down. Stain them ash black to provide a contrast with the bamboo fencing material.

Right: *Fine textile panels, held taut by thin battens at the top and bottom, provide shade without totally obscuring the light and the view.*

Creating the Mood

Screening does not have to follow a traditional route – contemporary alternatives can give a special look without departing from the natural theme that suits the contemplative style. It is invariably the distressed, the worn and the patinated surface that fits comfortably in a thoughtful, peaceful space, and even quite modern materials take on this quality over time. Metal panels can be used as backdrops or walls and, when oxidizing, can evolve into organic colours and textures. Copper will transform from its burnished hues to give a greenish, verdigris effect. Zinc will change from dark grey to a whitish, powdery finish that works well with subtle foliage, while steel will rust into delicious, orangy tones. Pressed metal panels constructed from aluminium, galvanized iron, copper or zinc can be used outdoors as a feature decoration on a foundation wall.

A glass screen, etched with a suitable design, can produce a visual pause in the garden, while not interrupting the view beyond. Textiles will deliver a similar effect if they are translucent and gauze-like, while dense fabrics will hide and enclose.

Bear in mind that any solid material will stop wind temporarily, while at the same time causing turbulence. Fixings should therefore be securely attached with some sort of spacing between the panels to aid the passage of strong breezes.

Above: *The wavy relief in this translucent glass screen suggests gently flowing rain.*

Above: *These succulents are attached to a wire mesh covered with a water-retentive fibre.*

Above: *Floaty muslin screens drift from this rustic pergola to create an intimate corner.*

IDEAS FOR BOUNDARIES IN A CONTEMPLATIVE COURTYARD

• *Keep the visual effect of enclosures light to avoid overpowering the garden.*
• *Screen walls can be made in sections of solid material, such as rendered blocks or painted marine ply, allowing planting spaces between.*
• *Fix cut bamboo to a timber framework to keep the canes from touching the wet ground; tie the poles in latticework layouts using black string to replicate Japanese designs.*
• *Plant newly pruned stems of willow such as Salix viminalis in winter to create a permanent living screen; weave it into a latticework design for extra density and interest.*
• *Panels of woven 'dead' willow make useful temporary screens.*

Above: *Fretwork trees echo the distant olive, creating interesting silhouettes to highlight the screen wall and planting beds.*

Below: *Solid walls can have figurative elements built in, and this imaginative example fits with a contemplative style.*

PLANTS AND CONTAINERS FOR A CONTEMPLATIVE RETREAT

Whatever other elements you have decided on, it is the inclusion of plants that will bring your contemplative courtyard to life. This does not necessarily require a profusion of greenery. An abstract and meditative design can be dramatically created with the sparing and symbolic use of tree and plant forms.

Above: *Spiky* Dasylirion serratifolium *and tropical* Vriesia *make interesting highlights.*

Designing with Neutral Spaces

To achieve a balance between planting and hard landscape, it is important to include areas of visual 'resting' space. In a Western garden, this function is usually fulfilled by areas of lawn, and sometimes with paving, but with an oriental interpretation an area of smooth pebbles can provide a similar calming effect. Movement and texture are achieved by raking them into a curved design to suggest an undulating landscape or ripples in a lake, as in a traditional Zen viewing garden. A variation on this theme might be to use large, carefully chosen containers and specimen plants to create graphic statements, rather than the traditional large-scale boulders that are associated with this garden style.

Balancing Hard and Soft

A purely stone garden can seem cool and impassive to Western eyes, so it is desirable to incorporate some living 'forest' elements for vegetative relief. Retain the original concept by restricting them to focus on sculptural accents, rather than spreading them around too liberally. Static, clipped evergreens and low mounds of green moss provide sculptural form, while clumps of *Festuca* and sedge grasses offer swaying movement.

Choosing Pots

Containers provide an important transition between the garden and the house, so select them in line with the oriental influences of the contemplative courtyard. There is a good selection of stoneware planters on the market, sometimes glazed in celadon green, smouldering blue and mysterious plum. Alternatively, deep, burned-brown raku glazes have the right weatherbeaten look for the effect you want to create. Stoneware is usually frost-proof, but do check.

Pots are sometimes made without drainage holes, making them suitable for water-loving species, such as papyrus grass or Marsh marigolds (*Caltha palustris*). A water-filled stoneware bowl will provide a miniature 'pond' if there is no space for the real thing and a lovely vessel for floating beautiful cut blooms. Don't leave water in containers in winter if it is likely to freeze. Tall, oriental water jars look handsome in their own right – not needing a plant for adornment – and make an excellent sculptural statement set among foliage.

Sculptured Forms

Trimming and pruning play an important part in creating sculptural forms. While in the West we commonly use topiary shrub forms, such as box and yew, the Japanese prune conifers into symbolic shapes, often referred to as 'cloud pruning'.

Evergreen pine trees are revered as symbols of stability and endurance. The Japanese black pine, *Pinus thunbergii*, and red pine, *P. densiflora*, are both available in dwarf cultivars and will stand up to the necessary training and pruning. Prostrate and pendulous forms of pines, such as *P. strobus* 'Nana' and

Above: *Low-growing clumping grasses give a soft interface between two paving areas.*

Above: *The streaky patina of the zinc planter combines well with the grey lavender.*

P. densiflora 'Pendula', are ideal for sculpted courtyards, particularly in conjunction with gravel and rock areas. Sculptural subjects can also be found among other conifers, with the spruces, *Picea* sp., offering attractive dwarf forms.

Dramatic sculptural form can also be provided by the New Zealand tree fern, *Dicksonia antarctica*, with its bold, fibrous trunk and broad canopy of fresh green fronds. Although they are considered tender, these ferns frequently flourish in the shelter of a courtyard. If suitable climatic conditions for *Dicksonia antarctica* do not prevail, the Chinese fan palm (*Trachycarpus fortunei*), and the Mediterranean fan palm (*Chamerops humilis*), offer a similar visual effect.

Right: *Sculptural planting, such as these clipped azaleas in a sea of gravel, brings poise and drama to the scene.*

PLANTING A GRAPE HYACINTH

Create a dreamy blue cascade by planting several varieties of honey-scented grape hyacinth (ones flowering at the same time) in each pot and lining the garden steps with them. Or, cluster the pots together to make a textural blue carpet to brighten the earliest weeks of the year. When the flowers are spent, don't discard the bulbs – take them out of their pots and plant them in clumps in the garden where they will flower happily next spring.

1 Line the base of a shallow pot with a layer of stone chippings to allow free drainage. Taller pots will need a deeper layer of drainage material. You can grow the bulbs in a sheltered corner of the garden before moving them on show. They are hardy and easy to grow.

2 Half-fill the pot with soil-based potting mix and place the bulbs, equally spaced, across the surface. Use seven bulbs for a 12cm (4¾in) pot; nine for a 15cm (6in) pot. Discard any bulbs that are shrivelled or soft. It is easier to make a pleasant arrangement using odd numbers of bulbs.

3 Fill to 2cm (¾in) from the top of the pot with more soil mix and firm lightly. Water the pots using a watering can with a fine rose. From planting time in early autumn, through winter, check watering needs. Top up with a layer of gravel or slate to acts as a foil for the bulbs when they flower.

4 A display like this will continue for several weeks if watered regularly and will attract the first butterflies and bees with their rich nectar. Once the flowers begin to fade, feed the bulbs with a high potash fertilizer, such as tomato food, to build them up for next year.

Contemplative Planting

A courtyard needs a strong base of evergreens to provide structure throughout the year, but a selection of deciduous species will reflect the changing seasons. The deciduous trees that most epitomize the oriental spirit are the flowering cherries and plums (*Prunus*), which sometimes offer beautiful bark as well as frothy spring blossom. In fact, nothing represents the transition to spring as aptly as cherry blossom. Just one small tree, such as pure-white 'Shirotae', deep-pink 'Cheals Weeping' or scented, shell-pink 'Takasago', is enough to lift the spirits after a long winter.

Space should be found for at least one elegant camellia, offering glossy, evergreen form with glorious blooms in spring. Rich double forms vie with extravagant singles boasting huge bosses of yellow stamens against petals of pure

Above: *Bamboo foliage diffuses light and makes a lovely rattling sound in the breeze.*

Above: *Deep red damask roses amongst a swathe of perennials herald the summer.*

white, rosy pink and deep red. Dwarf rhododendrons and azaleas are important, too, for their kaleidoscope of late spring flowers.

Autumn is the other transitional period, when flowers fade, fruits ripen and leaves prepare to drop. At this time, the brilliant maples (*Acer*) come into their own. Invaluable are the myriad varieties of *A. palmatum*, its deeply lobed foliage turning from bright, springtime green to vibrant tones of yellow, gold and red.

Plants that shiver in the breeze, creating dappled sunlight and evoking the natural landscape, fit perfectly into the contemplative concept. Statuesque bamboos, with their dense clumps of slender stems and wind-clattering leaves, make handsome screens or boundaries.

Ornamental grasses offer a similar effect of swaying stems and rustling leaves. Lower in height than most bamboo, they play an important role, both for edging paths and for making group statements. *Miscanthus sinensis* is a species that offers some of the most beautiful specimens, with fine, arching foliage and gleaming, feathery flower heads in late summer and autumn. Stripy leaved *M. s.* 'Zebrinus', slender 'Gracillimus' and arching 'Kleine Fontäine' are just a few examples.

Left: *Majestic tree ferns* Dicksonia antarctica *create an intimate enclosure with dramatic canopies of foliage.*

Above: *Japanese water iris (*Iris ensata*) is a good foil to the regal fern (*Osmunda regalis*).*

Above: *Large containers that can support a number of plants are ideal for terraces.*

Above: *A small cloud-pruned tree using Japanese holly (*Ilex crenata*).*

To show off their form and the delicacy of the flowers, place them where the low, setting sun provides backlight. For an airy effect, *Molinia arundinacea* and *Stipa tenuissima* both offer feathery pink flowers on arching stems. For contrast, the *Festuca glauca* cultivars offer low, tufted clumps of fine, blue-grey leaves, superb when planted in groups in a sunny spot.

For a still pool of water, low-growing hostas offer a magnificent range of colours enhanced by their deeply veined, glaucous leaves. Blue greens are shot through with acid yellow, spring green is brightened with splashes of cream and white.

Ferns offer sculptural elegance as fronds unfurl to reveal deeply dissected soft, green leaves that deepen in tone as they develop. For

the curiosity of its noduled stems, the horsetail *Equisetum hymale* is hard to beat, with *Juncus effusus spiralis*, the aptly named corkscrew grass, a close second. Among this boggy planting, add white-flowering calla lilies, *Zantedeschia aethiopica*, for their statuesque flower spathes, and Japanese water iris, *Iris laevigata* 'Snowdrift'. Above all, water lilies are transcendentally serene.

HOW TO PRUNE CLOUD TOPIARY

Choose a small-leaved evergreen shrub, such as box (*Buxus sempervirens*), Japanese holly (*Ilex crenata*) or privet (*Ligustrum delavayanum*). You may have a plant with the right 'bone structure', or framework of branches, already growing that would make a suitable candidate. See top right for a trimmed cloud-pruned box.

1 Open up the foliage with both hands to reveal the framework of branches. Ideally, you will have one or more main stems with strong side branches. A quirky branching pattern is ideal.

2 Cut out any unwanted branches, leaving behind more than you will actually need at this stage. Move around the plant and stand back regularly to see how the shape is evolving.

3 Strip the leaves and smaller branches off the lower parts of the main stems you intend to retain for the final shape. Use bamboo canes and wire to bend some branches to the desired shape.

4 Trim the selected stems and side branches at the stem tips to encourage compact growth. Leave bare stem between each 'cloud'. Clip once or twice in spring and summer to maintain its shape.

STRUCTURES AND FURNITURE FOR A CONTEMPLATIVE RETREAT

A garden is more than flat plane – tall plants and trees, changes of levels, boundaries and enclosures all play their part. To enjoy it fully, the space should evolve into a three-dimensional experience. A reflective space does not require clear divisions, but structural enclosures can create areas of solitude and privacy.

Above: *An archway of hornbeam focuses the view to the topiary forms beyond.*

Arches and Frames

Paths are a good starting point from which to view the garden, especially when they are framed by an archway or other entrance. When designing a garden with a suggestion of the Orient, curved forms provide an evocative vertical device. Frames tend to draw the gaze and can be employed to seduce the viewer to walk towards a destination. More unusual than building a regular, Western-style U-shaped frame, a classical Japanese-style arch would introduce an air of exoticism. The classical form used in temple gardens is based on bold, vertical posts, often round in section, surmounted by one or more carved, horizontal rails. They are sited to permit a symbolic passage from one world to the next. This style of arch is architecturally impressive when used singly, but when interpreted as a series it creates a pergola or covered walkway. This arch can also be adapted to form an enclosure around a bench or seat.

Circles, with their connotations of the Sun and Moon, are frequently used in oriental imagery, and a circular frame would make an effective device to bisect or terminate a pathway. A free-standing circle is quite a challenging object to create, so choose construction materials with care.

Blocks of sandstone or limestone could be used to make a circular frame to be set on a vertical axis. This would be a most impressive feature, although certainly not a construction job for a beginner. To provide a structural support mechanism, the circle would need to be integrated with a screen wall of the same material.

Steel provides the alternative method of construction. Strong and malleable, T- or H-sections can be welded into powerful circular shapes, even large enough to walk through. As with stone

Left: *This cast-iron structure wth a motif of vine leaves has a dream-like quality.*

Right: *Polished stainless steel is becoming a popular medium in the garden. This 'flying' arch creates a dynamic feature, reinforcing the circular patio and swirling mosaic design.*

construction, this should be a job for skilled experts. A single element would be very effective in its own right, but the nature of circles encourages you to site them in different ways. They can be set vertically or at an angle, singly as a frame or as series to suggest a path. They are fascinating formed in groups, especially when organized to achieve a three-dimensional, sculptural effect.

Flat sheet steel could also be used to achieve a different effect. By cutting circular openings in rectangular sections of metal, you can create layers of successive pierced screens.

A rusted look would appear natural in this type of garden, an effect achieved using Corten steel, expressly devised to take on a crusty texture of oranges and browns. You can see this material used in some outdoor sculptural works as well as cladding on some modern buildings.

Right: *Polished stainless steel is becoming a popular medium in the garden. This 'flying' arch creates a dynamic feature, reinforcing the circular patio and swirling mosaic design.*

Below: *A series of welded steel rings leads the eye directly to the stone circle sculpture.*

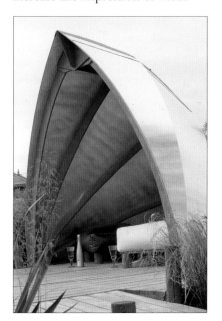

For a homemade alternative, go for a similar effect using heavy steel wire. This is easy to bend and can be built up in several layers to increase the impression of visual weight. Steel reinforcing rods and mesh, normally used in the construction of concrete slabs and walls, are another option, yielding excellent results. All these materials are inexpensive and easy to source.

The circle can be implemented in a number of ways and would make a compelling frame to reveal a secret garden. First divide your space with a solid screen and pierce it with an aperture to encourage the eye to peer through. A single opening works well if the path leads directly towards it, especially if a sculptural object or a specimen tree is revealed beyond. Alternatively, if the path progresses along the wall, a series of apertures could make an interesting walking experience – like a viewing at an art gallery of garden designs.

Left: *A V-shaped, timber-framed structure coated in steel shelters a seating area.*

Left: *A circular path is linked by a piece of curved timber, forming a bridge over this naturalistic pond.*

Paths and Bridges

To make your courtyard dynamic and interesting, you could include a passage through which you can walk and view the space from different perspectives, perhaps framed by a special entrance. A cabin could be both architecturally intriguing and a refuge or sanctuary in which to escape the stresses of daily life.

Another way to make a passage more of an adventure is to use a bridge in the design. This introduces changes of level and texture and can make a striking architectural feature. Even if there is no existing pond or stream, it can be equally interesting and easy to create a 'dry stream' that is represented by pebbles and rocks and the introduction of appropriate plants among them.

Right: *Sink reclaimed timber planks into a loose surfacing of pebbles.*

Far right: *A bridge of wooden blocks spans this dramatic water sculpture, featuring a wall cascade and formal pool.*

The style of the bridge will depend largely on the level of formality in the garden. A simple, organically styled bridge, suitable for a short span, can be easily created with two or three broad planks of timber. They should be thick enough to avoid twisting and long enough to provide a generous landing on each side of the gap.

Secure them underneath with cross beams to hold them in place and then fix them to posts sunk firmly into concrete foundations below.

Safety around water is an important consideration, so make sure that there is no possibility of movement or settlement. To avoid danger of slipping in wet or icy conditions, fix wire mesh over the surface of the planks.

Where there is a desire for a more sophisticated construction and more of a visual statement, timber and stone bridges offer many attractive possibilities. These would normally be based on classical designs with an arched form to support the bridge, which incidentally creates another circle when reflected in the water below. Practical details, such as steps and handrails, also offer further decorative possibilities.

Small bridges can be purchased off the peg – useful if you are dealing with a small water feature – but where you need to cover a wider span, you will need to commission something made to measure.

Above: *Caged and weathered timbers make an appropriate construction material for furniture in a wild, organic setting.*

Left: *An expressive, free-standing curved timber frame supports a hammock.*

A Sheltered Spot

To complete the calming effect of the contemplative retreat, you can provide a place of shelter, somewhere for meditation or a recreation such as reading and drawing.

You may aspire to a Japanese teahouse and thereby introduce an impressive garden focal point. If possible, site it beside a still pool, with the addition of a wooden deck cantilevered out over the water to bring you as close as possible to nature.

In classic Japanese style, the house would be constructed from beautiful timber posts and cladding, all sanded to a smooth perfection and furnished with a sloping roof and shady veranda. Cover the roof with overlapping wooden shingles instead of tiles and carry rainwater to the ground via delicate brass 'rain chains' in place of downpipes.

A less formal gazebo made of rough timber poles would be a shelter you could create yourself. To give it more of a weightless appearance, build it on a raised wooden platform secured in concrete foundations. Disguise the

base structure with a dense perimeter planting of ornamental grasses to suggest a water meadow. Use weatherproof roofing sheets to keep out the rain and cover them inside and out with a simple thatch made from bundles of willows, reeds or brushwood. Ready-made bamboo screening, supplied in rolls, would be adequate to create side walls to give shelter from sun

and light breezes, or fill the spaces with a denser screening material, such as wired heather matting.

Furniture should be selected to suit the style of shelter. Seating made from reclaimed timber and sawn planks would be ideal for the rustic gazebo. More formally, choose long, low stone or wooden benches for a traditional 'viewing platform' style of seating.

Above: *This tiny arbour is constructed from oversized square section timbers.*

Above: *A slate plinth creates a relaxing area for viewing and contemplation.*

ORNAMENT AND WATER FEATURES FOR A CONTEMPLATIVE RETREAT

A serene space needs ornaments that complement the atmosphere and stimulate the senses, with natural forms, soft colours and curving shapes. Water introduces calming, sensory qualities – dancing reflections, shifting shadows and the dreamy sounds of lapping, trickling, spurting or gushing water.

Above: *This display of fish creates a kitsch and amusing touch to a formal pool.*

Simple Approaches

Where space is limited, a modest bowl or container is all that is needed to make an ornamental statement. Borrow ideas for the terrace from tropical Eastern gardens, in which a carefully selected and positioned basin or jar can evoke a sense of perfection and balance. Fill it with water and decorate the surface with floating blooms, or supply a wooden ladle to encourage visitors to refresh themselves on a hot day.

The Sound of the Garden

Introduce sound and movement by attracting birds to the garden. Provide them with a shallow dish with a perching rim and simply take pleasure in watching them bathe. Another idea is bamboo and metal wind chimes, strung from a veranda, perhaps, or hung in the branches of a tree. These are not only attractive to look at, but they also send out gentle musical notes in even the lightest of breezes.

For something more personal, you can devise your own hanging decorations by stringing together found objects. Drill holes through pebbles, shells and pieces of driftwood to make fascinating and original organic sky sculptures. Rust-stained metal birds and insects associate well with informal gardens and introduce an amusing element when sited among the planting. Oriental-style objects, such as statues of gods and symbolic stone lanterns, make appropriate ornamental statements, while wall plaques extend the decorative possibilities of even the smallest space.

Still Pools

If space permits, then an expanse of water is an asset. You can site a formal pool in an open area untroubled by overhanging trees or shade from boundary walls and buildings. The resulting sheet of cool water will introduce a sense of calm, its surface reflecting light and moving cloudscapes. It creates a quiet place to relax and take in the natural world. The floating leaves of water lilies make ideal landing stages for frogs, pond skaters and dragonflies.

A shallow beach of pebbles bordering a more informal pond encourages wildlife, especially birds, into the water. Plant the edges with marginal moisture-lovers, such as iris, primula and Japanese rush (*Acorus gramineus*), to attract butterflies and other pollinating insects.

Above: *Bamboo wind chimes provide visual and aural texture in the garden.*

Above: *Bronze cranes look at home in this pond, among the giant gunnera leaves.*

Above: *Water bubbles up through a partially opaque Perspex tower.*

Above: *This arrangement of flat pebbles transforms them into an organic sculpture.*

Above: *Water lilies (Nymphaea sp.) won't tolerate running water or fountains.*

Above: *Rocks are used as symbolic mountains in oriental-style gardens.*

This pool could combine with a timber viewing deck, especially if it 'floats' out above the water supported by unseen posts. A canopy would make it a pleasant seating area finished off with a decorative collection of stone jars filled with water-loving grasses, such as papyrus and the graceful, white-spathed arum lily (*Zantedeschia*).

POND PRACTICALITIES

• *Formal water features require a clear area of level ground that is not overshadowed by deciduous trees.*
• *Informal ponds look most natural when they are sited with a background of shrubbery and moisture-loving plants.*
• *Create shallow planting ledges and boggy banks around ponds where planting is required.*
• *Filtration pumps are required for still water displays to keep it free from stagnation and algae.*

Safety note: *Take precautions to prevent children having access to ponds or water features.*

Above: *In this highly stylized, formal water feature, a snaking 'path' of Iris dissects a still pool; select* Iris ensata *'Southern Son', or other moisture-loving species.*

Right: *Cobblestone fountains appear at random throughout this seashore courtyard, bubbling up energetically between the pebbles.*

Moving Water

Where the sounds and textural effects of moving water are wanted, why not introduce a circulating pump into the pool? You can achieve an unusual and energetic effect by arranging the pump outlets so that the water is driven in a circular motion around the margin of the pond. Alternatively, low, gurgling spouts could appear, geyser-like, among a layer of cobbles near the edge of the beach, supplied by a series of small jets from the pump.

A natural-looking cascade would integrate well into an informal pool. Since it is often difficult to dispose of the spoil resulting from the pond excavation, use it to your advantage by creating a hillside. Cover this with a miniature landscape of boulders and rocks, interspersing them with a natural planting of dwarf shrubs, ferns and mosses. Build a water course through the hillside, pump the water up through hidden pipes to the top and then allow it to plunge through to the pool below, where the final delight would be a group of colourful koi carp playing in the eddies.

Taking up much less space than a pond, a gently moving rill would provide an appealing and graphic way to bisect the courtyard garden. Extra interest can be introduced by pumping the water over a bed of pebbles, in a shallow, snaking channel. More formally, a still, straight canal would provide a neutral, visual resting space between rectangular beds of mono-planted grasses. Line it with a narrow strip of stone or a dark-slate edging to emphasize the contrast between the movement of the plants and the stillness of the dark water.

Above: *A millstone fountain involves drilling through the centre of the stone and concealing a pump below.*

Above: *Pre-formed resin sections can be made up into hillside cascades; infill with bog plants to make them more natural.*

Above: *Cascading rills like these can be incorporated with a new construction, or built into an existing slope.*

INSTALLING A COBBLESTONE FOUNTAIN

The beauty of this type of cobblestone fountain is that it can be situated anywhere in the garden, regardless of whether a body of water exists. All you need is an electricity supply and you can position the fountain at ground level or within a raised bed. Create the gentle bubbling effect of a natural, life-giving spring within a shady meditation corner planted with ferns, hostas and bamboos, or in a more open part of the courtyard where the upwelling water will sparkle in sunlight and the wet cobbles will gleam. Use gravel, rocks and plants to disguise the electric cable connecting the hidden pump to the waterproof switch.

1 Mark out the diameter of the plastic water reservoir on the ground and dig out a hole slightly wider and deeper than its dimensions. Place a shallow layer of sand at the bottom of the hole and fit the reservoir into the hole.

2 Set the rim level with the surrounding soil and check that it is upright by using a spirit (carpenter's) level across the rim. Lift the reservoir to make any corrections. Backfill the gap with soil, ramming it firmly down with a length of dowel.

3 Place two bricks inside as a plinth for the pump. This prevents the pump's intake becoming clogged with debris. Check that the plastic pipe used for the fountain is high enough to extend up and just through the surface pebbles.

4 Shape the surrounding area into a shallow dish (to direct water back into the reservoir) and cover it and the reservoir with a polythene sheet. Cut a hole in the centre of the plastic to allow the pipe through. Fill the reservoir with water.

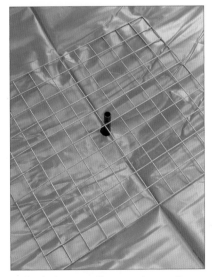

5 Check the water flow now in case it needs adjusting. Lay the polythene sheet back over the reservoir with the pipe protruding from the hole. Cover with a piece of rigid galvanized mesh large enough to rest on the rim of the reservoir.

6 Place a smaller mesh over the larger one to catch small pebbles. Add pebbles as necessary to cover the plastic and mesh. Make sure the tip of the delivery pipe is just clear. Connect the cable to a power supply and switch on.

LIGHTING FOR A CONTEMPLATIVE RETREAT

More than simply fulfilling a practical function, lighting can softly highlight night-time dining areas or draw your focus towards key garden elements – a specimen plant, perhaps, or a Japanese stone lantern. Uplighting bamboos, tree ferns and billowing grasses produces enchantment throughout the year.

Above: *Light simple, coloured glass candleholders along pathways.*

Natural Flame

There's something primal about fire that is utterly captivating. A fire pit could be the central focus of a garden, even in winter, drawing visitors close to stare into the flames and feel the heat. Small, free-tanding circular grates are available, but you could also build a sunken pit lined with firebricks to burn larger logs. In the daytime this could be covered with a decorative metal grid. Ask a local blacksmith to make one for you.

Solid church candles are ideal for use in the garden and they will last longer if you trim the wick after lighting them for the first time. Position them out of draughts – use terracotta pots set among the plants to provide shelter or stand them in wall niches. Small night-lights in coloured glass holders and lanterns also create an inspiring ambiance.

Use night-lights to illuminate a Japanese stone lantern or set them in rugged stone holders along a pathway. Make lighting the candles part of your winding-down ritual.

Modern Technology

The range of solar-powered lights has expanded tremendously and they now burn brighter and more reliably than previously. For the energy conscious, they are a very attractive and versatile alternative to mains powered lights. In some ways, solar-powered lights are more suited to the meditative garden because they follow the natural day-night rhythm and produce a softer effect, but you do need to position them where they can recharge.

New Age lighting effects and light sculptures can be the perfect addition to a meditation garden.

For example, you could use optical-fibre lighting fitted with a unit to create a twinkling starlight effect through decking or paving.

Lights running off a transformer are easy to install, but make sure the transformer has a waterproof housing. You should use a qualified electrician for installing mains-powered lighting.

Small LED spots in white or blue can be used to uplight boulders, large pieces of natural stone and driftwood, revealing the beautiful natural texture and form of these materials. Larger, more architectural plants also benefit from being lit from below and, if you like, these lights can occasionally be fitted with coloured filters. Lights camouflaged as rocks or as shells may also be of use in this type of garden.

Above: *A traditional stone lantern can be lit with an LED or candle.*

Above: *A curved sheet of Perspex creates a water-curtain effect lit by a coloured light.*

Above: *Dichromatic LEDs set into the timbers provide atmospheric lighting.*

Lighting Water

Since water plays a major role in courtyards designed to soothe, it makes sense to highlight these features at night. On a still, reflecting pool you could float candles, purpose-made oil lamps or clear electric globes that bob on the surface. Underwater pool lighting should be understated so that it does not interfere with the reflections of the night sky. If you use coloured light, pick one shade, such as a deep blue. Light oriental-style bridges to reveal their arcing shapes using tiny camouflaged LED spots or hang candle lanterns to light the way.

Cascades are best lit from below; in a terraced courtyard you could combine a water curtain falling over a sheet of transparent Perspex (Plexiglass)with gradually changing coloured light.

Above: *This pool has an integral abstract sculpture made of tall bamboo poles. The artistic lighting system transforms it into a dream landscape.*

LIGHTING PLANTS WITH UPLIGHTERS

Intriguing patterns and atmospheric effects can be created using low-voltage LED spotlights as uplighters. These spotlights run off a transformer and are variously positioned around the plants and pots to give different effects. In the set used here there are two spots with contemporary brushed-steel casings and optional wall brackets or ground spikes. When they are hidden among the foliage of pot plants or in a border you hardly notice them at all during the day. It is safer and more practical if you can switch the lights on and off from a convenient point indoors or from a shelter or retreat within the courtyard.

1 The lights are fixed into the containers by pushing the ground spike down into the compost (soil mix). The arrangement of differently sized pots gives more scope for experimenting with various effects, with spots set to give a combination of up- and down-lighting.

2 Fixing the lights behind a fern throws its fronds into relief. You can also shine one of the lights on to the wall behind to give more of a sense of depth and separation and, in this case, by glimpsing some of the purple wall colour you help to create a relaxing ambiance.

3 LED lights produce virtually no heat when they are on, so you don't have to worry about scorching your plant foliage. Here the potted sedge in the foreground looks almost like an optical fibre lamp popular in the 1960s with the light shining though its fine strands.

CASE STUDY: CALM OASIS

A thoughtful approach to balance and harmony in this enclosed city garden has resulted in a restorative haven that stimulates the senses. The garden design interprets the opposing forces of yin and yang, while reflecting four of the basic elements – metal, fire, earth and water – in the materials used in its construction and in the colours of the planting.

Above: *The Buddha statue provides a calming aid to focus meditation.*

A high terrace leading from the house provides a west-facing platform from which to view the overall scene, with a black metal table and chairs positioned on the paving where they can take full advantage of the summer sunsets. Steps descend to a slate path that divides the energetic, south-facing, yang side of the garden, with its hot and fiery planting, from the cool yin subjects that languish quietly on the opposite side of the path. The resulting effect is one of calm tranquillity and quiet harmony.

The path, which turns at right angles to create an indirect route through the garden, leads to a quiet pool traversed by stepping-stones. The pool is watched over by a contemplative Buddha, who sits calmly in front of a narrow mirror that rests informally against a wall.

The meandering journey taken by the path keeps visitors guessing at what will be around the next corner, thus giving the garden an element of mystery and surprise. A thick screen of rustling bamboo obscures the bottom of the garden completely from view.

Above: Cordyline australis *loves full sun; the spiky foliage provides a sense of energy and optimism.*

The path eventually culminates in a secret woodland glade where there is a reward waiting for anybody making the journey – a bamboo deckchair in which to rest, relax and meditate.

Dividing a garden into clearly defined sections, like this one, is an excellent way of disguising a long, narrow plot. The eye takes in only one discrete area after another, rather than seeing the whole garden in a single glance.

The garden plan for this Calm Oasis courtyard, shown overleaf, shows the visual dynamics of the space, and also includes practical sequences on making a slate path and planting an ornamental water plant in a pond, both features that are included here.

Right: *The generously proportioned raised terrace offers a delightful vista over the luxuriant planting throughout the garden.*

CREATING A CONTEMPLATIVE GARDEN

Flooring:
• *Keep hard landscaping to a minimum and use natural materials.*
• *Use curving, meandering, forms in paths and beds.*
• *Create stepping-stone paths through grass and gravel areas.*

Walls and Screens:
Create a sense of enclosure and privacy.
• *Plant the boundaries densely with tall shrubs and trees, such as bamboo or silver birch.*

• *Add screens made from willow or bamboo canes to break up areas and provide backdrops for set pieces.*

Plants and Containers:
• *Keep planting uncluttered by keeping to a small number of species.*
• *Concentrate on foliage effect, especially grasses, bamboo and other slender forms that have movement and make sounds in the breeze.*
• *Include some clipped evergreen cloud topiary for structure and form.*

Water Features:
• *Use water to achieve a calming effect, to introduce light and movement, and to encourage nature and wildlife.*
• *Features might include a gazing pool, a stream or a rill.*
• *Encourage birds with a shallow, water-filled drinking and bathing vessel.*

Structures and Ornament:
• *Create sheltered seating areas.*
• *Place symbolic sculptural statements at strategic points.*

CALM OASIS GARDEN PLAN

Buddha head

fence

brick wall

pool

stepping stones

timber edging

grey Snowdonian slate

Irish limestone flags

Right: *Irish limestone flags, used here for the raised terrace, are highly stain resistant.*

Plant list

1   *Equisetum hyemale*
2   *Holboellia latifolia*
3   *Euphorbia mellifera*
4   *Phormium tenax*
5   *Dodonaea viscosa* 'Purpurea'
6   *Trachycarpus fortunei*
7   *Sophora microphylla*
8   *Cordyline australis*
9   *Yucca rostrata*
10 *Albizia julibrissin* 'Rosea'
11 *Iris confusa*
12 *Yucca* sp.
13 *Astelia chathamica*
14 *Beschorneria yuccoides*
15 *Festuca glauca*
16 *Agapanthus africanus*
17 *Crocosmia* 'Solfaterre'
18 *Melianthus major*

19 *Euphorbia amygdaloides* 'Purpurea'
20 *Canna* 'Durban'
21 *Musa basjoo*
22 *Polystichum setiferum* 'Divisilobum'
23 *Phyllostachys aurea*

Left: *A number of cabbage palms (Cordyline australis) are positioned around the dining area in this courtyard. This plant thrives in full sun and semi-shade.*

Above: *Silver Spear (Astelia chathamica) are planted in two tall, angular stoneware urns that act as an informal entranceway to the planted areas beyond the flagstones.*

Above: *Feathery leaved* Albizia julibrissin *is a delicate small tree for a sheltered spot.*

Above: *Layers of bold architectural foliage create a sense of enclosure and privacy.*

Above: *The dramatic, silver-leaved* Astelia chathamica *is an evergreen perennial.*

LAYING A SLATE PATH

A slate path helps to create an atmospheric garden with a strong emphasis on natural harmony and organic materials. It is also satisfyingly crunchy underfoot. The dark colouring and interesting texture of slate makes a perfect foil for bamboo and other lush foliage plants and you can choose from a number of different shades and grades that will suit your purposes. Slate is more effective at preventing weed growth than gravel, due to weed seeds germinating in the surface layer, but being sharp-edged, it isn't kind to young children.

SLATE PATH CROSS-SECTION

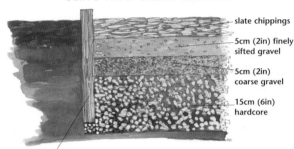

slate chippings
5cm (2in) finely sifted gravel
5cm (2in) coarse gravel
15cm (6in) hardcore

timber edging board, 30 x 2.5cm (12 x 1in)

1 Mark out the area with string and pegs and then dig out to a depth of at least 30cm (12in). Compact the surface by tamping it down thoroughly with a stout piece of timber or a garden roller.

2 Lay hardcore to a depth of 15cm (6in) and set tanalized wooden edging boards along both sides over a thin layer of hardcore, so that the boards finish at about 2.5cm (1in) above the adjacent ground. Screw the boards into stout

wooden pegs for stability. Compact the pathway with a post. The edging boards are approximately 30cm (12in) deep and 2.5cm (1in) wide.
3 Spread a layer of coarse gravel to a depth of 5cm (2in) and roll or tread all over it.

4 Cover the coarse gravel with a layer of finely sifted gravel, about 5cm (2in) deep.
5 Top with slate chippings as shown above, taking the path up to the ground surface. Soak with a hose to bind the gravel and wash away the dust.

PLANTING ORNAMENTAL HORSETAIL

The horsetail (*Equisetum hyemale*) adds an oriental flavour to a pool with its vertical, 1.2m (4ft) long stems and black banding. Miniature Cattail (*Typha minima*) would be

another good option. Use a perforated container for planting in water, as well as an aquatic compost (soil mix) and slow-release fertilizer pellets.

1 Line a perforated planting basket with hessian sacking to contain the aquatic compost (soil mix) while allowing the roots to penetrate. Pre-soak the young horsetail plants.

2 Set the plants on top of some compost so the surface is a little below the rim. Fill in between with more compost and firm. There is no need to remove perforated pots.

3 Cover the compost with washed pea gravel, to a depth of between 1.5–2cm (½–¾in). This helps to stop soil clouding the clear water and deters fish from uprooting the plants.

4 Lower the basket into the pool, resting it on stacked bricks if necessary, so the rim is just below the water surface. Try dark slate as an subtler mulch rather than pea gravel.

MODERN ZONES

The architecture of our living spaces should provide an antidote to the pressures of modern life. The contemporary courtyard, with its clean lines and low-maintenance approach, should have the same effect: a clear, uncluttered and relaxing perspective.

Hard landscaping plays a significant role in modern exterior design and the range of new materials available has changed many preconceptions about garden style. Industrial materials, such as stainless steel and concrete, are finding new uses in the garden, as are coloured Perspex, glass and 'intelligent' textiles.

The contemporary courtyard is an excellent vehicle to showcase avant-garde design, using clean backdrops and screens against which to display modern sculpture, dramatic water features and three-dimensional planting. It makes a stimulating setting for entertaining, a place to show off exciting forms of modern outdoor furniture, and has many possibilities for special lighting and sound effects.

Left: *This striking design uses strong colour contrasts and bold geometry. Coloured aggregates are used as decorative mulches – combined in this way they create a strong visual impression of three-dimensional form, from what is actually a flat surface.*

GARDENS FOR MODERN LIVES

A contemporary courtyard demands bold geometry of form, clean textures and crisp planting to create a garden with dynamic character and structure. A sensible approach is to use a formal design that echoes the appearance of the surrounding architecture, creating visual and physical links between the house and the hard landscaping outside.

Above: *Brilliant red and white Perspex is softened with the leaves of a giant gunnera.*

Reinterpreting the Classic

A contemporary garden will often be based on a classic formal design, using orthodox principles of order and arrangement, but reinterpreted in a fresh and original way. New types of construction materials make complex structures possible, and together with the use of bold, brilliant colours and unexpected textures, have turned many established gardening ideas on their head.

Traditional garden design principles can be used to formulate the basic structure, for example sculpting a hedge or designing a partition to mirror the form of a window, echo the scale of a door or follow the line of a roof. This approach helps to create a complementary external reflection of the building's proportion and style.

Above: *Weatherproofed screen prints introduce an unusual sculptural dimension.*

Modern Materials

The use of non-traditional and experimental materials will be a key feature of a contemporary space. Concrete is used to make polished, free-standing walls and sweeping steps, while stainless steel leaves behind its industrial roots and is translated into canopies, screens and sculpture; crushed, coloured glass or even crumbled, recycled rubber may take the place of traditional ornamental mulch. Coloured Perspex (Plexiglass) screens divert the eye and paving is employed to play visual tricks with perspective. A water sculpture created from fragments of glass can sparkle and glint in sunlight, while at night it can appear to glow with the help of carefully planned lighting.

The modern courtyard allows the urban dweller to have fun with a quirky selection of containers and associated planting, as well as in the choice of cutting-edge sculpture. Choosing intriguing, abstract pieces of art brings a whole new emotional dimension to the design, allowing for the expression of personal tastes and preferences.

Planting Choices

Since modern gardens rely heavily on architectural structure, when creating a smaller-scale courtyard scheme you need to retain the overall balance of the space. Too often, designers concentrate so much on the hard landscaping elements that the overall philosophy of the garden is lost. Crisp, minimal designs can be delightfully cool, while some modern materials are quirkily amusing, but also remember the value of planting to create ambiance, energy and character.

A clean-lined space provides a neutral vehicle to show off the wow factor of contemporary planting. The form, texture, colour and movement of trees, shrubs and perennials offers a huge palette of possibilities.

Low maintenance might be a requirement, but a balance can be struck. Tailored evergreens will normally be used to hold together the framework of the planting design; evergreens keep their leaves throughout the year and usually require a twice-annual trim. However, seasonal change is a valuable factor in planting design, so easy-care deciduous species should be considered, too.

A strong visual statement can be achieved using lines of identical trees, trained as standards with a clear trunk. Underplant them with clipped blocks of single-species low evergreens to create a living architectural statement of huge character. Formal cubist-style arrangements of this sort can be chosen from a huge diversity of planting, including grasses and bamboo, or seasonal flowers and bulbs, to change the look of the design throughout the year.

Right: *This sophisticated urban courtyard has permeable paving and is designed to divert water from the porch to irrigate a raised bed and eliminate water run off.*

FLOORING FOR MODERN ZONES

Your hard-landscaping choices can reflect the naturally occurring materials in your region. Alternatively, you can create a wild fantasy of unexpected colours, textures and materials. Clean lines and bold statements sum up the image of contemporary outdoor design, and flooring provides the first and most fundamental way to set the scene.

Above: *Grey slate highlights the turning corner of steps from the sandstone path.*

Left: *Grass is attractive but can be slippery and prone to wear. Square concrete paving slabs provide a secure walking surface and an attractive pattern.*

Straight grids of slabs will produce the most tailored effect. However, while a design of squares may work in small spaces, it may be monotonous over a larger area. Rectangles usually have a more sympathetic appearance and can help create an illusion of width or length where this is required. They tend to offer a better sense of movement and are normally used as identical-sized elements in a staggered pattern. Alternatively, they may be cut in random lengths, but in widths that are identical, or in no more than three varying widths to add interest and directional movement.

Ideas for Paving

Paving offers a wide choice of materials, colours and finishes. Natural stone slabs tend to offer the most elegant solution for a formal design, with a wide variety of tones and textures from which to choose.

Pale-coloured limestone is a popular choice for modern designs, especially in an urban location where its cool tones and light-reflecting qualities introduce calm and luminosity. It also has a fairly uncompromising look, so if you want something gentler, sandstone provides honey and golden hues. Slate has subtle variations of green, grey and plum, but may also be golden and fiery. Natural stone varies enormously in colour and texture.

It is tempting to order materials online, but it is always preferable to handle, examine and compare physical samples before purchasing. With so many products available, it is helpful to understand the differences in texture and colour. UK and European stone tends to be subtle in tone and texture, while material deriving from Africa, India and China can have a more fiery look.

The method by which the stone is cut and finished will alter the look of the paving scheme as well. Sawn slabs with crisp edges and a smooth surface are ideal for a modern style. The shape of the slab and the laying pattern are important, too: bold floor patterns will help to give the paving a crisp, clean appearance.

Above: *Stepping-stones of smooth sawn sandstone make a crisp, bridging pathway.*

LAYING PAVING SLABS

Neatly finished and perfectly level paving, using either square or rectangular units, is likely to be a major surfacing component in the modern courtyard. The choice of materials is personal and dependent on the specific style, but relatively plain, crisply finished slabs of either sawn natural stone, split slate, or concrete work well.

1 Excavate to a depth that allows for about 5cm (2in) of compacted hardcore or rubble topped with 5cm (2in) of ballast (sand and gravel), plus the thickness of the paving.

2 Place five blobs of mortar on the hardcore, one in the centre, the others near the corners. Bed the slab on the mortar, check it is level and tap with a rubber mallet to correct.

3 If creating a large area, lay slabs on a slight slope to ensure efficient drainage. Continue to lay the paving slabs on the mortar, until you have covered the whole area.

4 Space the slabs with pegs. After a couple of days, mortar the joints using a dryish mortar mix and a trowel, pushing it well down. Recess the mortar slightly.

Juxtapositions

Paths, steps and terraces can benefit from contrasting details to highlight elements. These do not have to be complicated: a dark-toned detail using slate or granite, combined with a pale limestone would give a sharp result, while an edging of honeyed sandstone produces a contrast that reinforces the design more subtly.

The use of plant material in conjunction with paving slabs will also produce a softening effect. Low-growing herbs in place of regular jointing would enliven a terrace; position slabs far enough apart to allow space for the planting. Alternatively, arrange square slabs in a grid pattern to make a formal, chequered design in a grass lawn.

There are many good examples of economy paving products, such as those made from tinted concrete or reconstituted stone dust formed in moulds taken from natural products. To stay in line with the contemporary concept, choose simple designs with a natural finish and colour.

Right: *A daisy floor pattern is achieved with contrasting cream and black setts.*

Left: *An agave with diminutive grey succulents and drought-resistant herbs help to animate this surreal desert landscape of crushed turquoise-coloured shells.*

laid on the surface after pouring. The surplus cement is then brushed off before it has completely dried to expose the granular material.

To prepare the ground area for concrete, it must be levelled and laid with a compressed hardcore foundation. The form and layout of the design is then set out using bands of shuttering material, such as marine ply. The concrete cement mix is poured in, tamped down to push out air, and then allowed to cure and set. For making steps and small areas of paving, concrete is poured into moulds formed on site using a system of shuttering to hold the shape in place. This is potentially a self-build project, as the system is economic and easy to create yourself with the aid of a cement mixer and levelling tools.

Creative Additions

Unusual and unexpected materials are frequently utilized as part of modern garden design. Coloured aggregates in the form of crushed glass, for example, and tinted stone chippings can play interesting roles

Detailing and Relief

Manufactured shapes are also made solely to add detailing to an area of paving such as edging. Ammonite and split-cobble forms, for example, can introduce an interesting relief to a plain design, especially effective when it is used in conjunction with a water feature or sculptural object. They might be introduced effectively in a sinuous, snaking line carefully cut through paving, or laid through a background of grass or contrasting stone chippings.

Poured concrete offers interesting solutions for paving and steps and it is the material to choose if you are

looking for an absolutely smooth, clear surface. Pure white cement makes a more refreshing alternative to the normal grey, or coloured pigments may be added to the mix to make a bold contrast statement.

Specialists now offer concrete with a polished surface that brings a super level of cool sophistication to a modern scheme. If you are looking for a more textured effect, then aggregates such as polished pebbles or coloured glass nuggets can be incorporated into the mix or

Right: *Concrete replica ammonites provide relief detail in this paving scheme.*

in flooring, for mulches and as decorative panels. They can be arranged in an infinite array of different designs and can be used to make up tantalizing geometric *trompe l'oeil* effects or chequered grids to create coloured 'set-piece' beds in place of traditional planting. They also lend themselves to more fluid, curvaceous shapes that might be incorporated with a scheme of tapestry-planting.

Granules of recycled rubber can surface pathways or be used in place of vegetative, moisture-retaining mulch. As well as neutral black, this material is available in many bright colours; because of its soft, rubbery qualities it is ideal for making up into animated designs suitable for children's play areas.

Futuristic Materials

Industrial steel grid panels are normally used for making steps and high-level decks, but they can also be used for ground-level paths. To achieve a minimalist effect, try setting them over natural gravel or coloured aggregate to create a startling contrast. Even more spectacularly, create a dramatic

Above: *Industrial steel mesh panels create paths across an area of tapestry planting.*

design feature by floating the grid panels over an area planted with diminutive succulent plants and ferns, to show off the foliage below. This creates a practical pathway, in this case to allow access for a car, that combines and contrasts geometric pattern with organic texture.

Solid sheet metal offers an alternative look for flooring. Stainless or anodized steel brings a

Above: *Green astroturf has a luminous quality, offset by the stark screen walls.*

sharp, edgy look to a crisp design scheme and it can be finished with a studded surface that is attractive and will also help to reduce slipping. Panels of this material are especially suited to being used as raised pathways or decks, perhaps over a water feature, or to span two separate parts of the garden.

Although functional, metal becomes hot to the touch in the sun and slippery in the wet – so you will need to exercise discretion in its use.

Often, timber planking can be used in place of metal to achieve the same objective, and this is especially suited to pool decking. Wood also lends a warm, organic feel to the garden and it is normally more practical. High-quality hardwoods such as maple, birch and ash are the best to choose, as they are more able to stand up to the rigours of heat, cold and wet. Make sure you use sustainable sources for hardwood. Alternatively, use naturally durable soft woods such as Western red cedar, Southern yellow pine, white fir or heavy planks of pressure-treated pine.

Above: *Splayed bands of timber accentuate the curves of this gravel path.*

Above: *This cube illusion is achieved with rectangles of glass and stone chippings.*

WALLS AND SCREENS FOR MODERN ZONES

Solid backdrops in the form of enclosing walls and screens can help to create an uncluttered setting for a formal modern courtyard. Concrete is probably the most versatile building material, but eye-catching solutions can also be achieved using metal, glass, stone and wood in an imaginative way.

Above: *A solid screen wall benefits from a large opening to view the garden beyond.*

Adaptable Concrete

Concrete is a superb material for a range of applications, from making the retaining walls for raised planting beds to the creation of formal, above-ground pools and water features. It can also be made into free-standing screens and other garden design features.

A solid screen could be incorporated into a water cascade, or it could function as a stand-alone backdrop to a piece of sculpture or artwork. In addition, a concrete screen makes an ideal support for lighting, with the wiring hidden out of sight inside, for special night-time effects.

As good as they are for creating privacy from neighbours, solid screens and boundary walls can be overpowering at times. When

Above: *Small, quirky details can do a lot to relieve a monotonous run of walling; colour-co-ordinated pots and a timber beam finish the opening effectively.*

Above: *These bold timber columns create a screen without closing off the garden.*

Above: *This wall of staggered wooden blocks achieves enormous textural interest.*

pierced with portholes or windows, however, their bulk is relieved and, where appropriate, you can benefit from views to the other side.

Concrete can be poured into shuttering moulds to create very elegant vertical features, but the more usual, and economical, method is to construct the wall with concrete building blocks, strengthened with reinforcing rods. A cement render is then applied to give the wall a smooth, even finish. For a permanent colour finish, incorporate special tinting pigments into the render; otherwise, you can use an exterior paint once the cement has completely dried. Stunning polished concrete effects can also be achieved in the hands of specialists.

CREATING A BOLD CANVAS

Depending on the colour you choose, a painted wall can act like a giant canvas hanging in your outdoor room. If selected with care, colour will add energy to a space, especially one used for entertaining, and either become a focal point in its own right or make a stunning backdrop to the courtyard. Before committing to a colour, use a sample to paint a small square area of heavy paper and view in position.

1 Begin by clearing a space around the wall so that you can work in relative comfort. Check that the rendering is sound and make any repairs before starting work. If it has never been painted before, seal the surface of the render with a PVA solution and allow it to dry.

2 If the render has been previously painted, prepare the surface for repainting by brushing it down with a soft-bristled hand brush to remove cobwebs and any debris, especially in corners and under the coping stones. Use a scraper and wire brush on painted brick to lift loose paint.

3 Having followed the manufacturer's instructions for preparing the paint, stirring it as directed, begin by applying a coat of paint to the edges using a small brush. Exterior-quality paints, including masonry paint, can be custom-coloured to match any colour sample.

4 Continue to work around the edges of the wall taking care to protect the flooring with a tarpaulin, dust sheets or plastic sheeting – it can be very time consuming to remove paint splashes, especially from textured surfaces. Use a smaller brush still for any narrow strips.

5 To paint the remaining central area of render, switch to a large brush or roller. Particularly with strong or deep shades, you may notice that the surface appears patchy as it dries. Leave it for the required amount of drying time, which varies depending on the temperature.

6 Once the first coat of paint is dry, apply the second, using the same technique. You may even need a little touching up after that. Comparing this scene with the first, you can see how dramatic the space has become. Add a finishing touch with the container plants and furniture.

Transparency and Colour

Glass is a superb screening material, able to block the wind without obscuring the view – an important feature for riverside and high-level terraces. Glass bricks can be useful in all or part of a boundary wall, to admit light with no loss of privacy.

Mirrored glass offers an illusory role, reflecting light into a shady area or multiplying images to give a false idea of space and dimension. It can be set into a wall to reflect an interesting feature or the façade opposite to create a double image. More inventively, a series of free-standing mirror screens set among low planting will reflect endless repeating images of foliage and skyscape to fantastic visual effect.

Colour produces a surreal effect in translucent materials, its intensity changing throughout the day as the lighting conditions vary. Coloured glass is especially suited to modern, stained-glass windows, providing relief and sculptural interest when set into a plain wall.

Alternatively, Perspex (Plexiglass) offers a tough, lightweight solution and is easier to handle and fix, so is attractive for large-scale applications.

A group of screens made in dazzling primary colours would make a striking sculptural statement; a single large screen composed of coloured panels could take on the look of a Mondrian painting, while throwing an evocative colour cast across its surroundings as light passes through it.

Light and Shine

Stainless steel can be polished to a mirror-like shine that will throw back light while creating interesting,

distorted reflections of planting or decorative objects beside it. It makes an excellent screening material for boundaries and backdrops, and it is especially useful for introducing an extra sense of dimension or for lighting up a shady area.

Steel sheets can be used in a solid mass where it is desirable to block a view or create a special effect. For partial screening, where you want a hint of the view beyond, intricate designs can be cut out using a laser.

Steel offers other solutions for semi-opaque screening. Industrial wire mesh provides the means to separate areas of the garden, or to make boundary enclosures that do not completely block a view. Rigid panels can be easily made by fixing the mesh in wooden frames, which can be screwed into timber posts set in the ground. Alternatively, it is possible to obtain stainless steel in sheet form with geometric perforations that produce a delicate relief. This produces an elegant solution for smaller, detailed effects within a screen.

Above: *An ephemeral screen uses clear Perspex floats strung on nylon cord.*

Above: *A curvaceous, stainless-steel screen makes an arresting modern backdrop.*

A MODERN PERGOLA

Using a basic pergola kit or self-build framework as a foundation (see page 133 for step-by-step construction), you can customize a pergola to create a feature that is more in keeping with the architecture and overall design theme of a contemporary courtyard. Traditional trellis panels don't always sit well against a modern backdrop, so you should explore other screening materials. These might include translucent or coloured panels of Perspex (Plexiglass) such as the ones used below. Alternatively, consider metal-framed units of lashed technical fabric.

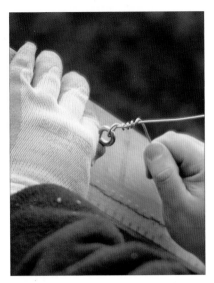

1 Using wooden crossbeams can give a pergola a heavy, weighty feel and make the overall structure look more traditional, or even rustic. As an alternative to this, screw in metal vine eyes and attach galvanized training wire. Secure the wire to the eyes and tighten.

2 Once they are all in place, the taut galvanized training wires form a versatile, lightweight 'roof' for the framework of the pergola. These wires are well able to support a tracery of climbing plants, outdoor lights or some form of temporary sun screening, such as a sail.

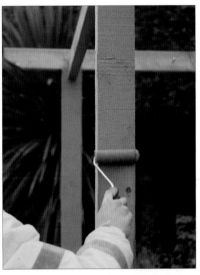

3 Coloured surfaces play more of a role in the modern courtyard garden, so you may want to paint the woodwork using an outdoor-quality paint. A small roller and paint tray make this a quick and easy task. Avoid overloading the roller and cover the ground to catch splashes.

4 To attach Perspex or Plexiglass prefabricated screens, drill holes at regular intervals through the frame and into the pergola's supporting timber upright and then secure the screen in position with galvanized screws.

5 To support the other side of the screen, either attach it to another pergola upright or fix a shorter post into the ground – which will be hidden behind the screen – and attach the frame of the screen to that.

6 The arrangement of screens shown here allows multiple entrances and exits to the patio area beneath the pergola, keeping the structure feeling airy and spacious. The floor is gravel laid over consolidated hardcore.

PLANTS AND CONTAINERS FOR MODERN ZONES

Geometry and scale are important design factors. In a minimalist design, all the bones are laid bare so the planting must play more than a supporting role. Clean architectural lines depend heavily on planting statements to introduce an organic equilibrium with the hard elements.

Above: *Architectural plants like this arum lily (*Zantedeschia*) make a bold statement.*

Left: *This ebullient architectural planting uses spiky foliage specimens that include palms, cycads and mature bear grass (*Dasylirion serratifolium*).*

Planting Choices

Bold planting statements are necessary in a contemporary garden, and structured blocks of single-species monoplanting help to achieve the right balance of weight and scale. They can aid a sense of progression through a space by means of sequential repetition or create focal points and special features.

The passage of a broad, uncluttered terrace or pathway can be reinforced by judicious planting choices. Trees trained with bare trunks to eye height and topped with a mop-head canopy make interesting vertical statements. Plant them in line, 3m (10ft) or so apart, on either side of a terrace to create a walkway. Underplant each specimen with a block of shrubs to give a sense of visual weight at ground level. This can be achieved

by depending entirely on evergreens to have a permanent year-round presence. Holly (*Ilex* sp.), Portuguese laurel (*Prunus lusitanica*) and *Elaeagnus x ebbingei* make good tree subjects. They all have the necessary height and the ability to tolerate regular trimming. *Buxus* and *Ligustrum* work well to make the cubes below, while green ivy will create a tight ground cover that is easy to maintain.

Trees and Shrubs

Although deciduous trees drop their leaves in winter, they have the advantage of changing foliage colour throughout the year, so altering the appearance of the garden season by season. Some have other special qualities, as they take well to forming and training, especially in a method known as 'pleaching'. Here

the canopy is trained on horizontal wires eventually to produce a long, unbroken block of foliage above head height, with the bare trunks showing beneath.

This rather grand style is particularly suitable for defining boundaries – either to reinforce a pathway, for example, or to frame a feature such as a pool or seating area. Lime (*Tilia*) is frequently used for its pale green leaves and scented summer flowers. However, hornbeam (*Carpinus betulus*) retains its rich, brown autumn foliage for a long time, adding an extra dimension in winter. It is useful for structural work, as it can be trained into hedges, archways and columns.

Above: *The bleached white trunks of silver birch trees frame low-growing box balls.*

HOW TO PRUNE BAMBOO

The grace and beauty of bamboo tends to diminish unless established plants are pruned annually. The aim is to be able to admire the line, colour and markings of the stems, or culms, by reducing congestion and removing debris. You can also control the spread of more invasive types by removing emerging shoots.

1 Cut out a proportion of the oldest stems at ground level. Those more than three years old tend to have dense whorls of leafy branches. In addition, take out some of the thinnest, weakest stems.

2 Avoid leaving short stumps of stems after pruning, as these go hard and take a long time to rot. Pull out any dead, rotted stems. A lot of dead stems may mean that the plant is dying after flowering.

3 Cut out any dead stems at the base as well as dead side shoots. Also remove stems that are crossing upright stems. Cut off the lower side shoots as close to the main stem as possible.

4 Leave the leaf litter at the base of the bamboo to allow the silica bound up in the dead leaves to be recycled. Apply a mulch of bulky organic matter in early spring to feed plants.

Small shrubs, such as fragrant, silvery *Santolina* and lavender, respond well to clipping into low, tight shapes suitable for edges and underplanting, but even better, they make excellent subjects for geometric tapestry designs. Taller-growing yew (*Taxus baccata*) and box (*Buxus sempervirens*) make good, dark evergreen subjects with excellent screening possibilities.

You can clip them into neat, rectangular blocks or rounded balls and spheres of foliage, which can be laid out in rows within a precise geometric template.

Low-growing bamboos also lend themselves to block planting and barrier edging; white-striped *Pleioblastus variegatus* and white-edged *Sasa veitchii* are both excellent candidates for this treatment.

Textural Planting

It is possible to create a range of adventurous optical effects that echo the architectural features of the courtyard design. Chequerboard and striped effects work well for tapestry planting when they can be easily viewed from above. Taller plants, used in regularly repeated patterns, can be employed to create screens and borders for paths. For low-level work, mat-spreading, mound- or tuft-forming evergreens make the best choice. Contrasting colours help to accentuate the display, with combinations of grey and lime, purple and black being extremely effective.

Interesting texture plays an important role. The black, blade-like foliage of *Ophiopogon planiscapus* 'Nigrescens' makes a gleaming and faintly sinister statement. In contrast, the needle-fine, grey-tufted grass *Festuca glauca* has a light and airy elegance. Ground-hugging succulents can be used to provide an exotic textural effect; the rosette-forming *Sempervivum* group and some of the hardy sedums are ideal.

Above: *White iris and frothy gypsophila complement this cool architectural design.*

Above: *Swathes of mono-planting add texture and movement.*

The colours of sedum, which vary from silver-grey through to reddish-purple, can be set off beautifully by a contrasting mineral mulch. White marble chippings, mauve slate and dark, polished river pebbles lend a sophisticated touch; by contrast coloured materials, such as crushed glass and plastics, can produce living pop-art displays.

Dynamics of Contrast

A tropical planting treatment can act as a foil to the cool, clean lines of contemporary architecture, introducing an energetic visual experience composed of exotic flowers, spiky leaves and tall, textured trunks. Palm trees, agaves and yuccas, phormium and cordyline, all have the architectural strength required to hold their own against a stark backdrop of bare walls and floors. A large specimen can be used singly to make a big, bold statement, though strong planting groups will create an exhilarating theatre of shape and form. Their sunlit shadows will dance by day, while judicious uplighting at night will throw their dramatic silhouettes in bizarre patterns against walls, screens and floors.

Containers for Planting

A courtyard garden can be dependent on containers, largely due to restricted space or lack of available ground for planting. In high-level projects, such as balconies and roof terraces, all the planting has, of necessity, to be in containers, either free-standing or built in. This is a high-maintenance form of gardening, requiring excellent soil quality, fastidious preparation and a very regular watering regime.

To complement the pared-down, minimalist style, planting containers should also be clean-lined and possess a bold, sculptural integrity. New shapes tend to have tall, narrower proportions than traditional pots, although still normally retaining a round or square shape. These forms work especially well when arranged in straight-lined groups, producing an elegant, sequential statement, to create a geometric backdrop or to line a pathway. Matching pairs can be used to frame a doorway or entrance, or mark a descent of steps. They do have one drawback, however; the height combined with a narrow base makes them unstable in exposed, windy sites and where children may be playing.

Above: *Bold green planting animates the soft grey of these weathered zinc containers.*

Cubes and wider, curved shapes are the solution to this problem. These offer potentially greater planting possibilities, too. The unusual height of a tall, slim pot must be balanced by squat planting to retain stability – an evergreen ball or cube of box, for example. Broad shapes in large sizes have the physical and visual volume to support a decent shrub or small tree, with their greater need for soil and root capacity.

Materials play an important role of course, and they should reflect and balance the ambiance of the hard landscaping. Terracotta, with its excellent cultural qualities, is the traditional material for plant pots. Its style has moved on over the centuries, however. The newest look uses white, grey or taupe-coloured clay to produce simple, but oversized containers with enormous integrity and elegance. The flat, matt finish ties in beautifully with both natural wood and the painted exterior joinery.

Glazed finishes offer an alternative look with the potential of a range of soft colours, but bear in mind that only stoneware (not terracotta) is suitable where there is a danger of frost.

Above: *A block planting of single species with co-ordinated colours.*

Above: *This large weathered pot is surrounded by tropical ferns and planting.*

Plastics offer the ideal solution where striking appearance and bold colour are required. Moulded containers in PVC, resins and fibreglass offer a variety of styles and sizes suited to very modern, extreme designs. Some are in shiny primary colours, up to 2m (6½ft) tall, and are sculptures in their own right. Others are more subdued – cubes and bowls in matt, translucent finishes that can even be adapted to lighting features.

Apart from their visual qualities, the huge advantage of these containers is their lightness – they are easy to handle and perfectly suited to roof gardens and balconies.

Zinc offers another lightweight container solution, with graciously elegant modern forms that retain a classic twist. Pure, round, classic shapes work in all situations, while cubes and tall rectangles can be juggled together to form an intriguing plant jigsaw. The best types

are acid treated to a sober, dark finish and double-skinned, to keep the root-ball (roots) protected from heat. This look mixes well with crisp designs in pale timber decking and cool limestone paving.

Oversized round and rectangular timber plant containers have a real contemporary edge. Made from European oak or tropical hardwood, they are an excellent foil for a garden dependent on darker stone surfaces.

POTTING UP A SEDGE

Grasses and evergreen sedges (*Carex*), as well as other plants with narrow, linear foliage, have the right look for modern outdoor spaces. Many require a minimum of

maintenance and have an airy, space-saving habit. Covering the compost (soil mix) with a sparkling and colourful decorative mulch adds to the contemporary feel.

1 Cover the drainage hole with a piece of tile or crock and pour 4–5cm (1½–2in) of gravel into the base. Cover the gravel with a little loam-based compost (soil mix). Soak the plant in its pot to wet the root-ball (roots).

2 Remove the plastic pot and try the sedge (here *Carex* 'Prairie Fire') for size. The finished compost level should be the same as the original nursery level, but leave space for a layer of mulch and for water to pool on top.

3 Gathering up the foliage of the sedge at the base, work in more compost to fill the gap around the root-ball. Check that there are no large air spaces by using your fingers to feed compost further down and firm lightly.

4 Choose a mulch of coloured glass chippings or acrylic chips. Work the chips around the base of the plant, covering the compost thoroughly. The finished plant should be watered well and stood in a bright or partially shaded site.

STRUCTURES FOR MODERN ZONES

The contemporary garden is an opportunity to use materials in new and unexpected ways. Three-dimensional structures within an outdoor space, such as an arch or a shelter, tend to loosely follow conventional approaches, but are interpreted in ways where the materials, execution, design and visual impact are more prominent than the purpose.

Above: *These curvaceous screens bring a new dimension to willow weaving.*

Left: *A tall screen strung with interwoven wires brings a sense of enclosure to one of a series of circular terraces on a sloping site, all enclosed by curving walls.*

Reinforcing rods used in concrete construction once more have a role to play. You can create a screen wall of vertical rods using a heavy wooden beam set on the ground – simply drill holes at 2–4cm (¾–1⅝in) intervals and push the metal rods in firmly. The rods might all finish on a single horizontal plane, or you can cut them into different heights to produce a wave effect. Stiff wire or even plastic rods could be used instead for a more ephemeral effect.

Wire and plastic mesh are versatile materials to incorporate into a semi-opaque structure. To create an intriguing feature, build a framework in the form of a

Establishing the Structures

Vertical elements add a crucial dimension to every garden design, introducing perspective and contrast between the planting and the house. These vertical elements may be purely symbolic in nature, or they could provide practical roles of shelter and retreat.

Spatial divisions provide an effective way to introduce focus, while creating real or illusory visual separations between different areas of the garden. Free-standing, vertical posts offer a host of opportunities to create impressive visual effects in a really simple way, by arresting the eye without affecting the overall view.

Install the posts in single rows to make a partition or backdrop, or double them up to accentuate a

pathway and organize directional flow so that the garden unfolds to visitors as you would wish it to be seen. Alternatively, they can be arranged in straight lines, grids, waves, curves or circles depending on the effect you want to create.

Construction and Finish

You can choose any vertical layout to suit your design format, but the construction material and finish will differentiate one concept of garden from another. A cool, architectural style would normally call for crisp, engineered materials, such as stainless steel or aluminium. In this case, posts would be formed from slim rods or hollow tubing. Metal with a rusted appearance provides a more organic look and one that is easier to produce at home.

Above: *This sweeping tunnel is formed from hoops of thin plastic film.*

Translucent "bubble effect" Perspex columns provide visually neutral support for the curved plastic "wave" canopy.

rectilinear cage, fixing the mesh all around it and on top. This would make an effective statement on its own, but an extra dimension could be achieved by the addition of a spreading deciduous shrub, such as *Cotoneaster dammeri*. During construction, plant the shrub on the inside of the structure, so that the framework of stems can be seen in winter.

Reinterpreting Traditional Materials

Wood is readily available and can be worked with the type of tools found in the home workshop. Timber posts have seemingly endless possibilities; arranged in groups, they provide an unusual way to create a simple and effective sculptural feature. It would be easy to create features for an organic-style design using bold, square timber sections from a sawmill, or you may be able to source the round poles used for supporting telephone wires. To introduce different textural effects, try

Above: *This futuristic raised terrace has satellite seating and an overhead shelter.*

wrapping them in heavy rope, perhaps leaving tassels to drift in the breeze. Try a contemporary swag effect, taking a closely banded series of taut ropes, passed through holes drilled in the uprights.

Another option is to make a pergola, attaching horizontal rails above head height. The pergola can be fixed to the house or a garden cabin, or build it as a free-standing structure over a pathway to draw the eye and emphasize a route.

A structure of bold posts and rails will cast shadows that change shape and direction as the sun passes across the sky, so adding to the dynamic effect of the arrangement. A roof of mesh material would offer a different strategy, providing structural support for climbing plants and a fixing point for lighting.

Metal elements can be combined with timber to alter the weight or style of the structure. Multi-stranded steel wire is immensely strong, but visually extremely light; it can be tensioned vertically or horizontally and then incorporated into a pergola structure, railings, gates or even screen doors.

Steel reinforcing mesh would offer the same structural function, but with an industrial and less elegant finish. Large sheets of this heavy, rigid mesh can be fixed flat to create a 'window' feature for a cabin wall, or it could be curved – perhaps to achieve a tunnel to support informal climbing plants.

A cabin is a desirable feature if there is space, offering a three-dimensional visual statement while providing the important features of shade, shelter and storage.

The structure may echo some architectural features of the house, or be created in free form, to accentuate the layout of the ground plan, for example. The style can be anything from hi-tech gleaming steel and glass to a low-key timber construction. The incorporation of a solid roofed veranda would provide shade from sun and shelter from light rain, making an ideal place for a viewing terrace to admire the garden. This would of course call for comfortable furniture as the location encourages lounging. It could also create a perfect place for a dining space.

FURNITURE FOR MODERN ZONES

Having planned the structural elements, you should now have a sheltered spot for your seating area. Don't choose 'modern' furniture just for the sake of it – select it to fit comfortably with the decisions you've already made. So look at the options available using both established and experimental materials – from wood and aluminium to concrete and plastic.

Above: *This moulded organic, free-form seat creates a striking sculptural form.*

Left: *An immaculately detailed bench and table system has been incorporated with the construction of this courtyard.*

Perhaps the most exciting recent development is a stranded plastic, which can be woven like basketware. Elegant and functional and, as a bonus, comfortable too.

Inviting, weather-resistant, outdoor furniture is available at last. Deep sofas and armchairs with matching occasional tables bring five-star hotel style to the home. For the ultimate luxury, choose a wonderfully sensual, circular double lounger, complete with a curvaceous, lidded canopy. A perfect hideaway.

At the opposite extreme, and following current trends in new uses for materials, furniture made from concrete is now available.

Material Options

Wood is the traditional material for exterior furniture and always looks at home in the garden. However, new designs incorporate other materials to give an edgier, lighter appearance, more akin to interior furniture and well suited to a crisp, modern garden terrace.

Aluminium frames, stone and slate tabletops and textile seats feature frequently. Moulded plastics in bright, pop colours offer comfortable and practical new-look seating. Lightweight and easy to store, a set of pink or lime-green chairs with a matching café table would introduce a cheerful note to a balcony or terrace.

Above: *A slab of limestone has been sculpted into a stunning feature bench.*

Above: *Translucent materials like glass and plastic make the most of the available light.*

Sometimes more functional than comfortable, it can, nevertheless, be found in organic forms that add an interesting sculptural feature to the courtyard. Polished finishes help to make the look attractive;

Above: *Armchairs of woven stranded plastic are lightweight and weather resistant.*

concrete can even be used for dining furniture, and the incorporation of fibre optics in the table surface will add drama to an evening's entertainment.

Creating Shelter

Shade from the summer sun is an important consideration for eating areas, and an overhead canopy is probably the most attractive solution where space allows. Where practical, these can be fixed to a convenient wall, but a free-standing model is another option. The most beautiful resemble curvy, floating sails, restrained by cables to the ground, creating an ephemeral sculptural statement in a modern garden setting. They may be made from canvas or from one of the innovative intelligent textiles that deflect the hot sun. Alternatively, a gazebo-style canopy makes a good semi-permanent solution that can be easily taken down and stored

Above: *Simple treatments yield big results. A long curving bench encloses this roof terrace, with folding chairs and a low table creating an intimate seating area.*

over winter. Washable textiles and integral curtains make these an appealing choice when a permanent structure is not feasible.

Parasols can be quickly erected wherever the need arises, but to be effective the canopy should be large and this tends to make them heavy and unmanageable.

Oversized shades with aluminium frames and winding devices are a practical choice, especially when fixed permanently to the ground. The best can be orientated according to the position of the sun, avoiding the need to move them about. Summertime lunch can then become a pleasurable experience, while evenings can be illuminated by lighting strings incorporated into the frame.

ORNAMENT FOR MODERN ZONES

The clean, cool space of a modern courtyard can be seen as an outdoor gallery, providing a theatrical context for contemporary sculpture. A terrace may provide only enough space to display a single statement piece of work, while a larger courtyard garden could stage a varied collection of different sculptural elements, or a large installation that dominates the whole area.

Above: *A decorative spiral of recycled, crushed windscreen glass.*

Modern Displays

Outside, flooded with natural light, the texture of a decorative piece alters from an interior display. Another interesting relationship is how ornamental elements link to a landscape with shrubs and trees. A piece of stone, when carved and polished, becomes an evocative and sensual form, and by exposing its ancient strata lines and colour a connection is made between the rock and its natural origins.

Wood, too, has a powerful connection with the natural world. Once rooted in the earth, it now gives up its innermost secrets to the artist's chisel or saw. Or, suggesting a period of prehistory, an ancient root burr might stand alone, its unworked, natural form interpreted as a piece of abstract sculpture.

Above: *This humorous Mediterranean-style feature suggests both pool and boules – water not required.*

Above: *This dramatic metal sculpture is enclosed by a curved, free-standing wall.*

Above: *Glass slivers in a curling framework of steel wire create an ephemeral effect.*

A construction that is formed from strands of wire has the effect of being just light and air; it seems to drift on the breeze, a gossamer vision to be caught only by chance. Mirrored glass possesses similarly elusive qualities and can be used to clever effect by multiplying images to present a constantly changing series of views to the onlooker. A group of tall, free-standing mirror panels might form the central focus to a courtyard, catching the skyscape by day, but appearing ghostly by night with subtle moonlit effects.

WATER FOR MODERN ZONES

Water is an important element of a contemporary courtyard. As well as providing calm and serenity, it animates a space and offers exciting sculptural possibilities. Much of the emphasis of garden design in recent years has been on innovative water features – spinning crystal orbs vying with shimmering towers of glass or pyramids of bright steel.

Above: *The finest vertical jets of water bisect a brilliant circle of tubular steel.*

Tumbling Water

The tumbling cascade has long inspired the imagination of the gardening world. You may lack the space to having a swimming pool on a terrace, but this is an easy technique to adapt as either a built-in or free-standing feature.

In terms of space, all you require for a cascade is simply a small, formal reservoir pool backed by a narrow wall. This is furnished with a simple spout or wide slot for the water to emerge through, which is pumped up from below.

A forceful cascade will break up the pool surface, creating dancing light and shadow. Another option is to fill the pool space with a bed of glass pebbles and light them from below to create a night-time glow.

Above: *This elegant cascade allows water to slip slowly overboard to a larger pool below. The upper ledge offers a good perching spot – conveniently beside the wine cooler.*

Above: *This low-key feature really proves that less can be more.*

Above: *Carefully organized chutes let water slip down gently from one to the next.*

Wall of Water

A chaotic water effect is not always appropriate in a courtyard, where noise can echo and reverberate, aggravating you and your neighbours. But using the basic cascade principle, you can achieve a gentle fall of water.

If water flow is reduced and then released in a broad sweep along the top edge of the wall, it will flow down slowly, hugging the vertical surface. This water curtain concept translates very well to a free-standing screen made of polished steel or translucent glass. It would make a magnificent visual conclusion to a long, narrow canal or a striking centrepiece for a formal terrace.

Shaping Water

Water moves smoothly over polished surfaces, making steel, marble and stone suitable candidates for a range of different water features.

Spheres and globes provide a sculptural opportunity that can be adapted in a variety of ways to suit the needs of your garden space. The curved form offers an effective way in which to combine an attractive shape with a beautiful material, allowing water to bubble up through a vertical tube inside. Spheres work very well in a shallow pool or in a small container of water that can be placed easily in a confined area. A large, silvery sphere would look mysterious as it seemed to rise out of a still pool, while a group of granite balls would make a striking feature in a paved area, with the reservoir and pump concealed in a container somewhere under ground.

The Lure of the Swimming Pool

In hot climates, swimming pools will often dominate the entire courtyard. Inside-out concepts allow pools to merge with the house, while plunge and lap pools are combined with shady, terrace verandas.

These ideas can be borrowed and adapted in cooler climates. A warm plunge pool or relaxing jacuzzi, ideally solar-heated, can usually be accommodated.

Safety note: *Children should be supervised at all times when near water. If you have an open-air pool consider security fencing, surface covers, alarms and motion detectors.*

Left: *Three tall steel cylinders spout freely to create a dynamic backdrop to a still pool.*

MAKING A STEEL WATER FOUNTAIN

This stylish and contemporary water feature is made from three stainless-steel tubes. The water tumbles from slits near the tops of the tubes, as well as overflowing from the tops and running down the sides. A steel fabricator should be able to supply standard stainless-steel pipes. The ones pictured here have slots cut with a hacksaw 5–10cm (2–4in) from the top of each pipe and each one is fitted with a baseplate for stability.

1 Clear and level a dish-shaped area to a depth of about 5cm (2in). In the middle, dig a hole to accommodate a plastic reservoir. Use a qualified electrician to set up a power supply, an outdoor socket or waterproof junction box.

2 After fitting the reservoir and ensuring that it is completely level, backfill around it with soil or sand. Line the cleared area and reservoir with geotextile fleece or sand. Cut a hole in the fleece over the reservoir.

3 Lay pond liner over the fleece and reservoir. Gradually add water to the reservoir to pull the liner into place. Stand the stainless-steel pipes on top of the liner next to the reservoir, making sure that they are vertical.

4 Place the pump in the reservoir, covering it with a galvanized metal grille. Cut a hole in the grille for the pipe to pass through. Then, to keep back finer particles, cover the grille with fine plastic shade netting.

5 Connect up a 2.5cm (1in) hose to the pump, securing it with a clip, and connect the other end to a three-way T-piece.

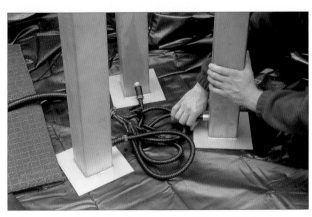

6 Connect each of the outlet pipes to a 1.3cm (½in) hose and flow taps. These are then, in turn, connected and secured with clips to the inlet pipes on each of the steel tubes.

7 Before completing the installation, test the water flow rate and make adjustments as required. Cover the floor with cobbles and rocks, concealing the hose and taps. Turn on the power.

LIGHTING FOR MODERN ZONES

Contemporary lighting ranges from functional low-level path and step lighting to works of art. Minimalism characterizes the design of most modern fitments, although softer, organic and abstract forms have inspired some outdoor light sculptures. And while the look of contemporary lighting is usually quite sophisticated, there is room for lightening the mood with fun and quirky effects.

Above: *A red uplighter among feathery* Stipa tenuissima *looks like glowing embers.*

Left: *Low-level recessed spots cast sufficient light for safety while highlighting various architectural elements and establishing a chic ambience.*

Metallic Lights
Wall lights, including pendant designs and uplighters, might be made from polished or brushed steel, copper or ceramic. The sleek shapes add sculptural interest to the modern courtyard garden and you can sometimes find other lighting elements, such as pathway or stairway lights, in the same design.

If you want to mix and match light fittings, it is usually best to pick ones made from the same material or that have some other element of conformity. Alternatively, combine very simple models, such as slender post lights, bulkhead lights, brick and paving block lights and metallic recessed lights. The latter, made with steel and chrome fittings, are unobtrusive and blend easily with decking boards and brick or rendered walls.

It is useful to consult a qualified lighting engineer at the beginning of any building work, as integrated lighting requires proper planning. White or coloured LEDs are extremely long-lived, making them ideal for less-accessible recessed fitments. Consider adding extra interest by using dichromatic or multicoloured units.

String and Rope Lights
With the advent of LEDs, outdoor fairy lights, or string lights, have become increasingly popular and specialist lighting firms offer a wide range. These include flower, fruit and leaf designs, insects and birds as well as more eccentric subjects. Simple neon-blue or white strings add a more romantic note to seating areas than fixed wall or recessed lights, and strings with

bunches of chilli peppers, for example, could enliven a small dining area on a roof terrace.

Another option for hi-tech courtyards are rope lights with clear plastic tubing containing lines of coloured lights. This flexible lighting can be wound into a sculptural form and lights can be programmed to give either a static display or a gradual fading from one colour to the next. Avoid the frenetic light-switching programmes.

Coloured Floods
When fitted with tinted covers, small halogen floodlights, or mini-floods, as well as spotlights allow you to colour-wash walls and trees.

Above: *Built-in lighting magnifies the dynamic effect of these water jets and extends the drama of the torch flares.*

You can totally transform the look and energy of a garden at night by adding colour to fine metal mesh or glass brick screens, or to garden buildings and pale rendered walls. And in winter, especially, coloured light can make the most of the sculptural qualities of a bare, deciduous specimen tree.

The Cutting Edge

Specialist lighting companies offer effects from stylish underwater lights to shimmering fibre-optic displays, and even light sculptures made from stacks of tempered glass.

Dichromatic and multicoloured units fitted with light-programming devices also allow you to change the mood of an area at the flick of a switch. More avant-garde examples allow you to project images on to bare walls or use laser displays. But whatever lighting scheme you choose, make sure that it is energy efficient and installed by a qualified electrician. Switch off lights when they are not in use to avoid light pollution and annoying your neighbours.

Above: *Here a highly theatrical effect has been created using a mirrored wall running alongside a flight of steps whose risers have been lit with neon blue fibre-optic piping.*

LIGHTING A PATHWAY

Low-voltage LED lights cast a clear, white light, ideal for illuminating a pathway or flight of steps in a contemporary courtyard. Designs vary, but there are many minimalist styles including small, sleek post lights such as the ones illustrated. These are robust and have a long life, making them practical for use in the garden.

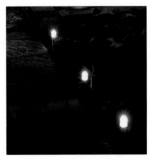

1 Push the spikes on each of the lamps into the ground, ensuring they are properly upright. There is usually plenty of cable between each unit to allow you to set them at the desired distances.

2 Use a trowel to dig a shallow channel along the edge of the pathway and then bury the low-voltage cable under the soil. Tuck the cable in neatly to avoid accidental damage.

3 The lights are partially camouflaged by the planting during the day, and they are fine to use in all kinds of locations around the garden in conjunction with hard or soft landscaping.

4 At night, these low-voltage lights cast a soft glow over the pathway, adding not only to the garden's safety, but also helping to create an appealing ambiance for however you use the area.

CASE STUDY: URBAN CHIC

This contemporary and sophisticated urban courtyard is an intimate retreat that cleverly optimizes the space within the confines imposed by a period building. Its distinctive modern feel is essentially minimalistic in concept and demonstrates an ability to cleverly reinterpret classical lines and symmetry using a range of modern materials.

Above: *Changes of level, using raised beds and steps, occur smoothly.*

In this contemporary urban courtyard, the garden room admits access to a lower terrace, which is partly enclosed by a vine-covered wall and overlooked by the home office – a stone-clad building with richly coloured roof tiles. Its exterior joinery is painted pale duck-egg blue, toning with the grey containers and subdued planting throughout the courtyard.

Reclaimed York-stone paving slabs make up the flooring, but a classically designed marble-tile mosaic detail has been incorporated, which creates a striking ground-level focal point in the central area. Positioned in front of glazed doors, it can be viewed from both indoors and out. The soft tile colours of cream, blue and grey pick up and reflect the tones of the other materials and finishes used in the courtyard garden.

Raised beds planted with structural evergreens, including *Pittosporum tobira* 'Nana', *Festuca glauca* and *Pittosporum tobira* 'Wheeler's Dwarf', form walls to line the steps to the upper level, which features a formal pool.

Above: Pittosporum tobira *'Wheeler's Dwarf' is grown as a neat, small-leaved foliage plant in this raised bed.*

On the boundaries, brick walls surround the garden, lined on one side by black bamboo (*Phyllostachys nigra*) and on the return by a bold, oak-framed pergola. Planting throughout the courtyard is in architectural blocks following the lines of the hard landscaping, with mop-head olive trees (*Olea europaea*) in aged zinc planters providing the main focal points.

The garden plan for this urban courtyard, shown overleaf, demonstrates how the character of the space is defined by the York stone paving and the subtlety of the planting elements. Practical sequences show how to lay a mosaic tile square and how to plant an olive tree in a steel container.

Right: *The insert of pale-coloured mosaic tiles creates a dramatic visual relief in the York stone paving. The tiles have been set flush with the surrounding flooring.*

CREATING A SMALL, MODERN GARDEN

Flooring:
- *Structure the hard landscaping into simple visual statements.*
- *Organize a clear route through the garden.*
- *Use the minimum number of different hard materials for a clear visual story.*

Walls and Screens:
- *Create an enclosure with walls, screens and planting.*

Planting and Containers:
- *Choose one style, formal or exotic.*

- *Plant in single-species blocks.*
- *Include evergreen and structural material for year-round interest.*
- *Allow for seasonal planting, especially spring bulbs and summer flowers.*
- *Choose co-ordinated planting containers that have sufficient volume to support large specimens if necessary.*

Structures and Furniture:
- *Co-ordinate the colour of exterior joinery with the landscaping.*
- *Incorporate at least one vertical structure to provide scale.*

Ornament and Water Features:
- *Include a small formal pool or rill, with a fountain to introduce elements of movement and sound.*
- *Use sculptural features.*
- *Co-ordinate the materials in colour, type and texture, allowing for one or two contrast details.*
- *Focus on water and sculpture features, architectural planting and wall textures.*

Lighting:
- *Introduce lighting to bring an extra dimension to the garden at night.*

URBAN CHIC GARDEN PLAN

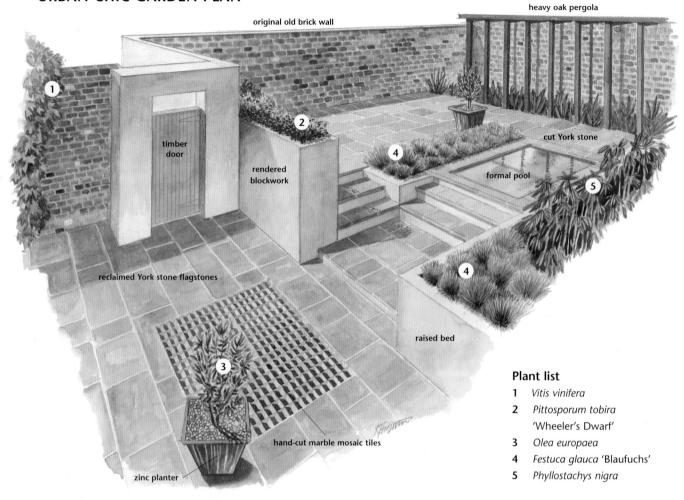

heavy oak pergola

original old brick wall

timber door

rendered blockwork

cut York stone

formal pool

reclaimed York stone flagstones

raised bed

hand-cut marble mosaic tiles

zinc planter

1

2

4

4

5

3

Plant list

1. *Vitis vinifera*
2. *Pittosporum tobira* 'Wheeler's Dwarf'
3. *Olea europaea*
4. *Festuca glauca* 'Blaufuchs'
5. *Phyllostachys nigra*

Left: *The formal zinc planters create elegant, understated focal points in this courtyard. See also the practical planting sequence shown opposite.*

Below: *The blue-grey foliage of Festuca glauca 'Blausilber' is used in the raised beds. The colour fits perfectly with the muted scheme.*

Above: *The mosaic tile inset creates a dramatic visual relief in the paving.*

Above: Vitis vinifera *'Purpurea' self-clings by suckers to the side wall.*

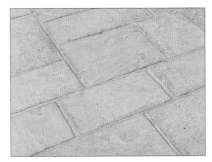

Above: *The whole composition is unified with the use of York stone paving.*

LAYING THE MOSAIC TILE SQUARE

The York-stone paving in the courtyard opposite has been embellished by the inclusion of a square inset of geometric blue and grey tiles directly outside the house. The mosaic tile square adds attractive detailing to the hard landscaping, breaking up the expanse of pale-coloured flooring. The following method shows how to create a similar effect. The tiles of the mosaic finish flush with the York stone so that furniture can be positioned anywhere without any change in level.

MOSAIC TILE SQUARE CROSS-SECTION

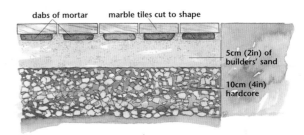

dabs of mortar   marble tiles cut to shape

5cm (2in) of builders' sand

10cm (4in) hardcore

1 Plan your design allowing for a 5mm (¼in) space between each tile for mortar. Calculate the number of tiles.
2 Mark out the area for tiling using string and pegs, making sure that the corners form exact right angles. Prepare the foundations by digging down to around 20cm (8in).
3 Add hardcore at least 10cm (4in) deep and compact with a sledgehammer or post. Spread a 5cm (2in) layer of builders' sand over the hardcore. Smooth with a rake.
4 Cut tiles to shape with an angle grinder, following safety regulations, and arrange in the desired pattern before laying.
5 Start at the centre and, working in small areas, dab mortar on the sand where each tile will lie. Position the tiles, adding a small dab to their edges. Tap down gently and check levels in both directions as you go.
6 Finish by working dark coloured mortar into the gaps, brushing surplus away before it dries.

PLANTING AN OLIVE TREE

Modern metallic containers with a weathered or satin finish work well in a minimalist urban courtyard. The look is perfected when planted with specimens that have a similarly muted colouring and simple profile. Increasingly popular and ideal for a sheltered courtyard are olive trees, with their handsome grey-green leaves.

1 Insulate the galvanized metal planter using sheets of polystyrene (Styrofoam) or bubble wrap/greenhouse insulation material. You could also pack insulation material around an inner plastic pot.

2 Cover, but do not block, the drainage hole with a crock and a layer of gravel, and add soil-based potting mix with extra grit. Having presoaked the olive tree, remove its pot and position the plant.

3 Finish off by adding a layer of mulch comprising fine-grade decorative golden gravel, slate chippings or coloured acrylic chips or beads.

4 Stand the planter in a sheltered spot, such as against a warm wall. In winter, water the olive tree sparingly and in prolonged cold and wet spells bring it under cover somewhere frost free.

PLANT DIRECTORY

Plants are the raison d'être of a courtyard garden. They can shape the design, create different moods and change through the seasons to provide constant interest. This directory does not set out to be exhaustive, but is instead designed to help you select some of the best plants for your style of courtyard. It focuses on all the important aspects of furnishing your outdoor room year round with leaves and flowers, including examples of architectural and dramatic specimens, heat- and shade-tolerant plants, ones suitable for container cultivation and ones for covering walls and trellis partitions. Though courtyards are often relatively small, a single specimen tree can transform the look and feel of the space, creating shade and an overhead canopy of branches, so enhancing the room-like quality. A range of evergreens gives a continuity of display, providing a backdrop to the ebb and flow of seasonal plants. They come into their own in winter and spring.

Left: *A cottage garden style display like this looks wonderful in summer, but for colour and interest throughout the year mix in evergreens and plants that bloom in other seasons.*

HOW PLANTS ARE NAMED

All living things are classified according to a system devised by the 18th-century botanist Carl Linnaeus. He gave plants two Latinized names to show their relationship to all other living things. A plant genus, the first of the two, is a group of plants containing similar species. A species, the second of the two, refers to a group of individuals capable of breeding with each other.

Above: *Dahlias are divided into groups that describe flower shapes, such as Cactus or Ball.*

Scientific Names

A plant's botanical, scientific or Latin name, though often derived from Latin, frequently also contains Greek and other languages. Some genera contain a number of species that may include annuals, perennials, shrubs and trees, and these may look very different from one another even though they are related. Others might contain just one species or a group of species that bear very obvious similarities.

A species is defined as consisting of individuals that are alike and tend naturally to breed with each other. Despite this simple definition, botanists and taxonomists (the experts who classify living things) often disagree about the basis on which a plant has been named. As the science continues to be refined, more old inaccuracies are coming to the fore. Having old names in common usage creates confusion, and plant names often distinguish the old name or synonym (syn. for short) by including it after the correct name.

Above: Cosmos bipinnatus *'Sonata Series'* has been given an award by the Royal Horticultural Society.

Understandably, gardeners often become frustrated with the seemingly constant name changing, but it is important to keep abreast of these changes. Update your garden library with a good, recently published pocket reference and take it with you when you go shopping for plants.

Variations on a Theme

In the average garden, you may grow a single species that is represented by small but pleasing differences such as variegated leaves, differently coloured or double flowers. The term for these variations is subspecies (subsp.), variety (var.), form (f) – similar to variety and often used interchangeably – and cultivar (cv). A cultivar is a variation that would not occur in the wild but has been produced and maintained by cultivation. Variations are given names in single quotation marks. So, a form of the Japanese apricot is *Prunus mume* 'Beni Chidori'.

Hybrids and Groups

When plant species breed with each other, the result is a hybrid. While rare in the wild, crossing is common among plant breeders and is done to produce plants with desirable qualities such as larger or double blooms, longer flowering time or greater frost resistance. A multiplication sign (x) is used to indicate a hybrid and the name often gives a clear idea of its origins.

A group is a cluster of plants with variations that are so similar they cannot sensibly be separated. Their names do not have quotation marks (for example, *Tradescantia* Andersoniana Group).

Awards

Look out for plants given awards and distinctions showing that particular species or cultivars have performed well in trials.

Above: Bougainvillea glabra

Above: Hydrangea anomala

HOW TO USE THE DIRECTORY

The plants in this directory have all been selected with the restrictions and advantages of courtyard gardens in mind. They represent some of the best choices and include climbers, accent plants, ground cover, and those with seasonal interest. This selection will help to furnish your courtyard with reliable, attractive and productive plants, through each of the four seasons.

Above: Iris 'Phil Keen' is an award winning tall bearded type, ideal for sunny borders.

Within this directory the plants are split into sections relating to types, such as trees for confined spaces, climbers, grasses and evergreens. There is also a section on striking architectural plants, to create a sub-tropical feel. Some of this group are tender, requiring winter protection, but the remainder are hardy, despite their exotic appearance. Other sections describe plants with seasonal highlights to enable you to plan colour and interest all year round.

Fragrance and aroma have long been associated with enclosed courtyards, and here there are plenty of examples to choose from. Problem-solving plants address issues of heat and drought as well as cool, shady corners where traditional sun-loving courtyard plants would suffer. While there isn't a section devoted to plants for containers, most of those listed can be grown in pots and planters for courtyards that do not have the benefit of beds and borders. For gardeners wanting to use the space more productively, there is a selection of easy-to-grow vegetables, fruits and herbs.

Each main entry features the botanical and common name, followed by an introduction to either the genus or the species described. More detailed notes are then given on the attributes of named varieties and the best forms to use in a courtyard. Notes indicate flowering time, where relevant, average size and preferred growing conditions, as well as information about the plant's hardiness.

CAPTION

A full or shortened botanical name is given with each photograph.

GENUS AND SPECIES NAME

This is the internationally accepted botanical name for a group of related plant species. This starts with the current botanical name of the plant which can refer to a species, subspecies, hybrid, variant or cultivar. If a synonym (syn.) is given, this provides the common alternative names for a plant.

COMMON NAME

This popular, non-scientific name may apply to the whole or part of the plant genus.

HEIGHT AND SPREAD

The average expected height and spread of a genus or individual plant are given, although growth rates may vary depending on location and conditions. Metric measurements always precede imperial ones. Where measurements diverge significantly, specific measurements are given. The dimensions of bulbs, annuals and perennials tend to be more consistent than those of shrubs, long-lived climbers and trees.

Above: Pelargonium

Pelargonium
Pot geranium

These popular plants flower prolifically all summer long, in all shades of pink, salmon, purple, red and white. Use them in borders, in hanging baskets, window boxes and any kind of container. There are too many hybrids to mention individually, but pelargonium groups include ivy-leaved types with thick, shield-like leaves on trailing stems, ideal for troughs and baskets; Zonal pelargoniums, for many people the typical pelargonium, have leaves banded or zoned a darker colour.

Height and spread: Usually to 45 x 45cm (18 x 18in)
Hardiness: Tender/Z 10
Cultivation: Grow in any well-drained soil in full sun. For pot plants, use any standard soil mix with added grit or perlite.

PHOTOGRAPH

A large number of entries feature a full-colour photograph, which makes identification easier.

GENUS DESCRIPTION

This provides a general introduction to the genus and may state the number of species within that genus. Other information may include general advice on usage, preferred conditions and plant care, as well as subspecies, hybrids (indicated by an "x" in the name), recommended varieties and cultivars (featuring names in single quotations) that are available.

HARDINESS

Hardiness zones give a general indication of the average annual minimum temperature for a particular geographical area. The smaller number indicates the northernmost zone it can survive in and the higher number the southernmost zone that the plant will tolerate. In most cases, only one zone is given. (See page 255 for details of hardiness symbols, zone entries and a zone map.)

CULTIVATION

This section gives the level of sun or shade that the plant either requires or tolerates, with advice on the best type of soil in which it should be grown. Where possible there are helpful tips on how to get the best from the plant.

TREES FOR SMALL SPACES

Good planting design depends on a strong framework, and, even in a confined space, trees are an essential part of the plan. When choosing a deciduous tree, pick one that will develop a striking winter profile, especially one with ornamental or edible fruits, flowers, coloured or handsomely shaped leaves and attractive bark. Some large trees make excellent hedging and green architecture.

Above: Crataegus laevigata *'Paul's Scarlet'* is an easy tree for city and country gardens.

Catalpa bignonioides 'Aurea'
Golden Indian bean tree
This luminous form of the Indian bean tree is ideal for adding an exotic touch to a sheltered courtyard or terrace. With its light canopy of broad, lime green, heart-shaped leaves, it creates a strong focal point in a garden right through summer and into autumn (fall).
Height and spread: 10 x 10m (33 x 33ft); much less if pruned
Hardiness: Hardy/Z 6–10
Cultivation: Prune this deciduous tree back hard every other year in spring to control its size and encourage the formation of even larger, more richly coloured leaves.

Cercis canadensis 'Forest Pansy'
Eastern redbud
A deciduous tree grown mainly for its heart-shaped leaves – which are a rich plum-purple in this cultivar – but also for its ability to form a graceful outline as it grows to maturity. The leaves turn yellow in autumn (fall) before falling.

Height and spread: To 10 x 10m (33 x 33ft)
Hardiness: Hardy/Z 5–9
Cultivation: Grow in fertile, well-drained soil in sun or light shade. Stake young trees for the first three years. Established trees may be cut back hard in spring to encourage larger leaves.

Cercis siliquastrum
Judas tree
This Mediterranean species thrives in a sunny courtyard, perhaps growing with the benefit of the shelter offered by a wall. The small and beautifully formed leaves are rounded with notched ends, and the curious clusters of purple-pink blossoms, which often arise directly from the bark of more established branches, show in spring either before or during the emergence of the leaves.
Height and spread: Eventually up to 10 x 10m (33 x 33ft)
Hardiness: Hardy/Z 7
Cultivation: Plant in well-drained loam, improved before planting if poor, in a warm, sunny or lightly shaded spot.

Cornus
Dogwood
Several of these slow-growing North American trees, including *Cornus kousa* var. *chinensis*, whose bracts fade to pink, the free-flowering 'China Girl' and conical 'Eddie's White Wonder', are noted for their suitability in confined spaces and long season of interest. As well as the showy 'flowers' there may be ornamental fruits and autumn (fall) leaf colour. In *C. alternifolia* 'Argentea' and the larger growing pagoda tree, *Cornus contraversa*, branches develop in a series of horizontal whorls or tiers. The cream variegated *C. c.* 'Variegata' is slow to establish and grow initially but worth the wait!
Height and spread: *Cornus kousa* 7 x 5m (23 x 16ft); *C.* 'Eddie's White Wonder' 6 x 5m (20 x 16ft); *C. contraversa* 'Variegata' 3–5 x 3m (10–16 x 10ft), and 8 x 8m (25 x 25ft) ultimately
Hardiness: Hardy/Z 5–8
Cultivation: Neutral to acid, humus-rich soil in sun or light shade and sheltered from wind.

Crataegus laevigata 'Paul's Scarlet'
Midland hawthorn
In late spring, clusters of rich carmine pink double blossoms smother this thorny deciduous tree. Although ideal for more relaxed, cottage garden planting, this is also a good specimen for cities, being tolerant of atmospheric pollution.
Height and spread: 6–8 x 5m (20–25 x 16ft)
Hardiness: Hardy/Z 4–7
Cultivation: Most soils will do but avoid waterlogged conditions.

Cupressus sempervirens Stricta Group
Italian cypress
These slender columns bring to mind sun-scorched slopes of Mediterranean hillsides and the formal gardens of the Italian Renaissance. A single plant adds just the right character to a terracotta-filled courtyard, but in larger terraces you can create striking vistas by planting in rows and avenues. On a smaller scale, try the hardy columnar juniper *Juniperus scopulorum*

Above: C. bignonioides *'Aurea'*

Above: Cercis siliquastrum

Above: Cornus kousa

Above: Cupressus sempervirens

Above: Olea europaea

Above: Magnolia x loebneri

'Blue Arrow' – a superior selection replacing the aptly named 'Skyrocket'.

Height and spread: 20 x 3m (70 x 10ft) at maturity; 'Blue Arrow' 6m x 50–60cm (20ft x 20–24in)

Hardiness: *C. sempervirens* hardy/Z 7–9; *J.* 'Blue Arrow' hardy/Z 3–7

Cultivation: Plant Italian cypress on free-draining ground. Water to establish, especially in poor dry soils, but avoid excess watering as this can cause the normally upright branches to splay out, spoiling the profile. Dislikes cold winds.

Fagus sylvatica
Beech

Along with hornbeam (*Carpinus*), beech can be clipped into large architectural elements within a formal courtyard, including boundary hedges, dividing walls and archways. Although deciduous, plants hang on to their dried coppery leaves through winter, providing a colourful backdrop for glossy evergreens. A good hedge for colder, more exposed gardens and cottage-style plantings. The copper beech, *F. s. f. purpurea*, has deep purple leaves.

Height and spread: As a hedge, beech is most often clipped to 1.2–3m (4–10ft) in height and up to 1m (3ft) wide

Hardiness: Hardy/Z 4–7

Cultivation: Any well-drained soil tolerating lime, in sun or light shade.

Magnolia x loebneri 'Leonard Messel'
Magnolia

A beautiful rounded tree, this variety produces pale lilac-pink blooms with relatively narrow petals in mid-spring. The contrasting effect of the pale flowers against the darker buds and bare branches is enchanting. The more upright 'Merrill' has white flowers.

Height and spread: 5–6 x 5–6m (16–20 x 16–20ft)

Hardiness: Hardy/Z 5–7

Cultivation: Grow on well-drained but humus-rich soil, ideally neutral to acid though some lime is tolerated. Sun or light shade.

Malus 'Evereste'
Crab apple

Though there are many varieties to choose from with late spring blossom, colourful autumn (fall) fruits and good autumn colour, 'Evereste' stands out as a fine example. This conical tree has fragrant white blossoms, which contrast with the red buds in late spring and an autumn crop of orange-yellow crab apples that develop red where they catch the sun. 'Red Sentinel' is similar to 'Evereste' but with dark red fruits.

Height and spread: 7 x 6m (23 x 20ft)

Hardiness: Hardy/Z 4–9

Cultivation: Grow on any well-drained but not dry soil in sun or light shade.

Above: Malus *'Evereste'*

Olea europaea
Olive

The European olive is gaining in popularity as a garden plant, though it is unlikely to fruit in cold climates. It naturally assumes a pleasing shape – usually dome-headed – and the narrow grey-green leaves are attractive. An olive is ideal for a container and makes a fine feature in a Mediterranean planting scheme. In frost-prone areas, some winter protection is necessary.

Height and spread: To 10 x 10m (33 x 33ft), but usually much less in cultivation

Hardiness: Borderline hardy/Z 8

Cultivation: Grow in fertile, well-drained soil in full sun.

Prunus
Ornamental cherry

This huge genus includes some of the best-loved spring-flowering trees. 'Snow Goose' has white flowers and 'Okame' shocking pink. *P. mume* 'Beni-shidori' (Japanese apricot) with deep pink flowers is ideal for wall training. A form of Yoshino cherry, *P. x yedoensis* 'Ivensii' has horizontal branches, white flowers and pink buds. *P.* 'Amanogawa' makes a pillar clothed in semi-double, shell pink flowers in late spring. *P.* 'Spire' is similar with good autumn (fall) colour. *Prunus subhirtella* 'Autumnalis Rosea' produces a light tracery of branches clothed from autumn until spring with sprigs of pale pink blossom.

Height and spread:
P. 'Amanogawa' around 8 x 4m (25 x 13ft); *P.* 'Spire' around 8 x 7m (25 x 23ft)

Hardiness: Hardy/Z 6–9

Cultivation: Grow in any moderately fertile soil in full sun; a little lime seems to suit the trees.

CLIMBERS AND WALL SHRUBS

This plant group is essential in a courtyard, where the boundaries and dividing screens play such a significant role in defining the space. With an appropriate balance of evergreens, flowering shrubs and ornamental vines, it is possible to swathe the walls and overhead structures of the courtyard with colour and texture that will last throughout the year.

Above: Abutilon megapotamicum *flowers look like Chinese paper lanterns.*

Abutilon
Flowering maple
These evergreen to deciduous flowering shrubs prefer the shelter of a warm wall unless grown in frost-free conditions. The wiry, lax stems of *A. megapotamicum*, with scarlet red and yellow bicoloured pendant blooms, or the cultivar 'Kentish Belle', which has apricot flowers, are best tied into horizontal wire supports. They flower through summer into autumn (fall). More tree-like are the earlier flowering cultivars of the hybrid *A. x suntense*, which have larger, dish-shaped blooms in shades of purple or white, together with *A. vitifolium*, the white form *A. v.* var. *album* and mauve 'Veronica Tennant'.
Height and spread: *A. megapotamicum* and *A.* 'Kentish Belle' 2–2.5 x 2–2.5m (6–8 x 6–8ft); *A. x suntense* 4 x 2.5m (13 x 8ft)
Hardiness: Frost hardy/Z 8–9
Cultivation: Grow in full sun, shelter and well-drained soil. Protect from frost with fleece.

Campsis radicans
Trumpet vine or creeper
Seldom seen in northern gardens, the orange-red, trumpet-like flowers of this vigorous, deciduous climber make an impressive show from late summer to autumn (fall) amid the profusion of pinnate leaves. The hybrid *C. x tagliabuana* 'Madame Galen' has larger blooms.
Height and spread: To 10 x 10m (33 x 33ft)
Hardiness: Borderline hardy/ Z 5–9
Cultivation: Grow in any fertile, well-drained soil in full sun. Provide initial support with wires on walls.

Ceanothus
California lilac
Few wall shrubs match the impact of these fast-growing shrubs when they are smothered with their small but densely clustered distinctive fluffy blue flowers. Colours range from pale powder blue to glowing indigo. There are both deciduous and evergreen forms, the evergreens being slightly less hardy and thus a riskier choice in a cold district, though neither form is long-lived. They flower either in late spring to early summer or in late summer. Spring-flowering evergreens include 'Delight', 'Italian Skies' and 'Puget Blue', all with rich blue flowers.
Height and spread: To 2 x 2m (6 x 6ft), or sometimes more
Hardiness: Borderline hardy/ Z 7–9
Cultivation: Grow in any fertile, well-drained soil in full sun. Prune after flowering, if necessary, but avoid hard pruning.

Chaenomeles
Ornamental quince, japonica
It is possible to train these somewhat intractable, thorny plants tight against a wall, but it is easier to tie them loosely to it and allow the stems to billow forward more informally. The cup-shaped flowers, which appear either before or at the same time as the leaves unfurl in spring, are charming. *C. speciosa* 'Geisha Girl' has apricot flowers and a neater habit than most. The hybrid group *C. x superba* includes a number of worthwhile selections

Above: Ceanothus

Above: Chaenomeles japonica

Above: Campsis radicans

Above: Clematis montana

Above: Clematis alpina

Above: Fremontodendron

in red, white and pink. Among the reds, 'Knap Hill Scarlet', with its large, bright red flowers, is perhaps one of the best. 'Crimson and Gold' has the added attraction of vivid yellow stamens, which contrast with the flowers. The small greenish yellow aromatic fruits, rich in pectin, may be used for jelly.
Height and spread: 1.5 x 1.5m (5 x 5ft)
Hardiness: Hardy/Z 5–9
Cultivation: Grow in fertile, well-drained soil in sun or light shade (north walls tolerated). Survives in most soils other than lime-rich or waterlogged ones.

Clematis
Clematis
It is possible to have a species or hybrid in flower during virtually every season of the year. Best known are the early and late summer-flowering hybrids. The showiest have large, flat blooms, plain or striped and often in strong, rich

colours, like the carmine 'Rouge Cardinal'. 'Marie Boisselot', is an excellent white. One of the best of the blues with a profusion of medium-sized blooms is 'Perle d'Azur', which flowers for weeks through summer into autumn (fall). For containers, try some of the new compact-growing large-flowered varieties like the double white 'Arctic Queen'. If you are nervous about pruning, forms of the later summer-flowering *C. viticella* group are easy and productive, and the bell-shaped blooms of *C. texensis* hybrids such as 'Gravetye Beauty' provide sumptuous displays.

The species have daintier flowers, though some are rampant growers. This makes them suitable for screening a large area (although only *C. armandii* is evergreen). The early spring-flowering *C. alpina* is elegant, with its nodding, bell-like flowers and ferny foliage. Selections are available

in blue, pink and white. *C. macropetala* is similar, with several pretty 'cottage garden' forms such as the double 'Markham's Pink'. The Mediterranean-looking evergreen, *C. armandii*, has long leathery leaves, and fragrant white flowers in spring. Also scented, especially 'Elizabeth', are selections of the rampant May-flowering *C. montana*, which will usefully adapt to a north wall or fence. Also shade tolerant but flowering later are the ferny leaved *C. tangutica* and *C.* 'Bill Mackenzie', with yellow, citrus peel, lantern-like flowers in late summer to autumn and silky whorled ornamental seed heads.
Height and spread: To 10 x 10m (33 x 33ft) (most species); to 3 x 3m (10 x 10ft) (hybrids and smaller species like *C. alpina*
Hardiness: Hardy/Z 4–9
Cultivation: Grow in most fertile, well-drained soils, preferably alkaline. Site in sun or (ideally) partial shade, making sure the roots are in shade. Pruning requirements vary with the different types, and you should refer to a specialist guide for details, but many late summer-flowering kinds (in pruning group 3), including *C. viticella* and *C.* 'Perle d'Azur', are easily dealt with: cut them to 30cm (12in) from ground level in late winter.

Eccremocarpus scaber
Chilean glory vine
This climber is often grown from seed as an annual, but can behave as a perennial, producing feathery foliage each year and bright orange tubular flowers until well into autumn (fall). Effective when allowed to scramble freely through an evergreen hedge or shrub.
Height and spread: 3 x 1m (10 x 3ft)
Hardiness: Borderline hardy/ Z 9–10
Cultivation: Grow in well-drained soil in sun, protecting the underground tubers in cold regions with a deep insulating mulch. Suitable for containers.

Fremontodendron 'California Glory'
Fremontia, flannelbush
The form 'California Glory' is a vigorous sub-tropical-looking wall shrub that can climb the façade of a house. It produces its large, saucer-shaped waxy yellow blooms from late spring to early autumn (fall). The dark green lobed leaves make a fine contrast but beware the rusty coloured bristle hairs, which can irritate skin.
Height and spread: 6 x 4m (20 x 13ft)
Hardiness: Frost hardy/Z 9–10
Cultivation: Any well-drained neutral to alkaline soil with sun and shelter. Cut off outward-facing shoots and tie onto wire supports.

Above: Humulus lupulus *'Aureus'*

Above: Hydrangea anomala

Above: P. quinquefolia

Hedera
Ivy
The ivies, all self-clinging, will bring green to even the most inhospitable parts of a terrace or courtyard, and there is more variety in leaf shape and colour than you might imagine. *H. canariensis* is a large-leaved species from the Canary Isles, usually grown in one of its variegated forms such as 'Gloire de Marengo', whose green leaves are irregularly margined with cream (deepening to yellow as they mature). It needs a fairly sheltered spot. For tougher locations, grow the similar looking *H. colchica* 'Dentata Variegata' or yellow-centred 'Sulphur Heart'. The smaller-leaved *H. helix* is tougher, in fact virtually indestructible: 'Glacier' has creamy edged grey-green leaves; 'Green Ripple' is vigorous, with distinctive, frilly-edged leaves and 'Buttercup' is slow growing and lime green.

Height and spread: *H. canariensis* 'Gloire de Marengo' to 4 x 4m (13 x 13ft); *H. helix* cultivars to 45cm–8m x 45cm–8m (18in–25ft x 18in–25ft)
Hardiness: *H. canariensis* 'Gloire de Marengo' borderline hardy/Z 8–9; *H. helix* cultivars hardy/Z 5
Cultivation: Grow in almost any soil. Variegated forms need some sun for the best leaf colour, while plain-leaved varieties do well even in deep shade.

Humulus lupulus 'Aureus'
Golden hop
This herbaceous twining climber is a prodigious grower. Once established, it will cover a wall or a pergola each year, making it useful for a seasonal curtain of foliage. Don't try to train it, apart from in its initial stages – just let the stems loosely support the yellow-green leaves. Clusters of hops form in later summer. The

bristly stems and leaves may irritate sensitive skin, so wear gloves when cutting back.
Height and spread: To 6 x 6m (20 x 20ft)
Hardiness: Hardy/Z 6–9
Cultivation: Grow in reasonably fertile, well-drained soil, in sun for the brightest leaf colour, though it also does well in shade. Avoid dry, windy conditions.

Hydrangea anomala subsp. *petiolaris*
Climbing hydrangea
The most commonly grown of the climbing hydrangeas is a useful plant for covering a north-facing or shady wall. These woodland plants cling to walls and fences via adventitious roots. The bright green heart-shaped leaves form a dense covering and foil for the creamy white frothy flower heads in autumn (fall). Butter yellow autumn foliage.
Height and spread: 15 x 15m (50 x 50ft)
Hardiness: Hardy/Z 5–8
Cultivation: Provide initial support for shoots of young plants to keep them in contact with the wall.

Parthenocissus spp.
Virginia creeper
These foliage plants are grown for their autumn (fall) colour and are ideal for covering large walls or for forming curtains over the sides of high retaining walls or pergolas. *P. henryana*

has dark green leaves veined and shaded with silver, turning red in autumn and is especially useful for north-facing aspects. Its spread is easily controlled by cutting back. *P. tricuspidata* is the well-known Boston ivy, and *P. quinquefolia* the Virginia creeper. Both are suitable only for larger gardens or for growing up into mature trees. *P. t.* 'Veitchii' has leaves that open purple in spring, mature to green, then turn red-purple in autumn given a sunny spot.
Height and spread: *P. henryana* 10 x 10m (33 x 33ft); *P. tricuspidata* 20m (65ft)
Hardiness: Hardy/Z 4–9; *P. henryana* borderline hardy/Z 7–9
Cultivation: Grow in fertile, well-drained soil in sun or partial shade.

Rosa
Rose
Few flowers can match the rose for pure, old-fashioned charm, and the modern repeat-flowering climbing forms are useful where space is limited. The following are all tried and tested. 'Madame Alfred Carrière', with an abundance of rather untidy but sweetly scented creamy white flowers in summer, is especially versatile, lighting up a wall, clambering through a mature tree or swathing a sturdy pergola or arch.

Above: Rosa *'Gloire de Dijon'*

'Félicité Perpétue' has dainty, crumpled flowers that open pink and fade to blush white. 'Gloire de Dijon' is early flowering and needs the shelter of a warm wall in frost-prone districts; it has large, bun-like, creamy apricot blooms. 'Constance Spry' has full, double, rich pink flowers. The repeat-flowering 'The New Dawn' tolerates shade and has blush pink perfectly formed blooms and healthy, glossy foliage. 'Compassion' is similarly long flowered with apricot-tinted blooms and a delicious scent.

Height and spread: Modern repeat-flowering climbers like 'Compassion' 3 x 2.5m (10 x 8ft). Others can be to 5 x 5m (16 x 16ft) or more, depending on the variety

Hardiness: Hardy/Z 4–9

Cultivation: Grow in very fertile, well-drained soil in sun or light shade.

Solanum
Potato vine

Preferring a sheltered spot, the semi-evergreen *Solanum jasminoides* 'Album' is a beauty with an airy habit and starry white flowers, each with a yellow 'beak'. The season extends over a long period through summer into autumn (fall). Similarly prolific but hardier is the Chilean potato tree *S. crispum* 'Glasnevin' with rich purple blooms. Tie the thin stems to their support.

Above: Rosa *'Constance Spry'*

Height and spread: 3 x 3m (10 x 10ft)

Hardiness: Half hardy to frost hardy/ Z 8–11

Cultivation: Grow in any well-drained soil in full sun. In cold areas, protect with a dry mulch over winter.

Thunbergia alata
Black-eyed Susan

This striking plant, which is usually grown as an annual in cold areas, is a climber that is also effectively grown in hanging baskets and allowed to trail down. The simple yellow or orange flowers have pronounced deep purple-brown throats – resulting in the highly descriptive common name, Black-eyed Susan.

Height and spread: 2m x 25cm (6ft x 10in); spreads more where it is grown as a perennial

Hardiness: Tender/Z 10

Cultivation: It will tolerate most soils in sun or light shade.

Wisteria
Wisteria

Mature specimens of wisteria are a sight to behold in late spring, when the fragrant, pendulous flowers first emerge. Wisterias usually flower best in full sun, at least in cold climates. The plant is hardy, but the wood needs a good roasting from the sunshine to ensure flower production, hence the value of pinning the main stems to a sunny wall. In late summer, cut back any wayward growth and trim again in late winter. Garden plants are usually selections of either *W. floribunda*, the Japanese wisteria (found in violet, white or purple forms) or its similar but more vigorous cousin, *W. sinensis*, the Chinese wisteria.

Height and spread: To 9 x 9m (29 x 29ft)

Hardiness: Hardy/Z 4–10

Cultivation: Grow in any well-drained but moisture-retentive soil, preferably not too rich, in sun or light dappled shade.

Above: Wisteria

Above: Thunbergia alata

BAMBOOS, GRASSES AND GRASS-LIKE PLANTS

Grasses and their look-alikes are very much plants of the moment. Their overall form ranges from low tussocks to tall, upright columns and the linear leaves make a satisfying contrast with broad-bladed specimens. Evergreens provide forms and colours suitable for Mediterranean, oriental or contemporary courtyards.

Above: Carex morrowii *'Variegata'* works well in a Japanese or contemporary setting.

Anemanthele lessoniana
Pheasant's tail grass
Formerly listed as *Stipa arundinacea*, this colourful evergreen grass has ribbon-like arching leaves forming substantial tussocks. Orange-brown tints develop during summer, intensifying through autumn (fall). With the long-lasting drooping panicles of purple-green flower spikes, this is certainly a grass for all seasons.
Height and spread: 90 x 120cm (3 x 4ft)
Hardiness: Frost hardy/Z 7–10

Cultivation: Tidy up in early spring by removing dead material and old flower stems. Grows on well-drained to heavier clay soils in sun or light shade. Suitable for containers.

Arundo donax var. versicolor
Variegated Giant Reed
The species is a statuesque, bamboo-like grass often seen around coastal Mediterranean regions, thriving in damp conditions and spreading to form thickets. The white variegated *Arundo donax* var. *versicolor* is especially showy and makes an impressive pot specimen for the summer terrace.
Height and spread: 2m x 60cm (6 x 2ft)
Hardiness: Half hardy/Z 8–10
Cultivation: Grow in sun with a plentiful supply of moisture. Cut back stems to ground level in spring.

Calamagrostis x acutiflora
Feather reed grass
This upright grass with long-lasting flower stems works effectively in groups and also when interplanted with broad-leaved perennials. 'Karl Foerster' has pinky-brown summer flowers that fade as autumn (fall) approaches and remain through the winter. 'Overdam' has the added attraction of pale yellow leaf margins.
Height and spread: 'Overdam' 1.2m x 60cm (4 x 2ft); 'Karl Foerster' 1.8m x 60cm (6ft x 2ft)

Hardiness: Hardy/Z 4–9
Cultivation: Cut down papery winter stems to ground level just as growth resumes. Best on moisture-retentive soil, rich in organic matter, in sun or part shade.

Carex
Ornamental sedge
These mostly evergreen grass-like plants offer many ornamental species and varieties, including the bronze-tinted group from New Zealand and the variegated Japanese sedges. Bronze carex include the low, arching *C. comans* forms, more upright *C. flagellifera* and varieties and the olive-coloured *C. testacea*, which includes the orange- and amber-tinted 'Prairie Fire'. The strongly upright *C. buchananii*, or leatherleaf sedge, has red-brown wiry foliage forming an upright fountain and works well in sheltered gardens or as a pot specimen, being somewhat tender. 'Frosted Curls' is pale green. Variegated *carex*, ideal for

Above: Arundo donax *var.* versicolor

Above: Calamagrostis x acutiflora *'Overdam'*

Above: Anemanthele lessoniana

Above: Deschampsia cespitosa

Above: Festuca glauca

Above: Fargesia nitida
'Nymphenburg'

lightening shaded spots, are *C. hachijoensis* 'Evergold', with low, arching tussocks of narrow, yellow-striped leaves; *C. morrowii* 'Fisher's Form', with cream-striped leaves, the diminutive *C. conica* 'Snowline', with white-edged leaves and the broad leaved, deciduous, moisture-loving *C. siderosticha* 'Variegata'.
Height and spread: 30–60cm (12–24in) x 35–45cm (14–18in)
Hardiness: Mostly frost hardy to borderline hardy except 'Evergold', which is hardy/Z 6–9.
Cultivation: Grow the bronze- and silver-leaved sedges listed on any free-draining but not dry ground and the variegated sedges on moisture-retentive soil with the exception of the moisture-loving *C. siderosticha*. You can cut bronze carex to near ground level in spring to encourage more brightly coloured regrowth; alternatively, just remove the long flowering shoots. Tidy any winter-scorched foliage on variegated forms in spring.

Deschampsia cespitosa
Tufted hair grass
This versatile grass makes an evergreen tussock of narrow, deep green leaves. In summer these produce tall, airy, arching panicles that will catch even the lightest of breezes. The flowers of the different cultivars (among them 'Bronzeschleier', *D.* c. var. *vivipara* and 'Goldschleier') eventually fade to pale biscuit by autumn (fall), providing a gossamer foil for late-flowering perennials.
Height and spread: 1.2 x 1.2m (4 x 4ft)
Hardiness: Hardy/Z 3–7
Cultivation: Grow on any neutral to acid free-draining to damp soil, incorporating plenty of organic matter at planting time. Best in sun or light shade. Excellent container specimen. Tidy plants in spring before new shoots appear.

Fargesia
Two dainty-leaved columnar to arching bamboos suitable for container gardening or smaller courtyards include the umbrella bamboo, *Fargesia murieliae*, which is sun and wind tolerant, and its forms, together with the shade-loving *F. nitida*, whose dark purple canes do not produce leaf whorls until their second year. *F. murieliae* 'Simba' is compact growing and ideal for large pots on the terrace.
Height and spread: *F. murieliae* 'Simba' 1.8m x 60cm (6 x 2ft); *F. nitida* 5 x 1.5–1.8m (16 x 5–6ft). Growth is less in containers.
Hardiness: Hardy/Z 6–11
Cultivation: Grow in moisture-retentive ground in sun or light shade. *F. nitida* needs wind shelter and dappled shade. Control spread by pruning (see pages 242–3).

Festuca glauca
Blue fescue
These tufty grasses, steely blue in colour, have a variety of uses. Grow them as a low border edging, in groups or to fill a pot. Look for varieties such as 'Harz', 'Elijah Blue' or 'Blaufuchs', which have strongly coloured leaves. The summer flowers are an added bonus but can be removed when they turn to biscuit as this can mar the display.
Height and spread: 30 x 30cm (12 x 12in)
Hardiness: Hardy/Z 4–8
Cultivation: Grow in any well-drained soil, preferably in sun. Tidy plants in spring by combing through with fingers to remove dead material.

Hakonechloa macra 'Aureola'
Japanese hakone grass
This yellow-striped *Hakonechloa* is a hardy deciduous grass with soft tapering leaves that arch to form a mound. Excellent as a pot specimen, it works well blocked in informal groups and mixed with other plants such as blue hostas and ferns for an oriental touch. Late summer and autumn (fall) tints are reddish, and airy flowers remain until late in the season.
Height and spread: 25–35 x 40–90cm (10–14 x 16–36in)
Hardiness: Hardy/Z 5–9
Cultivation: Grow on moisture-retentive but free-draining, neutral to lime-free loam or loam-based compost (soil mix) for containers. Tidy plants in spring by removing the dead foliage. Light shade prevents scorching.

Above: Miscanthus sinensis *'Zebrinus'*

Imperata cylindrica 'Rubra' syn. 'Red Baron'

Japanese blood grass

The deep crimson red-shaded leaves of this slowly creeping perennial grass are the main attraction. Grow it where it won't be overshadowed by other plants in the border or give it pride of place in a container. Plants can take a while to get going in a cold spring, and cosseting young plants pays dividends.

Height and spread: 40 x 40cm (16 x 16in)

Hardiness: Frost hardy/Z 5–9

Cultivation: Provide an insulating mulch through winter to protect roots from frost. Grow in moisture-retentive, humus-rich soil in sun or light shade.

Libertia peregrinans

New Zealand iris

Though not really a grass, this evergreen perennial is a look-alike with tufts of stiff, narrow leaves. These are amber-tinted and especially attractive when the light shines through them. New on the scene, 'Taupo Sunset' and 'Taupo Blaze' are even more brightly coloured and the foliage makes a fine foil for the small white blooms that appear on upright stems in spring and summer, before becoming orange seed heads.

Height and spread:
L. peregrinans 38 x 70cm (15 x 28in); 'Taupo Sunset' 60 x 70cm (24 x 28in)

Hardiness: Frost hardy/Z 7–9

Cultivation: Grow *L. peregrinans* in a warm, sheltered spot in full sun or light shade. Drought tolerant. Mulch in cold regions to protect roots in winter. 'Taupo Sunset' prefers more moisture.

Miscanthus sinensis

Eulalia

These elegant grasses, which range from tall, back of the border specimens to compact 'dwarfs', make arching clumps or upright columns of leaves topped by plumes of silvery, pinkish or brownish flowers that give a fountain effect in the courtyard. The selection 'Gracillimus', sometimes referred to as maiden grass, is especially fine, with slender leaves marked with a white midrib that curl pleasingly at the tips. 'Morning Light' is similar but slightly taller with a narrow white margin. 'Silberfeder' is tall with especially striking flower heads, but for small spaces try 'Kleine Silberspinne'. Of different character altogether is 'Zebrinus', with ribbon-like leaves, banded horizontally with yellow.

Height and spread: 'Gracillimus' 1.3–1.5 x 1.2m (4½–5ft x 4ft); 'Silberfeder' 1.8 x 1.2m (6 x 4ft); 'Kleine Silbespinne' 1.2m (4ft)

Hardiness: Hardy/Z 5–10

Cultivation: Grow in sun or light shade in any soil that does not become waterlogged or very dry.

Ophiopogon planiscapus 'Nigrescens'

Black mondo grass

This diminutive plant is not actually a grass, though it looks very much like one with its firm, strap-like leaves. The colour is the main point of interest – the closest there is in the plant world to a true black. It looks good in a gravel garden or against white marble chippings, which provide a contrast, and is both drought and shade tolerant. It slowly produces a carpet of black tussocks. The plain green *O. planiscapus* is a similarly tolerant and versatile ground cover plant.

Height and spread: 20 x 20cm (8 x 8in)

Hardiness: Hardy/Z 6

Cultivation: Grow in fertile soil, preferably lime-free or slightly acid, in sun or light shade.

Panicum virgatum

Switch grass

This prairie native has glowing autumn (fall) colour and long-lasting, airy seed heads forming a cloud-like effect above the foliage. Cultivars have glaucous or red-tinged foliage, colours often being reflected in the names, such as 'Dallas Blues', 'Heavy Metal' and 'Rotstrahlbusch', and usually offer the bonus of rich plum or crimson autumn tints

Height and spread: 1–2.5 x 1m (3–8 x 3ft)

Hardiness: Hardy/Z 4–9

Cultivation: Grows in most reasonably fertile and drained soils in sun or light shade. Cut back hard in spring.

Pennisetum

Fountain grass

Though not the hardiest of ornamental grasses, these graceful tussocks, with their arching, soft, bottlebrush heads, are much sought after.

Above: O.p. 'Nigrescens'

Above: Panicum virgatum

P. alopecuroides and the compact, earlier-flowering 'Hameln' are good performers in a sheltered courtyard, cascading over paved areas or making a fountain effect in a tall container. Purple- and burgundy-shaded forms of *P. setaceum*, such as 'Burgundy Giant', are eye-catching but harder to overwinter in cool climates.

Height and spread: 60cm–1.5m x 60cm–1.2m (2–5 x 2–4ft)

Hardiness: Frost hardy/Z 5–9; *P. setaceum* 'Burgundy Giant' Z 7–9

Cultivation: Grow in fertile, well-drained soil in full sun and use a dry mulch to insulate the roots in winter. Cut back top growth in early spring.

Phyllostachys
Bamboo

These elegant bamboos can serve as border or container specimens, as backdrops for smaller plants or as screening. Some are invasive, but their spread can be restricted by planting them in large containers sunk in the ground or by inserting deep barriers around their roots. New bamboo shoots can be cut off as they emerge. Handsome and generally well-behaved forms include *P. flexuosa*, the aptly named zigzag bamboo, *P. aurea* (fishpole or golden bamboo) and *P. aureosulcata f. auriocaulis*, both of which have golden yellow canes at maturity. The black bamboo, *P. nigra*, has greenish brown canes that turn an impressive lacquer-black with age – a truly dramatic plant.

Height and spread: 2–6m (6–20ft) x indefinite; less when grown in containers

Hardiness: Hardy/Z 6–10

Cultivation: Grow in fertile, well-drained but moisture-retentive soil in sun or light shade.

Pleioblastus
Bamboo

These slow-creeping bamboos make fine container plants where space is restricted. The white-striped low-growing *P. variegatus* looks well at the front of a border in an oriental setting and the taller, yellow-banded *P. auricomus* syn. *P. viridistriata* adds sparkle to dark and richly coloured perennials such as *Geranium psilostemon*. Both blend well with ferns and broad-leaved architectural plants in a cool leafy border.

Height and spread: *P. variegatus* 75cm x 1.2m (40in x 4ft); *P. auricomus* 90cm–1.5m x 1.2–1.5m (3–5 x 4–5ft)

Hardiness: Hardy/*P. auricomus* Z 8–10; *P. variegatus* Z 7–11

Cultivation: Grow in fertile, moisture-retentive soil, including clay, in sun or light shade. Cut back last year's stems in early spring to ground level to promote colourful new foliage. Curb unwanted spread by cutting through roots with a spade and discarding the unwanted material.

Stipa spp.

The stipas range in character from stand-alone specimens such as *S. gigantea*, otherwise known as golden oats, to the diaphanous *S. tenuissima*, whose tussocks of light green fading to biscuit, hair-like foliage are a perfect foil for so many flowering and foliage perennials. Its common names include Mexican feather grass and the descriptive 'pony tails'. *S. gigantea* adds height to a flat area of paving or gravel but has the advantage over shrubs and conifers of being see-through. Dot randomly through an area of low-growing plants, or use singly as a striking accent in a courtyard. The blue-green leaves of *S. calamagrostis* are topped in summer by feathery, arching, silvery buff flower panicles.

Height and spread: *S. gigantea* 2.5 x 1.2m (8 x 4ft); *S. tenuissima* 60 x 30cm (2 x 1ft); *S. calamagrostis* 1 x 1.2m (3 x 4ft)

Hardiness: Hardy/Z 7–10

Cultivation: Needs well-drained soil and a sunny spot. Cut back *S. tenuissima* and *S. calamagrostis* in early spring and tidy the evergreen basal clumps of *S. gigantea* after removing spent flower stems. Remove unwanted seedlings of *S. tenuissima*.

Above: Stipa gigantea

Above: Pleioblastus auricomus

Above: Phyllostachys nigra

Above: Stipa tenuissima

EVERGREENS

Evergreen shrubs, ground cover plants and foliage perennials are invaluable for the smaller garden where every part is on show year round. They help to create a feeling of restfulness and permanence, adding to the structure of the space, especially in the form of clipped hedges and topiary. Plain-leaved subjects act as a foil for brighter, more flamboyant seasonal plants.

Above: Choisya ternata *'Sundance'*
creates a bright splash in a dull corner.

Abelia
Glossy abelia

With its small, slightly glossy, dark green foliage, *Abelia* x *grandiflora* makes a handsome rounded shrub. It enjoys the shelter of a courtyard and rewards care with an abundance of dainty, tubular, fragrant, pink-tinged-white flowers between midsummer and autumn (fall). The somewhat less vigorous, semi-evergreen, arching form, 'Francis Mason', has attractive gold leaves streaked green.

Height and spread: 2.5 x 3m (8 x 10ft)
Hardiness: Borderline hardy/ Z 6–9
Cultivation: Fertile, well-drained soil in sun and shelter.

Bergenia
Elephant's ears

This plant tolerates less than ideal conditions from shade and heavy clay to heat and drought but generously rewards any extra care. The large, rounded and glossy evergreen leaves carpet the ground and contrast well with grassy leaves. In spring, stout flower heads packed with waxy tubular blooms in shades of white ('Bressingham White', 'Silberlicht'), through pink ('Wintermärchen') to deep magenta red ('Morgenröte', 'Abendglut') appear. Many develop striking red or deep mahogany leaf tints in winter.

Height and spread: 30–45 x 45–60cm (12–18 x 18–24in)
Hardiness: Hardy/Z 3–8
Cultivation: Tolerates a wide range of conditions but prefers fertile, moisture-retentive, humus-rich soil and sun. Remove dead leaves before flowering. Mulch with well-rotted manure or garden compost (soil mix) and periodically divide in early spring.

Buxus sempervirens
Common box, boxwood

Along with yew, this is one of the classic topiary plants, widely used for balls, domes, cones and spirals as well as for formal hedging. The dwarf form *Buxus sempervirens* 'Suffruticosa' makes intricate knots and parterres. Box works well in containers sited in shady, sheltered courtyards. Some cultivars of *Buxus microphylla*, e.g. 'Green Pillow', develop softly rounded forms without clipping. *Buxus sempervirens* 'Elegantissima' has creamy-white variegated leaves.

Height and spread: Dependent on shaping
Hardiness: Hardy/Z 6–8 (*B. microphylla* 7–9)
Cultivation: Clip in late spring/early summer. Remove all dead foliage and clippings to lessen risk of box blight. Grow in humus-rich, preferably slightly alkaline soil in light shade. Water containers well in summer. Feed with half strength liquid fertilizer to avoid scorching, or mulch with garden compost (soil mix).

Choisya ternata 'Sundance'
Mexican orange blossom

A buttery yellow leaved version of the Mexican orange blossom, 'Sundance' is not so floriferous. Flowers are open, white and fragrant. This shows its colour best in light shade, such as against a north-facing wall. Bright sunshine and frost can bleach or scorch the younger leaves, so shelter plants from cold snaps and intense midday heat.

Height and spread: 2 x 2m (6 x 6ft)
Hardiness: Hardy/Z 8–10
Cultivation: Shelter and light shade preferred. Improve dry soils prior to planting.

Above: Abelia *x* grandiflora

Above: Bergenia *cultivar*

Above: B. sempervirens *'Suffruticosa'*

Above: Euonymus fortunei

Above: Heuchera *cultivar*

Above: Laurus nobilis

Above: Photinia x fraseri

Escallonia laevis 'Gold Brian'
Hopley's gold

'Gold Brian' and its variegated counterpart 'Gold Ellen' are gems for the year-round garden. Both form compact domes of neat, golden yellow to lime green leaves, and in mid-summer have plentiful clusters of small, rich pink flowers.
Height and spread: 1.5 x 1.5m (5 x 5ft)
Hardiness: Borderline hardy/Z 7
Cultivation: Best in light shade, though the sun brings out golden tones. Any reasonably fertile soil. Prefers shelter.

Euonymus fortunei
Wintercreeper

Invaluable as 'fillers', for containers or as ground cover, variegated forms of *E. fortunei* such as the green and white 'Emerald Gaiety' and gold-splashed 'Emerald 'n' Gold' light up the garden in winter. The plain, glossy-leaved *E. japonicus* is upright and less hardy but adds a Mediterranean touch. Its white or gold variegated forms include 'Ovatus Aureus'.
Height and spread: 60cm (2ft) x indefinite; *E.* 'Ovatus Aureus' 3 x 1.5m (10 x 5ft)
Hardiness: *E. fortunei* hardy/Z 5–9; *E. japonicus* half hardy/Z 7–9
Cultivation: Any reasonably fertile soil. 'Emerald Gaiety' keeps variegation well in shade.

Heuchera
Coral bells

Now available in a wide range of subtly different forms, heucheras offer attractively coloured ground cover. These evergreen perennials have maple leaf foliage sometimes with ruffled or frilled edges and airy blooms from late spring. Deep purple-reds include 'Plum Pudding' and 'Chocolate Ruffles'. 'Pewter Moon' is overlaid with silvery marbling. There are also lime green and amber-coloured forms.
Height and spread: 40 x 30cm (16 x 12in)
Hardiness: Hardy/Z 4–8
Cultivation: Grow on fertile, moisture-retentive soil in sun or light shade. Remove fading heads of flowering heucheras and cut back damaged foliage in spring. Susceptible to vine weevil larvae.

Ilex aquifolium
Holly

The hollies are tolerant evergreens, usually with spiny leaves. Though they can eventually grow into trees, they can be clipped for hedging or simple topiary figures such as cones, domes and standards. Many selections have brightly coloured variegation. Only female forms will berry, and most need to be in the vicinity of a male. *Ilex* 'J.C. van Tol' and a few others are self-fertile.

Height and spread: To 3 x 3m (10 x 10ft), but depends on the form and/or pruning
Hardiness: Hardy/Z 6–9
Cultivation: Sun or shade. Use loam-based potting compost (soil mix) and large, heavy containers.

Laurus nobilis
Sweet bay

The bay can be grown either as a tree or shrub, its stiff, matt green crinkle-edged leaves having a sweet aroma. Clip to form a ball, cone or standard.
Height and spread: 3 x 3m (10 x 10ft), or less, depending on pruning
Hardiness: Borderline hardy/Z 8–10
Cultivation: Use potting compost (loam-based soil mix) for containers and place in sun or light shade. Clip in early summer.

Ligustrum delavayanum
Delavayanum privet

Similar to clipped box, this small-leaved privet is used for figurative and geometric topiary forms. Turn potted topiary regularly to avoid it developing bald patches on the shaded side.
Height and spread: Depends on clipping
Hardiness: Borderline hardy/Z 8–9
Cultivation: Clip in summer. Needs good drainage and best sheltered from cold, drying winds.

Photinia x fraseri 'Red Robin'
Fraser's photinia

This vigorous shrub produces flushes of glossy red leaves in spring or after pruning. It can make a large background shrub when left to its own devices or can be shaped into an attractive multi-stemmed form with domed head or lollipop standards. *Photinia serratifolia* 'Curly Fantasy' has wavy-edged leaves.
Height and spread: 4 x 4m (13 x 13ft) if not pruned
Hardiness: Borderline hardy/Z 7–9
Cultivation: Grows on most soils provided drainage is good. Spring growth may be frosted. Cut back to living wood.

Taxus baccata
Yew

One of the traditional evergreens used for topiary and green architecture, e.g. castellated hedging, archways and turrets. The surface of well-clipped yew resembles dressed stone in all but colour. Perfect for the formal or traditional garden, and shade tolerant. The Irish yew, *T .b.* 'Fastigiata', has a columnar profile; the slow- growing 'Standishii' makes a narrow, gold-variegated column.
Height and spread: Dependent on size and shape of topiary
Hardiness: Hardy/Z 6–9
Cultivation: Grow on well-drained soil in sun or shade. Improve dry soils before planting.

SCENTED AND AROMATIC PLANTS

Scent introduces another dimension. Try planting herbs such as rosemary and lavender close to paths where their fragrance will be released as you pass by. Different scents create different moods: the scents of roses and honeysuckle suggest a morning in the country, while the heady perfumes of lilies and tobacco plants can transform a sunny courtyard into a sultry paradise.

Above: Brugmansia, *also known as Angel's trumpets, has a heady evening perfume.*

Brugmansia x candida
Angels' trumpets, datura
All parts of this exotic plant are poisonous. Huge, trumpet-like flowers hang down from summer to autumn (fall), at night giving off an intoxicating fragrance. Some forms have white, yellow or apricot flowers.
Height and spread: 1.5 x 1.5m (5 x 5ft) or more
Hardiness: Tender/Z 10
Cultivation: Grow in fertile, well-drained soil in full sun. Trim potted specimens and keep frost-free in winter.

Choisya ternata
Mexican orange blossom
This evergreen shrub has aromatic leaves and scented white flowers in late spring. It gives a topiary effect without pruning. 'Aztec Pearl' has elegant narrow leaflets.
Height and spread: 2 x 2m (6 x 6ft)
Hardiness: Hardy/Z 8–10
Cultivation: Grow in fertile, well-drained soil. Choisyas tolerate moderate shade, but flower best in full sun.

Jasminum
Jasmine
The jasmines have a sweet, heady scent that epitomizes summer. In cold areas grow J. officinale, trained against a warm wall or over a pergola if winter temperatures drop only a little below freezing. The tender, pink-budded J. polyanthum flowers spring to summer in frost-free courtyards.
Height and spread: To 3 x 3m (10 x 10ft)
Hardiness: J. officinale borderline hardy/Z 7–10; J. polyanthum tender/Z 9–10
Cultivation: Grow in well-drained, fertile soil in sun or part shade.

Lathyrus odoratus
Sweet pea
This climbing annual varies in strength of fragrance. The highly scented old-fashioned varieties have made a comeback recently, though their colour range is limited. Train on obelisks or garden cane (stake) wigwams to give height. Pick or deadhead the flowers regularly to encourage more blooms.

Height and spread: To 2 x 2m (6 x 6ft)
Hardiness: Hardy/Z 1–11
Cultivation: Grow in any fertile, moisture-retentive soil in full sun. Sow in late autumn (fall) for early blooms or spring.

Lavandula
Lavender
Lavender flowers are adored by bees. English lavender, L. angustifolia, a cottage garden favourite, includes forms such as 'Hidcote' (deep purple); 'Nana Alba' (a compact white) and L. x intermedia (robust, with broader leaves and lavender flowers). Slightly less hardy is French lavender, L. stoechas. L. pedunculata subsp. pedunculata (syn. L. s. 'Papillon') flowers for months on end.
Height and spread: 45 x 45cm (18 x 18in) or more

Hardiness: Hardy/Z 6–9; L. stoechas Z 7–9
Cultivation: Grow in very well-drained soil, especially lime-rich or poor gravelly ground, in full sun. Keep bushy by clipping off old flower stems in early spring or as flowers fade in summer.

Lilium
Lily
In pots, try the tall trumpet-flowered African Queen Group (soft apricot), Pink Perfection Group or L. regale, with richly scented, white, waxy blooms, flushed purple outside. The Madonna lily, L. candidum, has white, widely flared blooms. Two more whites of note are L. formosanum with strong purple flushes on the outside of the blooms and L. longiflorum, which scents the night air.
Height: To 60–120cm (2–4ft)

Above: Jasminum officinale

Above: Lathyrus odoratus

Above: Lonicera periclymenum

Above: Nicotiana *Domino Series*

Above: Pittosporum tobira

Above: Rosemarinus officinalis

Hardiness: Hardy/Z 4–9
Cultivation: Provide good drainage, a cool root run and sunshine. Plant *L. candidum* shallowly in alkaline soil; *L. formosanum* needs moist, acid soil; *L. regale* is tolerant. Plant bulbs deep, using loam-based compost (soil mix) for pots.

Lonicera periclymenum
Honeysuckle
Honeysuckles are renowned for their scent, but not all are fragrant. *L. periclymenum* is one of the best for fragrance from dusk, and has two main forms: 'Belgica', sometimes called Early Dutch honeysuckle, has pink and red flowers in early summer; 'Serotina' (Late Dutch) has purple and red flowers from midsummer to autumn (fall). Both bear glistening red berry clusters. Honeysuckles can cover a pergola, make a scented arbour, or grow through a tree.
Height and spread: To 4 x 4m (13 x 13ft)
Hardiness: Hardy/Z 5–9
Cultivation: Any soil that is not too dry, with roots in the shade.

Matthiola
Stock
Most stocks can be treated as annuals or biennials, depending on the time of sowing. The white, pink, lavender or crimson flowers are lovely in cottage garden schemes. Brompton stocks are biennials; selected

strains include double forms and dwarfs. The Ten Week Series flower ten weeks after sowing, so staggering can result in a long season. Scatter seed of the headily night-scented *M. longipetala* subsp. *bicornis* amongst other plants.
Height and spread: 30 x 20cm (12 x 8in)
Hardiness: Hardy/Z 6
Cultivation: Grow in any soil in full sun. Sow seed from summer onward for flowers the following year and from late winter for flowers the same year.

Nicotiana x sanderae
Tobacco plant
As day temperature drops, the flowers of the tobacco plant release an incense-like fragrance. Tall, old-fashioned seed mixtures produce pastel flowers with a heady scent. Modern single-colour selections and dwarfs are less fragrant.
Height and spread: 30–90 x 25cm (12–36 x 10in)
Hardiness: Half hardy/Z 7
Cultivation: Grow in any soil in sun or light shade. Sow in a propagator in early spring.

Pittosporum tobira
Japanese pittosporum
This species has handsome, glossy foliage and clusters of sweetly scented star-shaped white flowers in late spring to early summer, later turning yellow. It makes a hedge in a

frost-free garden; elsewhere try growing it in containers.
Height and spread: 2 x 1.5m (6 x 5ft)
Hardiness: Borderline hardy/ Z 8–10
Cultivation: Grow in good, loam-based compost (soil mix) in sun or light shade. Prune or shape in late spring.

Rosa
Rose
There is a wide variation in the scent of roses; some have none and others release a fresh, spicy or deep, musk-like perfume. The climber 'Louise Odier', flowering in midsummer has strongly scented, double, bright pink flowers. 'Zéphirine Drouhin', also climbing, with magenta flowers, has a warmer fragrance. The Bourbon shrub rose 'Alba Semiplena' has very fragrant, milky white flowers.
Height and spread: Climbers to 3 x 3m (10 x 10ft); bush types 1–2 x 1–2m (3–6 x 3–6ft)
Hardiness: Hardy/Z 4–9
Cultivation: Grow in fertile, well-drained soil, ideally in full sun. Prune in early spring, if necessary. Deadhead regularly.

Rosmarinus officinalis
Rosemary
The aroma of this Mediterranean sub-shrub and culinary herb is especially strong in hot, dry weather. The species and its forms, with grey-blue to gentian blue flowers, bloom from mid-spring into summer. They can become long and bare, but respond well to light pruning,
Height and spread: To 2 x 1m (6 x 3ft)
Hardiness: Hardy/Z 7–9
Cultivation: Grow in free-draining, light soil in full sun. Prune after flowering.

Trachelospermum jasminoides
Star jasmine
An evergreen climber with pinwheel-shaped, divinely scented, white flowers in summer. More or less hardy, some form of winter protection is advisable in cold areas.
Height and spread: To 9 x 9m (29 x 29ft)
Hardiness: Borderline hardy/ Z 8–10
Cultivation: In containers, grow in loam-based compost (soil mix) in sun or light shade with support.

TROPICAL PLANTS

If you want to add a touch of the exotic and conjure scenes of tropical holiday destinations, then add some of the sculptural and large-leaved plants that are described here. Many of them are surprisingly hardy grown within the sheltered confines of a courtyard. For others, you can often provide sufficient protection from cold by wrapping in situ or mulching.

Above: Agapanthus *'Loch Hope'* is one of the more hardy and compact cultivars.

Above: Astelia chathamica

Above: Cordyline australis

Above: Dicksonia antarctica

Above: Eucomis bicolor

Acacia dealbata
Silver wattle, mimosa
The acacias are pretty trees or large shrubs with ferny, grey-green leaves and masses of fluffy, duckling-yellow flowers in late winter. *A. dealbata* is a delightful choice for a sheltered courtyard. Acacias are fast growers, but take well to pruning and are good wall shrubs.
Height and spread: 6 x 4m (20 x 13ft); less in a container or if wall-trained
Hardiness: Half hardy/Z 8–10
Cultivation: Grow in lime-free soil in full sun.

Agapanthus
African lily
These beautiful plants produce lush clumps of large, strap-shaped leaves before the heads of trumpet-like flowers appear in late summer. Spectacular but tender, so requiring winter protection, is *A. africanus*, an evergreen with deep blue flowers on tall stems. The borderline hardy *A. campanulatus* and forms are

a safer bet, or go for the truly hardy hybrids such as the deep blue *A.* 'Loch Hope'.
Height and spread: 60–120 x 60cm (2–4 x 2ft)
Hardiness: Borderline hardy/Z 7–10
Cultivation: Grow in fertile, reliably moist (but not boggy) soil in full sun. Protect with a dry winter mulch in cold areas.

Astelia chathamica
Silver spear
This New Zealand native looks like a metallic version of phormium. Though plants do sometimes flower in cultivation, it is the upright to arching strap-shaped leaves of silvery sage green that are the main feature of this striking evergreen perennial. *A nervosa* also has small, star-shaped flowers.
Height and spread: 1.2 x 1m (4 x 3ft)
Hardiness: Frost hardy/Z 8
Cultivation: Best in containers for ease of moving to shelter in winter. Use a moisture-retentive, peaty soil mix. Water freely in

summer but keep the plants very much drier in winter. This increases their hardiness. Grow in sun or light shade.

Canna x generalis
Canna lily
These exotic-looking plants have large upright leaves, often overlaid with bronze. The sumptuous, orchid-like flowers come in a range of colours, including bright red, white, yellow, orange and salmon, and appear from late summer to autumn (fall). Like dahlias, they can be lifted and overwintered in cold areas.
Height and spread: 1m x 50cm (3ft x 20in)
Hardiness: Half hardy/Z 7–10
Cultivation: Grow in fertile soil in full sun.

Chamaerops humilis
Dwarf fan palm
For warm courtyards only, this Mediterranean palm suckers from the base, making a bushy plant, well clothed with exotic-looking leaves of glossy green. It tolerates shade, and makes a

good choice for a courtyard. Sometimes grown as a houseplant or conservatory (porch) plant in cold climates, it is an impressive specimen.
Height and spread: 3 x 2m (10 x 6ft)
Hardiness: Half hardy/Z 9–10
Cultivation: Grow in fertile, well-drained soil in sun or light shade.

Cordyline australis
Cabbage palm
Often seen as a street tree in warm areas, the cabbage palm has a straight trunk topped with a symmetrical head of blade-like leaves, the central ones stiffly erect, the outer ones splaying outward and downward. Selections with reddish purple or variegated leaves are much less hardy.
Height and spread: 3 x 1m (10 x 3ft), sometimes more in both directions
Hardiness: Half hardy to frost hardy/Z 9
Cultivation: Grow in fertile, well-drained soil in sun. Remove dying leaves at the base of the crown. Excellent pot plant.

Dicksonia antarctica
Tree fern
These are the plants of the moment: dramatic as single specimens and when grown in groups. Tree ferns will thrive in large pots in a sheltered, ideally lightly shaded spot. In cold areas, pack the dormant crowns with straw or some other dry material in winter.
Height and spread: 2 x 4m (6 x 13ft)
Hardiness: Half hardy/Z 10
Cultivation: Grow in fertile soil or soil mix, preferably enriched with leaf mould.

Eucomis bicolor
Pineapple plant
This plant has pineapple-like flowers, with a tuft of green leaves at the top. Thriving in pots, it does best in a sheltered spot. It produces pale green or white flower spikes from late summer to early autumn (fall).
Height and spread: 20–30 x 60–75cm (8–12 x 24–30in)
Hardiness: Borderline hardy/ Z 8–10
Cultivation: Grow in moderately fertile, well-drained soil in full sun. Protect in winter.

Melianthus major
Honey bush
One of the most handsome of all foliage plants, this has divided, soft, silvery-grey leaves. It is best grown against a wall in cold areas. Although shrubby, it

behaves more like a herbaceous perennial in cold districts, dying back to ground level. Ideal for giving height to plantings of cannas, dahlias and half hardy annuals.
Height and spread: 2.5 x 2m (8 x 6ft)
Hardiness: Half hardy/Z 9–10
Cultivation: Grow in any fertile, well-drained soil in sun. In cold regions apply a dry mulch such as straw or bracken to insulate the roots.

Musa basjoo
Japanese banana
Bananas are grown for their exotic-looking, paddle-shaped, fresh green leaves. Away from the tropics any fruit produced is unlikely to ripen. The arching leaves create a jungle atmosphere. Also consider *Ensete* cultivars (Abyssinian banana).
Height and spread: 1.5 x 1.5m (5 x 5ft), or more in favourable conditions
Hardiness: Borderline hardy/ Z 9–10
Cultivation: Grow in fertile soil in full sun. In cold areas pack trunk loosely with dry straw in autumn (fall) as frost protection.

Phormium
New Zealand flax
Phormiums are handsome perennials with blade-like leaves that arch elegantly over. They need winter protection in cold areas. One of the tougher

selections, *P. tenax* Purpureum Group has bronze-purple leaves. A wide array of creamy yellow- and coppery pink-leaved forms is available – these require warmth and shelter.
Height and spread: 2 x 2m (6 x 6ft) or more; dwarf forms generally within 1 x 1m (3 x 3ft)
Hardiness: Borderline hardy/ Z 8–10
Cultivation: Grow in drained but moisture-retentive soil. Use a loam-based compost (soil mix) for containers. Sun or light shade. Protect with a deep dry mulch in cold areas.

Trachycarpus fortunei
Chusan palm
The hardiest palm, this is useful for bringing the exotic to cool-region courtyards. Stiff, pleated leaves making impressive fans can be 75cm (30in) across.
Height and spread: To 3 x 1.5m (10 x 5ft)
Hardiness: Borderline hardy/ Z 8–10

Cultivation: Grow in loam-based compost (soil mix) and place in sun or light shade. Shelter plants from strong winds in winter.

Washingtonia filifera
Desert fan palm
This tender palm is similar in appearance to *Trachycarpus fortunei* but with a more open habit – leaf stalks can be 1.5m (5ft) long or even more on mature specimens – and a trunk swollen at the base. As the lower leaves die back, a 'thatch' develops on the trunk. This is a fire risk and so should be removed. Suited to planting in dry urban landscapes.
Height and spread: 3 x 1.5m (10 x 5ft), or more in either direction
Hardiness: Tender/Z 9–10
Cultivation: Use loam-based compost (soil mix) with added leaf mould and sharp sand, and place plants in full sun.

Above: Phormium tenax *cultivar*

Above: Melianthus major

Above: Trachycarpus fortunei

HEAT-LOVING PLANTS

In areas that have hot dry summers or corners of the courtyard that are sizzling sun traps, you must have a set of plants that will thrive as the temperature climbs and will not create unreasonable demands for watering. The following selection includes brightly coloured sun-worshippers, intricately shaped and textured succulents and striking architectural plants.

Above: *The blue heads of* Cynara cardunculus *can be cut for drying.*

Above: Bougainvillea glabra

Agave americana
Century plant

These eventually huge succulents, with rosettes of leathery, waxy-coated, toothed-edged leaves, also have spectacular flower spikes. Flowering results in the death of the central rosette, but fresh plants develop around the base. Remove and grow on until they too reach flowering size. *A. a.* 'Marginata' has leaves edged with creamy yellow – a variegation reversed on 'Mediopicta'.

Height and spread: 2 x 2m (6 x 6ft)
Hardiness: Tender/Z 9–10
Cultivation: Use standard cactus potting compost (soil mix) and site in full sun. Provide winter protection in cold areas.

Bougainvillea
Paper flowers

These are rampant, thorny-stemmed climbers for warm climates only. The 'flowers' – actually coloured bracts – are long-lasting. *B.* x *buttiana* is a large group of hybrids with flowers in shades of white, yellow, purple or red. The species *B. glabra* has white or magenta flowers, which often have wavy edges.

Height and spread: 10 x 10m (33 x 33ft)
Hardiness: Half hardy/Z 9–10
Cultivation: Grow in fertile, well-drained soil in full sun or light shade. Train over pergolas or against walls. Can be planted in large pots to grow up posts where there is no soil border.

Cistus
Rock rose

These Mediterranean shrubs have sticky, aromatic shoots and a succession of crinkled, papery flowers in summer. *C.* x *aguilarii* 'Maculatus' has white flowers, blotched blackish maroon at the centre, and *C.* x *pulverulentus* has rich cerise flowers.

Height and spread: To 1.2 x 1.2m (4 x 4ft)
Hardiness: Borderline hardy/ Z 7–9
Cultivation: Grow in very well-drained soil, including poor gravelly areas in sun.

Convolvulus cneorum
Silverbush

This beautiful plant is related to bindweed. The silky silver leaves alone make it worth growing, so the clear white flowers are an added bonus in summer. It revels in hot, dry conditions and, like many silver-leaved plants, looks best in gravel.

Height and spread: 60 x 60cm (2 x 2ft)

Above: Ipomoea indica

Hardiness: Hardy/Z 8–10
Cultivation: Grow in very well-drained soil, preferably gritty, in full sun.

Cynara cardunculus
Cardoon

A dramatic perennial, for use either as a specimen or in imposing groups at the back of a large border, if you have enough space. It has huge, jagged-edged leaves of silvery grey and, in summer, large, thistle-like flowers at the tops of sturdy stems.

Height and spread: 2 x 1.2m (6 x 4ft)
Hardiness: Half hardy/Z 9–10
Cultivation: Grow in well-drained soil in full sun.

Euphorbia characias subsp. *wulfenii*
Spurge

This shrubby euphorbia is distinguished by its domed heads of lime green flowers that last for a long period over late spring and early summer. 'Lambrook Gold' has particularly vivid flowers but

Above: Pelargonium

Above: Passiflora *'Amethyst'*

Above: Plumbago auriculata

Above: Sempervivum *'Raspberry Ripple'*

those of 'John Tomlinson' are even more yellowish. Unnamed seedlings may not be so distinguished. Cut individual stems to the base after flowering, leaving new shoots to replace old. Handle with care as the sap is an irritant.
Height and spread: 1.5 x 1.5m (5 x 5ft)
Hardiness: Borderline hardy/ Z 7–10
Cultivation: Grow in well-drained soil, preferably in full sun, though this euphorbia tolerates light shade.

Ipomoea nil
Morning glory
Best known for its sky blue trumpet-like flowers, which last only a day, this annual climber also comes in purples, reds and white. *I. indica*, the Blue Dawn flower, has funnel-shaped, purple-blue flowers.
Height and spread: To 3–4 x 3–4m (10–13 x 10–13ft)
Hardiness: Tender/Z 10
Cultivation: Grow in moderately fertile, well-drained soil in sun.

Passiflora caerulea
Blue passion flower
Most passion flowers are hothouse plants, but the species described is reliably hardy in a sheltered spot in cold areas. The distinctive summer flowers, which are white with a central boss of violet filaments, are striking,

and are sometimes followed by fleshy egg-shaped yellow fruits. The selected form *P. c.* 'Constance Elliot' is a real stunner, with fragrant, creamy white flowers.
Height and spread: To 3 x 3m (10 x 10ft)
Hardiness: Borderline hardy/ Z 8–10
Cultivation: Grow in any fertile, well-drained soil in full sun. Protect in winter in cold areas. Provide support for tendrils.

Pelargonium
Pot geranium
These popular plants flower all summer long, in all shades of pink, salmon, purple, red and white. Use them in borders, in hanging baskets, window boxes and any kind of container. There are too many hybrids to mention individually, but pelargonium groups include ivy-leaved types with thick, shield-like leaves on trailing stems, ideal for troughs and baskets; zonal pelargoniums, for many people the typical pelargonium, have leaves banded or zoned a darker colour.
Height and spread: Usually to 45 x 45cm (18 x 18in)
Hardiness: Tender/Z 10
Cultivation: Grow in any well-drained soil in full sun. For pot plants, use any standard compost (soil mix) with added grit or perlite.

Plumbago auriculata syn. P. capensis
Cape leadwort
This South African gem is grown for its appealing sky blue flowers, produced over a long period in summer on a mound of lax stems. The plant does not climb unaided, but needs to be tied to a support. In cold areas, move containers into a conservatory (porch) over winter.
Height and spread: 1.5 x 1.5m (5 x 5ft), more in a favourable site
Hardiness: Tender/Z 9
Cultivation: Grow in well-drained soil in sun or light shade.

Sempervivum
House leek
Though not as showy as the maroon-black *Aeonium* 'Zwartkop' or blue-leaved *Echeveria*, these rosette-forming succulents have the advantage of being remarkably hardy and extremely drought tolerant. Coming in a very wide variety of purple-, red-, green- or grey-leaved species and cultivars, sometimes overlaid with a cobweb of pale hairs, each 'parent' becomes surrounded

by a colony of smaller individuals, which survive after the parent dies. These new offsets encrust the soil surface or spill out over the edges of pots.
Height and spread: 8–10 x 30cm (3–4 x 12in)
Hardiness: Hardy/Z 3–8
Cultivation: Grow in clay pots or alpine pans (wide, shallow terracotta pots) filled with a sharply draining, reasonably fertile compost (soil mix), and stand in full sun. Cut off old flower stems.

Yucca filamentosa
Adam's needle
This bold foliage plant, with its firm, blade-like leaves, has spikes of white flowers, usually in late summer to autumn (fall), but not necessarily every year. Yuccas create a symmetrical effect in a container. 'Bright Edge' is gold variegated.
Height and spread: 1 x 1m (3 x 3ft) (height doubled when in flower)
Hardiness: Hardy/Z 5–10
Cultivation: Use loam-based compost (soil mix), and place in full sun or very light shade.

SHADE-LOVING PLANTS

While it can seem that all the interesting plants need sun, many beautiful specimens will tolerate light or dappled shade. The ground beneath shrubs and climbers can be colonized with a handsome array of shade-loving foliage perennials such as hostas and ferns. And in heavily shaded courtyards, clusters of large planted containers make luxuriant displays.

Above: Leucothoe *'Scarletta' syn 'Zeblid'* *has rich red and mahogany foliage.*

Aucuba japonica
Spotted laurel

This shade-loving, pollution-tolerant shrub has several fine gold-splashed cultivars, and female forms such as 'Crotonifolia' also produce crops of large red berries. Few shrubs brighten up a gloomy corner in a city courtyard so well.

Height and spread: 2–2.5 x 2–2.5m (6–8 x 6–8ft)

Hardiness: Hardy/Z 7–10

Cultivation: Any reasonably fertile and moisture-retentive but drained soil. Cut off frost-damaged shoots mid-spring.

Begonia
Begonia

Shady containers and baskets rely on the floriferous but tender begonias for colour through summer into autumn (fall). Tuberous-rooted pendulous begonias come in shades of white, pink, red, orange and yellow. The orange *B. sutherlandii* is a dainty choice. New on the scene, 'Dragon Wing Red' has deep glossy green architectural leaves and copious scarlet blooms.

Height and spread: 60 x 30cm (2 x 1ft); *B. sutherlandii* 45 x 45cm (18 x 18in)

Hardiness: Frost tender to half hardy/Z 8–10

Cultivation: Grow in moisture-retentive compost (soil mix) sheltered from wind. Protect from vine weevil. Dead head regularly.

Cyrtomium
Holly fern

Less dainty than some other ferns, cyrtomiums are especially useful for providing a strong contrast to the more flamboyant plants in the courtyard border. *C. fortunei* has upright fronds, while *C. falcatum*, known as the Japanese holly fern, makes a good houseplant, although it can also be grown outdoors in sheltered areas.

Height and spread: 60 x 60cm (2 x 2ft)

Hardiness: *C. fortunei* hardy/Z 6–9; *C. falcatum* borderline hardy/Z 7–9

Cultivation: Grow in fertile, moist but well-drained soil in any degree of shade.

Dryopteris
Male or Buckler fern

The dryopteris are robust ferns, invaluable for providing clumps of trouble-free greenery among other plants. *D. filix-mas*, the male fern, is technically deciduous, but usually does not die back completely in autumn (fall). *D. erythrosora* is best in a moist, sheltered site. Its triangular fronds are glossy coppery pink when young. *D. affinis* 'Cristata', known as the king of ferns, has striking upright fronds.

Height and spread: 60 x 60cm (2 x 2ft)

Hardiness: *D. filix-mas* hardy/Z 4–8; *D. erythrosora* hardy/Z 5–9

Cultivation: Grow in fertile, humus-rich soil in shade.

Fatsia japonica
Japanese aralia, false castor oil plant

Fatsias are hardy enough for outdoor use in most areas. Their large, hand-like leaves give a tropical, jungle look. White pompon flowers in autumn (fall) are followed by black fruits.

Height and spread: 3 x 3m (10 x 10ft)

Hardiness: Borderline hardy/Z 8–10

Cultivation: Grow in any well-drained soil. Prune in spring to remove frost-damaged wood and pull off dead leaves.

Fuchsia
Fuchsia

A huge group of tender and reasonably hardy species and cultivars ranging in height and form from tall shrubs suitable for

Above: Begonia sutherlandii

Above: Fuchsia *'Tom Thumb'*

Above: Cyrtomium fortunei

hedging to small pendulous plants for baskets. Individual flowers can be breathtaking and vary from slender tubes and single blooms with elegantly protruding stamens to sumptuous two-tone confections with semi or fully double flowers. Among the smaller borderline hardy fuchsias are the arching 'Lena' with white and magenta double blooms, the bushy single red and purple flowered 'Tom Thumb' and taller, similarly coloured 'Mrs Popple'.

Height and spread: 'Tom Thumb' 30 x 30cm (12 x 12in); 'Lena' 30–60 x 75cm (12–24 x 30in); 'Mrs Popple' 1 x 1m (3 x 3ft)

Hardiness: Frost hardy to borderline hardy/Z 9–11; 'Mrs Popple' Z 8

Cultivation: Grow in moisture-retentive but drained soil or compost (soil mix) and keep pots well watered in summer. Deadhead and liquid feed with flowering formula fertilizer.

Hosta
Hosta, plantain lily

Gradually increasing in size each year, hostas make striking specimens. They are like caviar to slugs, but growing in pots stood on gravel provides some protection. Moderately slug-resistant large-leaved hostas include *H. sieboldiana* 'Frances Williams', an old variety, with puckered, thick, glaucous green leaves, margined with creamy

Above: H. sieboldiana elegans

beige, and *H. sieboldiana* var. *elegans* with thickly puckered, glaucous, bluish-green leaves and almost white flowers.

Height and spread: To 60 x 60cm (2 x 2ft) or more, depending on variety

Hardiness: Hardy/Z 4–9

Cultivation: Grow in fertile, humus-rich, reliably moist soil.

Impatiens hybrids
Busy Lizzies

Flowering profusely in shade, these will brighten dull corners. They are difficult to raise from seed, so buy them as bedding plants or as 'plugs' in early spring. Colours include white, pink, red, purple and orange.

Height and spread: To 30 x 30cm (12 x 12in)

Hardiness: Tender/Z 10

Cultivation: Grow in moisture-retentive but drained fertile soil. Avoid overhead watering.

Lamium
Deadnettle

A groundcover perennial with evergreen foliage, 'White Nancy' combines silvery white leaves with short spikes of hooded white flowers. Good container plant.

Height and spread: 15 x 15cm (6 x 6in); roots as it grows

Hardiness: Hardy/Z 3–8

Cultivation: Sun or shade. Improve thin, dry soils with copious organic matter. Cut back periodically to encourage fresh foliage and flowering.

Above: Pieris japonica

Above: Impatiens *hybrid*

Leucothoe
Fetter bush

These ericaceous shrubs include the cream and pink marbled *L. fontanesiana* 'Rainbow', with its arching branches clothed in elegant tapered leaves and sprays of white, lily-of-the-valley like blooms in late spring. Relatively new on the scene are compact shrubs with much smaller, mahogany red-tinted leaves such as *L.* 'Scarletta', 'Carinella' and the compact crinkled leaf form *L. axillaris* 'Curly Red'. All suit shady courtyard containers. Foliage colour intensifies through autumn (fall) and winter.

Height and spread: 1.5 x 1.5m (5 x 5ft)

Hardiness: Fully hardy/Z 5–8

Cultivation: Requires ericaceous compost (acid soil mix). Shade preferred, though sun tolerated.

Pieris
Lily-of-the-valley bush

Pieris are woodland shrubs and so do best in a lightly shaded position on the patio. Attractive as the bell-like spring flowers are, most are grown for their foliage, most striking as the new growth appears in spring.

P. japonica 'Flaming Silver' has bright red new growth, edged with a pink that rapidly fades to silvery white. 'Blush' has pink buds opening white but retaining a pinkish cast. 'Valley Valentine' has deep purple-red flowers opening from crimson buds.

Height and spread: 2 x 2m (6 x 6ft)

Hardiness: Borderline hardy/ Z 7–9

Cultivation: Use ericaceous compost (acid soil mix) for containers, ideally with added leaf mould.

Polystichum
Shield fern

These evergreen ferns make useful container specimens. *P. munitum* (sword fern) has shining green fronds. *P. aculeatum* (hard shield fern) looks elegant through winter and the highly divided fronds of *P. setiferum* Divisilobum Group (soft shield fern) are lacy in effect.

Height and spread: 1 x 1m (3 x 3ft)

Hardiness: Hardy/Z 4–9

Cultivation: Grow in humus-rich, preferably alkaline soil in shade.

EDIBLE PLANTS

It is remarkably easy to raise vegetables and herbs, even on the tiniest terrace. At the simplest level, fill some pots or hanging baskets with herbs, salad leaves or tomatoes. Blueberries and figs both grow well in containers, and many fruit trees, including apples and plums, come in dwarf forms. Try growing a potted grapevine over a pergola and squashes or runner beans up a trellis screen.

Above: *Cherry tomatoes in patio pots are too delicious not to sample!*

EASY VEGETABLES

Many vegetables are suitable for growing on patios and in courtyards, either in containers or raised beds, and some are extremely decorative. A number of reliable varieties that crop well and have good pest and disease resistance are listed here, but for a wider choice, consult seed catalogues regularly. New varieties, including increasing numbers designed for container growing, are introduced each year.

Allium cepa
Onions
These are usually grown from 'sets'. These are produced by sowing onion seeds very thickly, which then grow into small plants that produce small bulbs (the 'sets'). Plant in autumn (fall) and spring to ensure continuity of cropping. 'Giant Zittau' is a good variety for autumn planting and keeps very well. Reliable varieties include 'Red Baron' and 'White Prince'. Don't try to store onions with a thick neck as they will rot.

Beta vulgaris Cicla Group
Swiss chard
Sow this decorative vegetable in late spring for cropping from late summer. Swiss chard has large, glossy, crinkled leaves with white stalks. Those of ruby chard are brilliant red and the leaf beat mixture Bright Lights has red, yellow, orange and white stems. Pick young leaves to eat raw in salads and steam or stir-fry larger leaves picked from the outside of plants. Cover crowns with a dry mulch for winter protection.

Brassica oleracea
Cabbage, kale, borecole
'Marner Early Red', with its beetroot- (beet-) red leaves, eaten raw or cooked, is one of the first cabbages to crop. 'Vertus' and the purple-tinged 'January King' are frost tolerant Savoy cabbages. 'Castello' and the quick-maturing pointed cabbage 'Greyhound' are for summer cropping. Curly kale or borecole provides 'greens' from autumn (fall) through till spring. Sow spring for summer transplanting.

Capsicum annuum
Sweet or bell pepper; chilli pepper
These need a long growing season in a sheltered spot. 'Redskin' is compact and will grow in pots on the patio; 'Bendigo' grows in an unheated greenhouse and other excellent varieties include 'Hungarian Wax', with long, pointed, yellow fruits, and 'Cayenne', with very hot fruits that can be used fresh or dried. Also try 'Gold Spike' and 'Serrano Chilli' as well as the patio pot chillies, 'Apache' and 'Fatalii'.

Cucurbita pepo
Courgettes (zucchini)
Don't put plants outside until the last frosts have passed unless you can protect them with cloches. Courgettes are usually grown as bushes whilst the related squashes, such as acorn, are often grown over supports. Sow under glass from late spring to early summer, harvesting from midsummer onwards for courgettes, late summer and autumn (fall) for squashes. Varieties of courgette include 'Ambassador', 'Burpee Golden Zucchini', 'Early Gem' and 'Gold Rush'.

Daucus carota
Carrot
Can be sown in succession for cropping throughout the year. 'Flyaway' is an early maincrop variety that has been bred for resistance to carrot root fly. Try the short cylindrical and round varieties e.g. 'Amsterdam Forcing', 'Sytan' and 'Parmex' in pots.

Lycopersicon esculentum
Tomato
The ideal patio crop, tomatoes revel in warm sunshine and thrive in large containers or growing bags. For cherry tomatoes try 'Super Sweet 100', 'Gardener's Delight', the yellow 'Sungold' or (if using hanging baskets) 'Tumbler'.

Phaseolus coccineus
Runner (green) beans
Grown as annuals and tolerating some shade, runner beans need to be trained on a structure such as a twiggy tripod. They have attractive flowers. Good varieties include 'Sunset' and 'Czar'. French beans can outperform runner beans in difficult conditions.

Solanum tuberosum
Potatoes
These are divided into early and maincrop types. Tubers are traditionally sprouted or chitted in a light, cool, well-ventilated place prior to planting, but can be planted as sold with similar

Above: *Onions*

Above: *Chilli peppers*

Above: *Runner beans*

Above: *Pears*

Above: *Grapevine*

Above: *Chives*

results. Grow new potatoes (earlies) in large, deep tubs, gradually adding more soil as the shoots appear. Crop when the plants begin to flower. 'Charlotte' is nice in salads.

CONTAINER GROWN AND WALL-TRAINED FRUITS

A sunny wall is a gift to any fruit-lover. Espaliers, cordons or fans make the most economical use of space, and trees can be bought ready-trained. If a wall is shaded for much of the day, try the Morello cherry.

Ficus carica
Figs
Figs thrive in containers, making them ideal patio crops. In cold areas, only the fruits that emerge right at the start of the season will ripen. Remove any small figs that appear in mid-summer and towards the end of the growing season. Protect by bringing pots under cover in colder areas.

Malus domestica
Apples
These thrive well in cold areas as they need low temperatures in winter to ensure good flowering.

Prunus cultivars
Plums
Plums are hardy in a range of climates. Grow hardy varieties in an open site, less-hardy types against a warm, sunny wall to

protect the spring blossom from frost. Dessert plums include 'Victoria', 'Belle de Louvain', with large purple fruits, and sweetly flavoured 'Greengage'. Cooking plums include 'Laxton's Cropper' and 'Pershore Yellow'.

Prunus persica
Peaches
Peaches make excellent wall crops, but in cold districts the blossom needs shelter from early frosts. The related nectarines (*P. persica* var. *nectarina*) and apricots (*P. domestica*) have similar needs. In frost-prone areas, a plum can be a safer bet. Peaches and nectarines fan-trained against a wall provide a decorative feature but both need a warm, sunny protected site to thrive.

Pyrus communis
Pears
Like apples, pears are good in cold areas, since they also thrive on low winter temperatures. Pears need a reliably warm summer and autumn (fall) for the fruit to ripen fully. Look for varieties grafted on to dwarfing rootstocks if space in the courtyard is at a premium.

Vaccinium corymbosum
Blueberry
Best cropped in its second year – take off the flowers in the first year of pot growing to allow plants to strengthen. Grow in

ericaceous compost (acid soil mix) and water well throughout summer as the crop develops. A range of varieties will ensure heavier yields and longer cropping times. Net against birds.

Vitis vinifera
Grapevine
These make handsome plants, whether trained against a wall or over a pergola, and can be grown solely for ornament. For edible crops, thin fruit trusses as well as the grapes within each truss to produce larger fruits.

HERBS AND SALAD LEAVES

Most herbs and salads can be grown in containers, making them ideal patio crops. Make sure some are within arm's reach of the kitchen door: it's so rewarding to pick a selection of fresh herbs from outside to use in cooking.

Herbs don't usually have high nutrient requirements so are undemanding and can be fed and watered sparingly. Sage, rosemary, thyme, marjoram and French tarragon are especially drought tolerant. Chives (*Allium*

schoenoprasum) are also suitable for growing in a container, and the small pink flowers are a bonus. Mint is invasive, so is best kept to its own container, rather than mixing. Ensure you have plenty of potted parsley, coriander (cilantro) and basil waiting in the wings as these annual herbs tend to get used up quickly. The tall, architectural and feathery-leaved fennel and its annual relative dill are best grown in the ground.

Leafy vegetables suitable for growing on the patio include all varieties of lettuce, particularly the continental or cut-and-come-again types, which regrow after cutting, such as 'Bionda Foglia'. 'Little Gem' is a quick-growing dwarf that soon produces hearts. Mixtures of lettuce, endive, beetroot (beet), baby spinach, chicory and parsley will provide a delicious mixed salad. Coriander and rocket (arugula) add zest and the latter is best sown in succession from spring to late summer, keeping the ground well watered in hot weather to prevent plants running to seed.

SPRING PLANTS

Don't ignore the potential of deciduous shrubs and perennials in favour of an evergreen-based design. Such optimism is felt as early bulbs break the dark days of winter and presage the arrival of spring. Choose early flowers such as *Crocus chrysanthus*, *cyclamineus* daffodils and 'Tête à Tête', and follow with hardy dwarf tulip cultivars and *Muscari*. Elegant and flamboyant late tulips herald summer.

Above: *The vigorous Dutch crocus looks good planted in naturalistic drifts.*

Anemone
Windflower

The showy flowers of *A. coronaria* appear from late spring to early summer, depending on when they are started off. Plant a few pots together for a spectacular display. The two main hybrid groups are the double-flowered St Bridgid and single-flowered De Caen Group in red, pink, violet-blue or white. The dainty daisy-flowered *A. blanda* bloom from early to mid-spring, and though tubers are often sold as mixtures, planting single colours like 'White Splendour' creates more impact.
Height and spread: 30–40 x 15cm (12–15 x 6in)
Hardiness: Hardy/*A. coronaria* Z 8–10; *A. blanda* Z 6–9
Cultivation: Use loam-based potting compost (soil mix) and keep in a sunny spot.

Camellia
Camellia

Spring-flowering camellias are generally forms of *C. japonica* or the hybrid group *C.* x *williamsii*.

Above: Anemone coronaria

These shade-loving woodlanders produce showy blooms in white, pink and red, with a huge variety of flower forms, including single, double, peony and anemone forms.
Height and spread: To 3 x 3m (10 x 10ft), depending on the variety
Hardiness: Hardy/Z 7–9
Cultivation: Grow in lime-free, moisture-retentive but drained soil rich in organic matter. Tolerates sun, with some shelter from midday heat. Avoid a site receiving morning sun. Shelter from wind.

Crocus
Crocus

With their goblet-like flowers, crocuses are reliable spring heralds. Most sturdy garden varieties are grouped under the late winter-flowering *C. chrysanthus*, which includes 'Cream Beauty', 'Snow Bunting', the striped 'Ladykiller' and 'Advance' with yellow and violet blooms, or *C. vernus* with 'Jeanne d'Arc', a pure white, and the stripy purple 'Pickwick'

Above: Muscari armeniacum

Above: Leucojum vernum

being popular choices. Plant in drifts or in shallow bowls and troughs.
Height and spread: 8 x 5cm (3 x 2in)
Hardiness: Hardy/Z 3–8
Cultivation: Grow in any but waterlogged soil in sun.

Leucojum vernum
Snowflake

Looking like Tiffany lamps, the snowflakes are among the most elegant of the spring bulbs, with nodding, bell-like flowers on tall, narrow stems. Each petal is delicately marked with green or yellow. They are especially effective when planted overhanging water.
Height and spread: 35 x 15cm (14 x 6in)
Hardiness: Hardy/Z 4–8
Cultivation: Snowflakes like reliably moist soil in sun or light shade.

Magnolia stellata
Star magnolia

The shrubbiest of the magnolias, its slow rate of growth makes it ideal for even the smallest courtyard. The spidery white flowers open well before the leaves in early to mid-spring, but the shrub, with its airy habit, fades into the background when not in bloom.
Height and spread: 1.2 x 1.5m (4 x 5ft)
Hardiness: Hardy/Z 5–9
Cultivation: Grow in fertile, well-drained soil in sun; in frost-prone areas, some shelter from strong early morning sun at flowering time is desirable.

Muscari
Grape hyacinth

These charming bulbs are easy to grow and some spread like wildfire. *M. armeniacum* is the

Above: *Dwarf* Narcissus cyclamineus

Above: Rhododendron yakushimanum

Above: Tulipa *'Queen of Night'*

most commonly grown species, with dense clusters of deep purple-blue flowers. The less vigorous *M. botryoides* 'Album' has slender spikes of scented white blooms.

Height and spread: To 20cm (8in) x indefinite

Hardiness: Hardy/Z 2–9

Cultivation: Grow in any well-drained soil in sun or light shade.

Narcissus
Daffodil

The huge range of hybrid forms are divided into groups according to their flower shape. The double-headed, white 'Thalia', lovely with fritillaries, and 'Tête-à-Tête', a reliable dwarf with very early, bright yellow, multi-headed blooms, are two of the best. The fragrant 'Actea' has white petals and short orange-rimmed cups. For fragrance also try the double cream 'Sir Winston Churchill'. The early, low-growing *cyclamineus* daffodils have swept back petals and a long narrow cup and include the weatherproof hybrids 'February Gold', 'Peeping Tom' and 'Jetfire'.

Height: *N. cyclamineus* 20cm (8in); *N.* 'Thalia' 30cm (12in); *N.* 'Tête-à-Tête' 15cm (6in); *N.* 'Actaea' 45cm (18in)

Hardiness: Hardy/Z 3–9

Cultivation: Grow in any well-drained soil, preferably in full sun.

Pulmonaria
Lungwort

Stems bearing clusters of gentian blue, pink, mauve or white bell-shaped blooms appear before the ground-covering leaves of this woodlander open fully. Some, like *P. saccharata* 'Mrs Moon', have a two-tone effect with pink buds opening to purple petals. The similarly coloured Argentea Group develop leaves that are almost completely silver. For white flowers and silver-spotted leaves try *P. officinalis* 'Sissinghurst'.

Height and spread: 30 x 60cm (12 x 24in)

Hardiness: Hardy/Z 4–8

Cultivation: Grow on moisture-retentive soil rich in organic matter in shade. In midsummer, cut foliage to ground level, feed and water to encourage a fresh flush of leaves to last through untill autumn (fall).

Rhododendron
Rhododendron

Though many of the species and hybrids would overwhelm a courtyard garden, dwarf evergreen rhododendrons, including the Japanese azaleas, are ideal. Most form neat, shallow domes with small glossy leaves often taking on red and purple tones and studded with bright

blooms in mid- and late spring, e.g. *R.* 'Vuyk's Scarlet'. *Rhododendron yakushimanum* is a slow-growing, larger-leaved species, with a rounded habit, and the new growth is covered in an attractive cinnamon felting. The large blooms are white-tinged pink. Related are a series of compact and colourful hybrids known as Yaks.

Height and spread: *R.* 'Vuyk's Scarlet' 75cm x 1.2m (2½ x 4ft); *R. yakushimanum* 1.2–1.5 x 1.2–1.5m (4–5 x 4–5ft)

Hardiness: Hardy/Z 5–8

Cultivation: Grow in containers in ericaceous compost (acid soil mix) or in borders of humus-rich, lime-free soil in sun or light shade, avoiding hot, dry locations. Water pots well in summer, preferably using rainwater.

Tulipa
Tulip

Available in a vast array of sumptuous colours and forms, tulips are ideal for containers. 'Spring Green' is creamy white, broadly striped with green – a marked contrast to the almost black 'Queen of Night'. The dwarf *greigii* tulips are all easy to grow and include 'Red Riding Hood', with early scarlet blooms over maroon-striped leaves. Try with primroses, dwarf daffodils and blue violas. Particularly elegant are the later-flowering tall, lily-flowered tulips, including the golden yellow 'West Point'.

Height: To 60cm (2ft)

Hardiness: Hardy/Z 3–8

Cultivation: Grow in any drained soil in full sun with shelter from strong winds. Best results are often achieved by planting new bulbs each autumn (fall).

SUMMER PLANTS

As we spend more time outside, the colours, varied flower forms and perfumes of summer blooms heighten the sensual experience. The exuberance of early summer 'cottage garden' plants and the arrival of bees and butterflies sweeps away memories of winter. From mid-summer, tender perennials or patio plants add flamboyant touches to pots and planters and many perform well into the autumn.

Above: Salvia verticillata, *particularly 'Purple Rain', flowers through the summer.*

Allium
Ornamental onion

These produce striking heads of blue or purple, white or yellow flowers, followed by decorative seed-heads. The early summer-flowering *A. christophii* has large, lilac-purple flowers in spherical heads that glint with a metallic sheen. *A. hollandicum* 'Purple Sensation' has smaller, deep purple drumsticks.

Height and spread:
A. christophii 60 x 18cm (2ft x 7in); *A. hollandicum* 'Purple Sensation' 1m x 10cm (3ft x 4in)
Hardiness: Hardy/Z 6; *A. christophii* borderline hardy/ Z 4–10
Cultivation: Grow in any well-drained soil in sun, though they will tolerate some shade.

Argyranthemum
Marguerite daisy

As well as the familiar marguerite daisy – a tender perennial with a profusion of single white daisy-like blooms and divided grey-green leaves – there are a host of others, some with double or anemone-centred blooms and coming in shades of yellow, pink and crimson. Compact plants are available for containers.
Height and spread: 30–100 x 30–100cm (1–3 x 1–3ft), depending on variety
Hardiness: Half hardy/Z 10–11
Cultivation: Grow in free-draining potting mix (soil mix) or fairly fertile border soil in full sun. Clip over to deadhead after each flush to maintain a bushy habit.

Brachyscome
Swan river daisy

The compact, mossy leaved *B. multifida* has powder-blue daisies and is a tender perennial, ideal for baskets. Recent breeding has created a range of pastel-coloured annual daisies with good drought resistance that work well in courtyard beds, e.g. the black-eyed Bravo Series (blue, purple and white blooms).
Height and spread: To 45 x 45cm (18 x 18in)
Hardiness: Half hardy/Z 8b–11
Cultivation: Grow in free-draining but moisture-retentive compost (soil mix) or drained, fertile soil in sun.

Cosmos atrosanguineus
Chocolate cosmos

Smelling of delicious melted chocolate, the single, blood-crimson flowers of velvety texture are produced over a long period from midsummer to autumn (fall). Site so that you can put your nose to the flowers!
Height and spread: 75 x 45cm (30 x 18in)
Hardiness: Borderline hardy/ Z 7–9
Cultivation: Grow in moderately fertile, well-drained soil in sun. Winter protection is advisable in cold districts. Excellent for pots.

Cosmos bipinnatus
Garden cosmos

With one of the longest flowering seasons of any annual, cosmos are of unquestioned value. Apart from the distinction of the glistening flowers and feathery foliage, they are excellent for cutting and make a fine show *en masse.*
Height and spread: To 1m x 45cm (3ft x 18in)
Hardiness: Half hardy/Z 9

Cultivation: Grow in any soil in sun. Seed can be sown *in situ* after frost has passed. Deadhead regularly to prolong the display.

Crocosmia 'Lucifer'
Montbretia

The king of crocosmias, this robust plant has stiff, pleated leaves with large heads of brilliant flame-red flowers from midsummer. The leaves are also effective in flower arrangements.
Height and spread: 1.2m x 8cm (4ft x 3in)
Hardiness: Borderline hardy/Z 5–9
Cultivation: Grow in any garden soils, in sun or light shade, but avoid sites that are too hot and dry or windy. Light staking may be necessary.

Dahlia cultivars

These plants bring colour and flamboyance to the late summer and early autumn (fall) garden. The current vogue is for dark-, bronze- or black-leaved cultivars. Flowers can be huge, cactus- or waterlily-like; pompons or balls, in eye-catching shades of white, cream, pink, yellow, orange, red and purple.
Height and spread: To 1.2m x 60cm (4 x 2ft), depending on the variety; dwarfs to 45cm/ 18in tall
Hardiness: Half hardy/Z 9
Cultivation: Grow in well-drained but rich, moisture-retentive soil, in full sun. Excellent in containers. Stake taller varieties. Pinch out the growing tips for bushiness and deadhead. Tubers may be left in the border in mild regions.

Above: Allium christophii

Above: Cosmos atrosanguineus

Above: Dahlia

Above: Tropaeolum majus

Above: Diascia 'Rupert Lambert'

Above: Lilium 'Eros'

Diascia
Twinspur
Recent breeding of both diascia and the related nemesia genus has created a range of colourful, long-flowering plants, many of which will survive the winter in a sheltered spot outdoors. Ideal for containers, diascias carry sprays of delicate shell-shaped blooms in shades of pink, orange and salmon. Brick pink *D.* 'Ruby Field' is one of the hardiest.
Height and spread: 25–30 x 60cm (10–12 x 24in)
Hardiness: Frost hardy/Z 7–9
Cultivation: Grow in moisture-retentive compost (soil mix) and deadhead any spent flower stems regularly. Given sharp drainage, survives winter as a basal carpet of evergreen leaves.

Hemorocallis 'Stella de Oro'
Daylily
A compact free-flowering daylily with grassy leaves and rounded flared blooms of golden yellow produced in early summer and repeating in flushes. Always neat and requiring little maintenance.

Height and spread: 30 x 45cm (12 x 18in)
Hardiness: Hardy/Z 4–9
Cultivation: Easily grown on moisture-retentive, fertile loam or clay in sun or light shade.

Knautia macedonica
Knautia
A stalwart perennial, flowering through the second half of summer, this knautia has deep crimson pincushion flowers on wiry stems that mingle perfectly with other blooms. For a range of colours grow 'Summer Pastels'.
Height and spread: 60–80 x 45–60cm (24–32 x 18–24in)
Hardiness: Hardy/Z 5–9
Cultivation: Any well-drained soil in full sun. Deadhead.

Lilium
Lily
Hybrid lilies such as the compact orange 'Enchantment' are the easiest to grow. More exotic examples include the scented turkscap types 'Black Beauty' (deep red) and 'Eros' (pinkish-orange). 'Brushmarks', an Asiatic hybrid, makes sturdy plants with large flowers – rich orange marked with red.

Height: To 1.2m (4ft)
Hardiness: Hardy/Z 4–8
Cultivation: Grow in well-drained soil in sun (ideally in a position where their roots are shaded). Suitable for containers.

Rhodanthemum hosmariense
No common name
This low, creeping, sub-shrubby plant with finely cut silvery green foliage seldom stops flowering. Wiry stems carry large white daisies with a bold yellow centre. 'African Eyes' is a petite, bushy form.
Height and spread: 15–30 x 30–45cm (6–12 x 12–18in)
Hardiness: Frost hardy/ Z 6–9
Cultivation: Grow in any free-draining soil in sun. Deadhead regularly.

Salvia
Ornamental sage
Salvias are a huge genus with many excellent plants. Drought resistant kinds include *Salvia* x *sylvestris* 'Mainacht', with slender branched spikes of dark purple-blue flowers, in early to midsummer. The later flowering *S. verticillata* 'Purple Rain' is looser in habit with abundant whorled blooms into autumn (fall).
Height and spread: 70 x 45cm (28 x 18in)
Hardiness: Hardy/Z 5–9
Cultivation: Grow in moderately fertile, well-drained soil in sun or light shade.

Tropaeolum majus
Nasturtium
These familiar annuals are among the easiest to grow. Vigorous trailing varieties are used in hanging baskets or trained as climbers, but modern compact forms and the dark-leaved, red-flowered 'Empress of India' are lovely in pots or alternatively for filling in around other plants.
Height and spread: To 3 x 3m (10 x 10ft) (trailing forms); other strains often within 30 x 30cm (12 x 12in)
Hardiness: Half hardy/Z 8
Cultivation: Grow in any well-drained, preferably poor, soil in full sun.

Verbena bonariensis
Purpletop vervain
Tall, rigid, lightly branched stems carry rounded heads of tiny violet-purple blooms. Self-seeding scatters plants through borders, but the effect is light and airy. The plant is a magnet for bees and butterflies, with flowers continuing through summer and well into autumn (fall).
Height and spread: 1.2–2m x 45cm (4–6 x 1½ft)
Hardiness: Frost hardy/Z 7–9
Cultivation: Any free-draining soil in full sun. Though the mother plant may die in winter, seedlings produce fresh crops.

AUTUMN PLANTS

With the shortening days and evenings, and mornings becoming cooler, summer draws to an end. Autumn compensates, with its rich foliage colours highlighting the remaining blooms and providing a backdrop for glistening fruits and berries. Many tender, summer-flowering plants continue till the frosts and some flowers emerge only late in the year, one final fling before the new cycle begins.

Above: *Some forms of Japanese maple (Acer palmatum) produce glowing autumn hues.*

Above: Cotoneaster horizontalis

Above: Aster x frikartii *'Mönch'*

Above: Cyclamen hederifolium

Acer palmatum
Japanese maple
The fleeting but vivid autumn (fall) leaf display varies depending on the weather. Soil type can make a difference, with most acers colouring best in acidic conditions. Plants in the *A. p.* var. *dissectum* group have dainty filigree foliage. *A. p.* 'Sango-kaku' has lacquer-red stems and golden yellow autumn foliage and is an excellent small multi-stemmed tree.
Height and spread: 1.2–8m (4–25ft), variety dependent
Hardiness: Hardy/Z 5–8
Cultivation: Grow in any soil, preferably leafy and fertile, with some overhead shade. Protect from winds and spring frosts.

Anemone x hybrida
Japanese anemone
These upright perennials bring elegance and a spring-like freshness to the late summer garden, with their white or pink dish-shaped flowers atop wiry stems and contrasting yellow stamens. Spreading to form large clumps in time, they are ravishing in the dappled light beneath deciduous trees. Cultivars include 'Lady Gilmour' and 'Honorine Jobert'.
Height and spread: 1.5m x 60cm (5 x 2ft)
Hardiness: Hardy/Z 6–8
Cultivation: Grow in moisture-retentive soil in shade or sun; lighter, drier soils are tolerated.

Aster x frikartii 'Mönch'
Aster
The flowers of this daisy-like perennial appear in late summer and early autumn (fall) and are violet blue with yellowish orange centres. 'Mönch' has long-lasting, lavender blue flowers from midsummer, is disease-resistant and doesn't require staking.
Height and spread: 70 x 40cm (28 x 16in)
Hardiness: Hardy/Z 5–9
Cultivation: Grow in well-drained yet moisture-retentive, moderately fertile soil in full sun.

Ceratostigma willmottianum
Hardy plumbago
This cobalt blue-flowered deciduous shrub with a low domed habit works wonderfully against the backdrop of autumn (fall) leaves. Blooming from late summer, its leaves start to turn red as autumn approaches.
Height and spread: 1 x 1.5m (3 x 5ft)
Hardiness: Hardy/Z 7–9

Cultivation: Grow in a sunny, well-drained spot. The plant is usually cut back by frost, so remove dead stems in spring close to ground level.

Cotoneaster
Cotoneaster
The cotoneasters are tolerant of many situations that other plants abhor. Among the best for late interest is deciduous herringbone cotoneaster, *C. horizontalis*. The leaves turn a vivid red before falling at the same time as the berries ripen to red. Another good choice for late colour is the evergreen, ground-covering *C. salicifolius* 'Gnom' with vivid red berries.
Height and spread:
C. horizontalis 1 x 1.5m (3 x 5ft), taller trained against a wall; *C. s.* 'Gnom' 30cm x 2m (1 x 6ft)
Hardiness: Hardy/Z 5–8
Cultivation: These shrubs with their varied size and habit are tolerant of a wide range of conditions, including cold and exposure. Remove unwanted seedlings.

Cyclamen hederifolium
Cyclamen
This little Mediterranean cyclamen, formerly *C. neapolitanum*, blooms mid- and late autumn (fall) in shades of pink or white. The first flowers appear as the heart-shaped, marbled leaves open out. These last for months, making attractive ground cover. Freely seeding, large colonies soon establish beneath trees and larger deciduous shrubs.
Height and spread: 10 x 15cm (4 x 6in)
Hardiness: Hardy/Z 5–9
Cultivation: Tolerant of a wide range of conditions but soil must be well drained. Needs summer shade. Mulch with leaf mould or ground composted bark when the leaves die down in summer.

Hibiscus syriacus
Hibiscus
These upright deciduous shrubs with their trumpet-shaped blooms, each with a boss of stamens protruding from the dark-hearted centres seem too exotic to be hardy. Colours range from dusky pink 'Woodbridge' and rich blue 'Bluebird' to white or purple, and plants flower from late summer into autumn (fall).
Height and spread: 2.5 x 1.5m (8 x 5ft)
Hardiness: Hardy/Z 6–9
Cultivation: Well-drained, neutral to mildly alkaline soil with maximum sun and shelter.

Hydrangea
Hydrangea
Though many of the shade-loving mop-head or lace-cap flowered *H. macrophylla* and *H. serrata* cultivars begin flowering in summer, the blooms mature, change colour and often reach a peak of beauty through autumn (fall). The summer-flowering *H. paniculata* types such as

'Pink Diamond' and 'Unique', with creamy white, lacy, cone-shaped heads, also frequently develop pink or red shading.
Height and spread: To 1–1.5 x 1–1.5m (3–5 x 3–5ft), depending on cultivar
Hardiness: Hardy/Z 6–8
Cultivation: Excellent in large pots. Use loam-based compost (soil mix) or plant in humus-rich, moisture-retentive soil. Flowers may be pink-purple or blue, depending on the soil – acid or ericaceous is necessary for blue tones. Leave papery flower heads on over winter and cut back very lightly in spring to a pair of swollen buds. *H. paniculata* may be pruned hard in spring.

Kniphofia
Red hot poker, torch lily
Together with the familiar burning poker effect of yellow deepening to orange or red, there are cultivars blooming into early autumn (fall) that have predominantly single-coloured blooms, like the greenish-yellow 'Percy's Pride' or flame 'Prince Igor'. The blooms of *K. rooperi* are egg-shaped and two-toned. Site the clump where early frosts won't mar the display.
Height and spread: Around 1–1.2m x 60cm (3–4 x 2ft), depending on the variety
Hardiness: Hardy/Z 5–6 (most pokers, although some are borderline)

Cultivation: Grow in soil that does not dry out in summer but that remains well drained in winter. Full sun.

Pyracantha
Firethorn
Among the toughest of garden plants, the firethorns are ideal for screening. They froth over with creamy white flowers in early summer, and develop clusters of orange, yellow or red berries in autumn (fall). Magnificent trained against a wall, but beware of planting them too near a walkway, as the stems are armed with barbarous spines. 'Orange Glow' has vibrant orange berries, while those of 'Soleil d'Or' are golden yellow.
Height and spread: 1.8 x 1.5m (6 x 5ft), more if wall-trained
Hardiness: Hardy/Z 6–9
Cultivation: Grow in almost any soil, in sun or moderate shade.

Rudbeckia fulgida
Orange coneflower
This plant makes a vivid display in autumn (fall), with stiff yellow-orange daisy flowers, each with a black eye, above mounds of dark green foliage. Leave the heads in place through winter in larger courtyard borders.
Height and spread: 60 x 30cm (2 x 1ft)
Hardiness: Hardy/Z 4–9
Cultivation: Grow in most soils in sun but avoid dry spots as the plant needs moisture.

Sedum spectabile
Ice plant
Above their fleshy, grey-green leaves, ice plants produce flat heads of pink flowers in autumn (fall), loved by butterflies and bees. The flowers last for a long period, gradually turning a rich brown. 'Herbstfreude' has darker brick pink blooms.
Height and spread: 45 x 45cm (18 x 18in)
Hardiness: Hardy/Z 4–9
Cultivation: Grow in reasonably drained soils, including clays in sun or light shade.

Sorbus
Rowan
The rowans are good trees for the urban courtyard, casting little shade and tolerant of pollution. *S. aucuparia* 'Fastigiata' is narrowly upright, useful where space is at a premium, with orange berries enhanced by red or yellow autumn (fall) leaves. 'Joseph Rock' is similar with amber berries. The Kashmir rowan, *S. cashmiriana*, has large, pearl-like white berries that persist after leaf fall. For a small space try the dainty *S. villmorinii* with ferny leaves and clusters of small pale pink berries turning crimson.
Height and spread: To 10 x 7m (33 x 23ft); *S. cashmiriana* 4 x 3m (13 x 10ft)
Hardiness: Hardy/Z 5–8
Cultivation: Grow in any well-drained soil in sun or light shade.

Above: Hibiscus syriacus *'Diana'*

Above: Kniphofia *'Alcazar'*

Above: Rudbeckia fulgida

WINTER PLANTS

While in winter the garden lacks the exuberance of warmer months, the skeletal structure of deciduous shrubs and trees makes a pleasing contrast with evergreen forms. The glowing reds of foliage and stems punctuate the greenery and highlight the predominantly yellow and white winter blooms. Sculptural seed-heads decorate the borders, and pots of early bulbs signal the start of the new gardening year.

Above: Skimmia japonica *'Rubella'* is a form with tight crimson cones of flower buds.

Above: Cyclamen coum

Betula utilis jacquemontii
Himalayan birch

A multi-stemmed specimen of this beautiful tree can become a striking focal point for the garden in winter when the bark peels to reveal the white trunks. Selected forms, e.g. 'Jermyns', are even more beautiful. Relatively slow growing.
Height and spread: 15 x 7.5m (49 x 24ft)
Hardiness: Hardy/Z 4–7
Cultivation: Grow on well-drained but moist soil in sun. Wash algae from the bark with a sponge and mild soapy water.

Clematis cirrhosa 'Freckles'
Fern-leafed clematis

One of very few winter-flowering climbers, this clematis has nodding, bell-like, creamy white flowers, spotted with maroon,

during any mild spell in winter, but is at its best as the season draws to a close. In sudden cold snaps, the foliage may acquire bronze tints.
Height and spread: 6 x 6m (20 x 20ft)
Hardiness: Hardy/Z 7–9
Cultivation: Grow in fertile, well-drained, ideally alkaline soil in sun or light shade. Best against a sunny wall in cold areas.

Cyclamen coum
Sowbread

The hardy cyclamen provides close ground cover in dry shade. The dainty flowers, with their back-swept petals, appearing in winter and early spring can be purple-violet, pink or, in the case of 'Album', white. The leaves are marbled.
Height and spread: 8 x 10cm (3 x 4in)

Hardiness: Hardy/Z 5–9
Cultivation: Grow in moderately fertile, moist but well-drained soil in partial shade; drier soils are tolerated.

Daphne bholua
Lokta

For fragrance in the sheltered winter garden, these reliable Himalayan daphnes are hard to beat. The upright stems are scattered with rounded clusters of waxy tubular flowers (white flushed pink and purple) in late winter. *D. b.* var *glacialis* 'Gurkha' is deciduous and slightly tougher than the evergreen 'Jacqueline Postill'.
Height and spread: 2 x 1.5m (6 x 5ft)
Hardiness: Borderline hardy/Z 7
Cultivation: Grow in sun or light shade on humus-rich, moisture-retentive ground or in large pots.

Erica carnea
Winter heath

Varieties of the lime-tolerant *E. carnea* and *E. x darleyensis* are invaluable as groundcover beneath deciduous shrubs in

winter and make good pot specimens, acting as a foil for early bulbs. A range of pink and purple shades is available, but whites tend to be most popular. The carpeting *E. c.* 'Springwood White' blooms for weeks over fresh green foliage, while *E. x d.* 'Silberschmelze' is taller with cream-tipped growth in spring.
Height and spread: 'Springwood White' 20 x 55cm (8 x 22in); 'Silberschmelze' 30 x 75cm (12 x 30in)
Hardiness: Hardy/*Erica carnea* Z 6–8; *E. x darleyensis* Z 7–8
Cultivation: Grow in sun on humus-rich, moisture-retentive but drained soil.

Galanthus
Snowdrop

Among the first bulbs to flower in winter, snowdrops are universally loved. *G. nivalis* is the most usual species, but they hybridize so freely that there are many forms. 'Flore Pleno' has honey-scented double flowers, the tips touched with green. *G.* 'Atkinsii' has elongated petals and broad, grey-green leaves.

Above: Daphne bholua

Above: E. carnea *'Eileen Porter'*

Above: Galanthus nivalis

Height and spread: 10 x 10cm (4 x 4in)
Hardiness: Hardy/Z 3–9
Cultivation: Grow in reliably moist soil, preferably where they will be shaded when dormant – beneath a deciduous tree or shrub is ideal.

Helleborus
Hellebore
The hellebores are long-lived plants that gradually make more and more impressive clumps. *H. niger*, the Christmas rose, produces glistening white flowers in the very depths of winter, though it can be difficult to establish. Slightly later flowering *H. orientalis* is easier and plants often self-seed. Flowers are subtly coloured in a predominantly dusky range of purple, pink and creamy white (often the flower centres are spotted with purple). Especially desirable are the rare yellow and clear red forms.
Height and spread: 30 x 30cm (12 x 12in)
Hardiness: Hardy/Z 5–9
Cultivation: Grow in any moist but not waterlogged (preferably alkaline) soil in sun or shade.

Mahonia x media cultivars
Mahonia
Wonderfully architectural plants for the winter garden, forms of this mahonia hybrid have whorls of long, glossy, pinnate leaves, each stem crowned with upright or arching yellow flower

Above: Helleborus orientalis

sprays. The most popular is the strongly upright, autumn (fall) to early winter-flowering 'Charity', but 'Winter Sun' is certainly worth seeking out, its well-formed flower heads being more frost resistant. With a little pruning after flowering, it also has a more bushy and compact habit. Others to consider include the handsomely flowered 'Lionel Fortescue' and 'Underway'. The heavy crops of blue-black berries are a boon for birds.
Height and spread: 4 x 4m (13 x 13ft)
Hardiness: Hardy/Z 8–9
Cultivation: Grow on reasonably fertile well-drained but moisture-retentive soil. Drought-tolerant in shade once established. Cut back shoot tips after flowering to promote bushiness.

Sarcococca hookeriana
Christmas or sweet box
These compact, rounded evergreens have small pointed leaves and through winter, bear tiny white blooms with a powerful fragrance, captured and concentrated in the shelter of a shady courtyard. Black fruits follow. The leaves of the hardier form *Sarcococca hookeriana* var. *digyna* are elegantly tapered and the shoot tips of the aptly named 'Purple Stem' are flushed purple, its flowers pink tinted.
Height and spread: To 1.5 x 1.5m (5 x 5ft)

Above: Viburnum tinus *'Gwenllian'*

Hardiness: Hardy/Z 6–8
Cultivation: Once established tolerates dry shade but preferably grow in moisture-retentive but well-drained, humus-rich soil and shade.

Skimmia japonica 'Rubella'
Skimmia
The skimmias make satisfying mounds of evergreen foliage with clusters of sweetly scented flowers in late winter, followed by berries on female forms. The unopened buds on the male form are deep crimson.
Height and spread: 1.2 x 1.2m (4 x 4ft)
Hardiness: Hardy/Z 7–9
Cultivation: Grow in fertile, well-drained soil in sun or light shade; most skimmias do best in slightly acid conditions.

Viburnum tinus
Laurustinus
The shrubs in this genus provide interest throughout the year. Some are grown for their flowers in winter or spring, others for their berries, some for both. The evergreen *Viburnum tinus* has white flowers in shallow domed heads in late

winter and early spring followed by bluish-black berries. 'Eve Price' is a reliable selection with pink buds and 'Gwenllian', a pretty form grown for its pink-tinged white flowers, opening from dark pink buds.
Height and spread: 3 x 3m (10 x 10ft)
Hardiness: Hardy/Z 8–10
Cultivation: Grow on any drained but moisture retentive soil including clay. Tolerates lime and partial shade.

Viburnum x bodnantense
Bodnant's viburnum
Selections of this deciduous, upright viburnum include 'Charles Lamont', 'Deben' and 'Dawn', all of which carry small, pink-shaded pompon blooms in flushes through winter, when there is a mild period. Their fragrance travels far and is a blend of honey and almond. The plants sucker mildly from the base but need little attention.
Height and spread: 2.5 x 1.5m (8 x 5ft) or more
Hardiness: Hardy/Z 7–8
Cultivation: Grow on any drained but moisture-retentive soil including clay. Tolerates lime and partial shade.

MAINTENANCE

Whether you are a regular gardener or only occasionally get your hands dirty, time outdoors among the plants is both refreshing and restorative. Courtyards tend to be easy to maintain. Often there is no lawn to cut or large hedges to trim. And, with raised beds and containers, heavy work such as digging may not be necessary. Even watering can be done automatically. But regular feeding of plants in pots and planters and feeding the soil is essential.

Touching up paintwork, treating wooden furniture, ensuring borders and paving are weed-free, as well as regular deadheading, will keep your courtyard spick and span. In a limited space, the careful pruning, shaping and supporting of plants becomes especially important, and spring is a busy preparation period for the season ahead. By the time autumn arrives, the gardener's focus turns to sweeping up fallen leaves, protecting tender plants, patio furniture and terracotta pots from the cold of the coming winter. And pools, pumps and filters also need attention at this time.

Left: *A courtyard display such as this will need daily nurturing, and once or twice a year the courtyard should have a thorough springclean.*

PLANT UPKEEP

In a small garden, essential regular maintenance should include supporting plants and tying in shoots, removing faded blooms and investigating yellowing leaves. With good, fertile soil you may grow strong, healthy plants with plentiful flowers and fruits, but courtyard gardens often have poor, impoverished ground and plants need additional help in the form of feeding and mulching.

Above: *Climbers need different levels of support. Clematis prefer a wire lattice.*

Above: *Cut off unwanted stems and check that existing ties aren't too tight.*

Above: *Creating a framework of stakes and twine will give a plant extra support.*

Above: *When a mass of flowers goes over, such as marguerite daisies and lavender, use hand shears to deadhead them.*

Supporting Plants

Herbaceous perennials, herbs and lax shrubs may need support and this is best added as new shoots start to come through, so that the underlying support structure is eventually camouflaged. Support ranges from pushing in a few twiggy sticks to create a framework of stakes and twine or using purpose-made climbing frames, wall trellis or wires. Climbers and wall shrubs produce numerous new shoots and you will need to select the ones you want to keep and train and tie these on to their supports. Fan the stems out or train along horizontal wires to stimulate increased flowering and fruiting. Don't pass stems behind trellis panels or wires; rather tie them on to the front of the support. This ensures much easier maintenance.

Deadheading

This process prevents plants using up their valuable resources by setting seed. It also tricks the plant into producing more blooms in an effort to reproduce, and so

Above: *For large rose heads, cut back to the stalk base or just above a joint.*

Above: *Plants rarely recover a good, natural shape after having collapsed in the wind and rain, so early support is essential.*

lengthens the flowering season, especially for annuals. There are several ways to deadhead depending on the plant (see pictures below). Leave some sculptural seed-heads for autumn and winter decoration.

Above: *Once faded, small blooms may be pinched out between finger and thumb.*

Feeding

Regular feeding, especially when flower buds are developing and plants are in bloom, is essential. Check fertilizer packets to find the right balance for your flowering or foliage plants as well as for crops in the productive garden. Nitrogen (N) makes leafy growth, phosphorous (P) develops roots and potassium (K) promotes flowering and fruiting. These are expressed as an N:P:K ratio.

If you are looking for a feed for leafy vegetable crops, for example, you would choose one with a relatively large amount of nitrogen.

Just as with a good multivitamin tablet, you will also see additional trace elements listed on packs and bottles, including iron, manganese, and boron. These additional nutrients can help ailing plants suffering from deficiencies in their diet, which show up as discoloration of leaves and other abnormalities.

Tomato feed, which is high in potassium, works well on sparsely flowering plants producing leaves at the expense of bloom, while rose fertilizer is a tonic for other flowering shrubs and climbers, such as clematis and hydrangea. Use specially formulated ericaceous feeds for plants that need to grow in acid soils. And before the foliage of spring bulbs and lilies starts to fade, build flowering reserves using a high potash feed.

Above: *High-performing displays in containers and small raised beds need regular summer feeding. Nutrients are limited due to the small soil volume.*

Above: *Weekly liquid feeds between mid-spring and late summer are best, but top dressing with a granular, slow-release fertilizer in spring and midsummer suffices.*

Above: *Some fertilizers can be mixed with water from a hose and simply sprayed on to plants. This saves time and avoids heavy watering cans.*

Top Dressing

Using well-rotted manure, spent mushroom compost and garden compost (soil mix) for top dressing conserves moisture and improves soil texture and fertility. Apply the mulch thickly (8–10cm/3–4in) deep) in autumn (fall) or late winter on to moist soil, keeping it away from the stem bases to prevent rotting.

Rejuvenating Plants

Some quick-growing herbaceous plants and established bulb clumps may become overcrowded, causing poor flowering. To rejuvenate, lift and divide in autumn or spring (or, in the case of spring bulbs, after flowering). Improve the soil and replant the smaller vigorous portions, discarding the old, congested centre.

Plants in pots should be replanted into a larger container before they become pot bound to give the roots space to develop. If you want to keep a specimen in a specific pot, scrape off the loose top layer of potting mix and replace with fresh, adding slow-release fertilizer or a layer of organic mulch. If you can get it out of its pot, do so and scrape off loose compost from the root-ball. Cutting the mat of roots back slightly stimulates new growth. Ensure that compost (soil mix) is properly worked in down the sides of the pot.

Above: *Ease a pot-bound plant out, pushing through the drainage hole.*

Above: *Always feed after pruning shrubs and climbers to replace lost resources. Winter pruning can often be accompanied by mulching with manure or compost.*

Above: *Agapanthus is moved into a larger container without disturbing the roots.*

PRUNING AND TRAINING

A small garden that is planted with shrubs and climbers can soon look unkempt and overcrowded if regular pruning and training is not carried out. It is helpful to keep a diary of which plants need dealing with at particular times of year so that you don't inadvertently cut something back at the wrong time and spoil its flowering display or fruit production.

Above: *For best results prune wisteria in late summer and again in late winter.*

Left: *Shrubby mallow (Lavatera x clementii) dies back after frost, so in the spring cut to the new shoots at the base.*

Right: *Mock orange (Philadelphus) and other spring and early summer flowering shrubs are pruned back once flowering is over.*

When to Prune

Long-lived shrubs and trees, such as magnolias, Japanese maples and evergreen azaleas, are typically slow growing and need very little pruning or trimming. In contrast, fast-growing shrubs, and ones that produce an abundance of flowers and fruit, are often relatively short-lived. Examples of this type include buddleia, broom (*Cytisus*), lavender, abutilon and shrubby mallow (*Lavatera*). The mallow benefits from annual radical pruning in order to keep it in an artificial state of youthfulness.

If you can't judge when fast-growing deciduous plants, such as shrubby potentilla, need pruning, it is usually safe to cut out around a third of the oldest stems in spring. A good rule of thumb (with the exception of *Hydrangea macrophylla*) is to prune plants that flower before the longest day of the year just after flowering, and to prune those that flower after that in the spring.

The first group includes spring and early summer-flowering shrubs, such as mock orange (*Philadelphus*), forsythia, weigela and deutzia. Remove a large proportion of the flowered wood (especially the oldest branches) and leave newer shoots to mature and flower the following year. These plants are described as flowering on second year wood.

The second group of plants includes buddleia, lavatera, abutilon, caryopteris, *Hydrangea paniculata*, bush roses and late-flowering clematis, such as the viticella types. These can be pruned hard back to a framework of branches because they have time to produce mature wood through the early part of the year.

Above: *The vigorous* Buddleia davidii *forms should be pruned back hard to a low framework of branches in spring.*

Above: Hydrangea paniculata, *when pruned strongly, will produce large and well-formed flowers.*

Above: *Prune bush and patio roses hard back in late winter. Remove dead, diseased, weak or crossing branches.*

Maximizing Growth

With some plants, the harder you prune, the larger the flowers will grow, as in the case of *Hydrangea paniculata*, or the bigger and brighter the foliage or winter stems, as with gold- and variegated-leaved shrubs such as sambucus and coloured-stem dogwoods. Correct pruning of climbers, such as wisteria, or fruit trees, such as apples and pears, promotes the production of short-flowering and fruiting spurs.

Removing Dead Wood

As well as pruning to promote flower and fruiting, you also need to cut out damaged or diseased wood and old or unproductive branches on flowering or fruiting shrubs and climbers. If you are pruning to reduce or maintain the size of a plant, try to mirror its natural habit. If you clip just the ends of branches it forces the plant to shoot from dormant buds further down the stems, turning shrubs into congested mounds. Instead, reach into the plant to cut out whole branches.

Training and Pruning Soft Fruit

After harvesting soft fruit such as raspberry and blackberry, prune old canes out and tie new canes into supports. Most bush fruits are pruned to maintain an open shape with no crossovers or congestion. Many can be trained to save space as cordons, espaliers, fans and, in the case of gooseberries, as standards. These forms need more maintenance but fruit picking is often easier. Follow individual pruning requirements, as timings and techniques vary.

Training Wall Fruit

Pruning can be tricky with plants that flower early and bear fruits late. With the pyracantha, for example, it is best to tie it into a support framework, trimming back new, unwanted growth after flowering. If you cut the blossom off you won't get any fruits.

Above: *It is often easier to prune bare branches in the winter or spring as you can easily see what needs to come out.*

Above: *Prune mature blueberries in late winter or early spring when flower buds are visible. Thicker, strong shoots fruit best.*

Above: *The thorny stemmed evergreen firethorn (Pyracantha) can take up a lot of room and is best when espalier trained.*

Shaped and trained apple trees are normally pruned twice a year – once in midsummer and again in winter. Summer pruning controls the amount of new growth produced, sends energy back to the developing fruits and increases light for ripening. Winter pruning consists of thinning overcrowded fruiting spurs on old plants and removing dead or diseased wood. Don't winter prune plums.

Above: *Take out crossing branches and old, flowered wood (the latter often appears 'twiggy' and highly branched).*

Above: *Blackberries are easy to grow but vigorous. After fruiting, cut out old canes and slant new shoots down to fix to wires.*

Above: *Training branches closer to the horizontal, such as with wall-trained roses and fruit trees, promotes flowers and fruit.*

PRUNING TIPS

- *Cut above buds to prevent die-back.*
- *Remove thin, unproductive shoots and crossing or rubbing branches.*
- *Thin branches to allow light and air to circulate.*
- *Sterilize cutting tools regularly to prevent disease spreading.*
- *Keep tools sharp.*

WATERING TECHNIQUES

Watering can be tricky in courtyards. Not only do house and boundary walls create a rain-shadow effect, but there may also be little exposed soil for water to drain into. The amount of plants growing in a small plot can also put a strain on resources. And if you are growing mainly in pots and raised beds, some form of automated watering system could be very useful.

Above: *Plan your watering techniques according to the courtyard's requirements.*

Conserving Water

Plants are tougher than you might think, and once established they should need watering only during periods of drought. Newly planted specimens, especially shrubs, need watering throughout hot, sunny or dry spells in their first year because their root system won't be large enough to cope with demands from the leaves.

On free-draining, sandy soil or when gardening in containers and raised beds, concentrate on drought-tolerant plants rather than water guzzlers such as lush herbaceous perennials. Mulching with moisture-retentive organic materials, such as bark, well-rotted manure and garden compost, helps to seal in moisture, but make sure the ground is thoroughly moist before you apply it.

Don't water overhead using a hosepipe. Much of the water will be wasted and run off the foliage

Above: *A thick layer of bark mulch helps to conserve water already in the soil.*

without penetrating the ground to reach the roots. Short bursts of general watering also encourage shallow rooting. Deep roots seek out moisture and allow plants to fend for themselves during dry spells. Try and water in the cool of the morning or the evening to reduce evaporation.

Hand and Automatic Watering

Using a watering can, perhaps filled from a water butt, will make you think about where the water is being used and thus reduce wastage.

If you are away for more than a few days at a time in the summer, a willing neighbour or an automatic watering system is essential. Such a system can be efficient if it is properly adjusted and monitored.

Most automatic irrigation systems include special accessories for watering wall containers and baskets as well as patio containers, and they are easy to put together or extend.

Above: *Use drought-resistant plants such as these house leeks (*Sempervivum*) and other succulents in dry, sunny areas.*

Above: *When watering small plants and seedlings, use the watering can's rose fitting, otherwise the flow of water will disturb the soil and may uproot plants.*

Above: *Take the rose off the watering can spout, unless watering seedlings and young plants, and put the spout under the foliage close to soil level to direct the water.*

Above: *A hosepipe with various attachments can speed up watering and make it easier to reach wall containers and baskets.*

Above: *A simple system for newly planted borders, and beds used for crops, is a leaky or perforated hose attached to an outdoor tap.*

Water Capture

Provide a ready supply of rainwater by running the downpipes from the main house roof into water butts. Water from guttering on sheds, summer houses and greenhouses can also be captured in this way.

You can now buy butts designed for fitting into confined spaces, or to maximize the amount of water captured, consider fitting an extension to divert excess water from one butt to an adjacent one.

Plastic water butts aren't the most attractive containers but you can usually camouflage them to a degree by using screens made of trellis covered with climbers.

When building your courtyard garden, ensure that the paving slopes slightly to direct water into beds and borders, especially in low-rainfall areas and where the soil is free-draining. You can also divert rain from guttering directly into the beds if the flow is not too great.

Above: *Divert water run-off from paving directly into borders to keep them watered.*

Above: *Trellis screens in position around a butt, ready to be planted up.*

Above: *Drought-tolerant herbs like lavender are ideal for free-draining ground.*

SETTING UP A WATERING SYSTEM

It isn't costly to set up an automatic watering system, and starter kits with add-on packs are available. There are no special tools and the work is reasonably straightforward.

Measure the lengths of piping required, adding extra for leeway. Soak the tubing ends in hot water to soften the plastic and allow easier fixing on to the connectors.

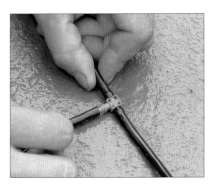

1 After laying a main pipe around the site that attaches to an outdoor tap, small spaghetti-like tubes or side branches are fitted to take water to specific plants.

2 With the tap turned on, the water comes out of an adjustable drip-feed nozzle positioned where the best water penetration to each plant's roots is assured.

3 Use a watering computer to set watering times and check that each plant is receiving the right amount. You may need to adjust individual nozzles.

SEASONAL JOBS

Small garden spaces demand careful upkeep because your attention is focused within that confined area and everywhere is on show. Many general maintenance jobs can be done in a matter of minutes and could become part of your daily or weekly routine, along with watering and deadheading, but once a year it is good to have a really thorough spring-clean.

Above: *Spring brings many maintenance tasks, but don't forget your spring flowers.*

Spring

Traditionally, perennials were cut down in autumn as the garden was 'put to bed' for the winter. But long-lasting seed-heads, stems and leaves provide shelter and food for beneficial insects and birds as well as thermal insulation for cold-sensitive roots and shoots. The dead remains of many plants, including ornamental grasses, also continue to look attractive, especially when outlined in frost. In early spring the dead material pulls away easily and at this time you can deal with overwintering weeds or annuals that may have sprouted during mild winter spells.

Once you have tidied your border, top dress with well-rotted manure or garden compost (soil mix) to get plants off to a good start, or refresh worn areas of bark mulch to keep down weeds.

Once spring has arrived, sub-shrubby specimens, such as penstemon, cotton lavender (*Santolina*) and Russian sage (*Perovskia*), will show signs of

Above: *Leave sculptural seed-heads for winter garden decoration. Cut back in spring.*

Above: *Top up bark mulch annually, especially where it is starting to wear thin.*

new growth on their lower stems. Cut back the old woody growth to just above where you can see regeneration taking place.

The warmer days of late spring and early summer are ideal for retouching exterior paintwork and applying coloured wood stains to

freshen up fences and trellis, as well as other painted or stained wooden structures.

Scrub unwanted algae and mud splashes from the base of rendered walls, garden statuary and bird baths and hire a power washer to lift algae, moss and grime from porous paving.

Above: *Cut penstemons back in April or May to where you can see the new growth sprouting lower down.*

Above: *Treat woodwork and trellis panels to a fresh coat of paint or stain in the spring or early summer.*

Above: *Use a pressure washer to remove grime and algal build-up on paving. It is advisable to wear waterproofs.*

Above: *In summer, remove floating and submerged pond growth using a net or cane.*

Above: *Top up ponds and features running from small reservoirs to protect the pump.*

Above: *Keep part of the water surface clear to maximize reflection.*

Summer

During summer, give hardwood furniture at least a couple of coats of teak oil, or similar, or re-apply exterior varnish or paint. Wrought- and cast-iron furniture should be treated with a rust-proofing paint after removing loose flakes with a wire brush and/or power washer.

At this time of year you may need to top up water levels in ponds and take action if blanket weed becomes a problem or if oxygenating plants are becoming too vigorous. Pull out excess weed and compost it. Water lilies and marginal plants may also become overcrowded and should be thinned as necessary. Keep a good proportion of the water surface clear in order to maximize reflections.

Autumn

Falling autumn leaves can rapidly accumulate and should be cleared frequently to prevent them smothering delicate plants and making surfaces dangerously slippery. If you have room to make leaf mould (a good soil conditioner), pack leaves into a perforated refuse sack and store them in a shady corner for a year.

If your garden has lots of autumn leaf litter, consider covering pools and ponds with netting to prevent leaves fouling the water. Before icy winter weather descends, clean and maintain any pond pumps and filters. You may need to lift them for dry storage over winter – check the manufacturer's instructions.

Winter

Over the winter months, protect wooden and metal furniture using waterproof fabric covers. If possible, move wooden chairs and tables into a shed or summer house, because covers can cause condensation to build up underneath, which damages the timber.

Terracotta pots and ornaments are vulnerable to frost damage, especially if they are classified only as frost resistant. The raised detail on pots and decorative rims and handles is particularly at risk. Move them to a sheltered corner or take them under cover or protect them *in situ* using bubble plastic insulation (see page 249) or hessian stuffed with straw.

Pumps and filters in ponds should be switched off for winter as fish or amphibians survive in zones of warmer water, and the activity of the pump mixes warm and cold together. If the pond surface freezes over it can trap poisonous gases given off by decaying vegetation and fish waste, and this can kill ornamental fish and other aquatic wildlife. Prevent this by using an electric de-icer or by placing a floating plastic container in the water. If the pond freezes, lift out the container to allow gases to escape.

Above: *Decaying leaves look untidy and can become slippery in the wet, so sweep them up regularly.*

Above: *Pumps and filters need to be kept free from blanket weed and other debris that will block inlets and restrict water flow.*

Above: *Netting pools in autumn prevents leaves from fouling the water, and can be removed once all the leaves have dropped.*

PLANT PROTECTION

In the sheltered confines of a courtyard garden you may be tempted to grow all kinds of tender plants. Although they may thrive during the summer, keeping them alive in winter can be more difficult. Plants in containers are particularly vulnerable. But don't worry if you don't have a greenhouse or conservatory. It is possible to protect many plants where they stand.

Above: *Provide extra protection for tender wall shrubs such as* Ipomoea hederacea.

Protection from Frost

Some of the worst damage to soft new growth is caused by late spring frosts. Plants most vulnerable to frost are soft woods, bloomers that are still growing and potted plants. Frost can have a devastating effect on the flowering of *Hydrangea macropylla* cultivars (mophead and lacecap hydrangeas). Japanese maples, camellia and pieris are also vulnerable. The greatest threat of frost is during the night when the temperature drops enough to freeze the moisture on plants. Signs of frost damage include darkened, yellowed or mushy leaves or leaf curling. So if frosts are forecast protect the flower buds and shoot tips by draping the plant. You will need to attach horticultural fleece or bubble plastic to a horizontal batten temporarily fixed above the plant. Stretch the fabric over the plant and secure it at the base with a heavy piece of timber or a few bricks. Alternatively, tie the fleece over the plant using pegs or string. Mulch the base of the plant with bark to protect its roots.

Mulching Border Plants

Less hardy perennials, tuberous plants and bulbs can often be protected in the border simply by applying a thick mulch of bark. However, take care not to pile this material up against the base of shrubs, climbers or semi-woody plants, such as penstemons and Mediterranean herbs, as the accumulated moisture can cause rot. In many regions now, dahlias and canna (Indian shot) can be left in the ground rather than being lifted and stored in a frost-free greenhouse.

House and Conservatory (Porch) Plants

Houseplants, orchids and cacti kept in the courtyard garden for the summer should be moved back indoors in late summer or early autumn (fall) before night temperatures fall too far. Before doing this, give each plant a thorough check and search for aphids and other pests, such as slugs and snails. Tender fuchsias and marguerites, as

Above: *In late summer, move houseplants and rot-susceptible succulents indoors.*

well as potted figs, can stay outside a little longer, but they must be brought in before the first frosts. Don't overwater at this time. Figs can be stored in the darkness of a garage or cellar once leaves have dropped.

Tender bulbs and tubers, such as begonias, lifted for the winter, need not take up a lot of space and can be overwintered in a frost-protected coldframe, garage or shed. Store them in barely moist compost (soil mix), checking for pests, such as vine weevil, or evidence of rot beforehand.

Above: *Drape evergreen camellia, pieris and rhododendron with horticultural fleece to protect them against frost.*

Above: *Protect tender bulbs and perennials in situ by heaping on dry leaves, bracken or bark.*

Above: *Use fleece to prevent frost damage to flower buds and tender shoot tips on magnolia and hydrangea.*

PROTECTING TENDER SHRUBS

Potted evergreens, such as the Mediterranean bay tree shown below, may suffer in some regions unless protected from cold winds and frost. You need to insulate the roots as well as the leaves. Wrapping the pot protects terracotta or ceramic from splitting and flaking due to water in the clay body freezing and expanding.

1 Fix a number of bamboo canes, taller than the plant, into the pot. Cut a piece of greenhouse insulation or bubble polythene to fit round both the top growth and container.

2 Wrap the plant around with the plastic or use a couple of layers of horticultural fleece. Overlap and secure the covering with twine at various intervals, starting at the base.

3 Continue to tie the plastic around the plant, but keep the top open to allow moisture to escape and air to circulate. Unwrap in spring during mild weather when the danger of frosts has passed.

4 Cluster vulnerable plants together against a warm wall for added protection, paying particular attention to protecting the root-balls (roots). Drape fleece over the tops in frosty spells.

5 Standard topiary pieces, such as this rosemary, need special attention. Protect the main stem using plumbers' pipe insulation, or lagging, and wrap the base with bubble plastic.

PLANTS TO WINTER WRAP

- *Astelia chathamica* (silver spear)
- *Callistemon* species and cultivars (bottle brush)
- *Cordyline australis* (cabbage palm), red-leaved and variegated forms
- *Ensete ventricosum* (Abyssinian banana)
- *Eriobotrya japonica* (loquat)
- *Hebe* (large leaved cultivars)
- *Leptospermum scoparium* cultivars (manuka, New Zealand tea tree)
- *Metrosideros excelsa* (Christmas tree)
- *Musa basjoo* (Japanese banana)
- *Myrtus communis* (myrtle)

Above: *Give tropical-looking loquats* (Eriobotrya japonica) *winter shelter.*

Above: *New Zealand tea tree should be wrapped until the last expected frosts.*

Above: *Protect wall-trained Australian bottle brush* (Callistemon) *in situ.*

USEFUL SUPPLIERS

AUSTRALIA

Anston Paving Stones Ltd
60 Fussell Road
Kilsyth, Victoria 3137
Tel 1300 788 694
www.anston.com.au
Paving

Cotswold Garden Furniture
42 Hotham Parade, Artarmon
New South Wales 2064
Tel (02) 9906 3686
www.cotswoldfurniture.com.au

Diamond Valley Garden Centre
170 Yan Yean Road
Plenty, Victoria 3090
Tel (03) 9432 5113
www.dvgardencentre.com.au

Heaven In Earth
77 Hakea Close
Nowra, New South Wales 2541
Tel (02) 4423 2041
www.heaveninearth.com.au
Garden accessories and ornaments

Mary Moodie's Pond, Pump and Pot Shop
Southern Aquatic Garden
Centre, 110 Boundary Road
Mortdale
New South Wales 2223
Tel (02) 9153 0503

North Manly Garden Centre
510–512 Pittwater Road
North Manly
New South Wales 2100
Tel (02) 9905 5202
www.greengold.com.au
Furniture, containers and sculpture

Outdoor Creations
Heidelberg Road, Ivanhoe,
Melbourne, Victoria
Tel (03) 9490 8000
www.outdoorcreations.com.au
Landscaping and sculpture

Peakhurst Garden Centre
874 Forest Road, Peakhurst
New South Wales 2210
Tel (02) 9533 4239
info@peakhurstgardencentre.
com.au
www.peakhurstgardencentre.
com.au

Wagner Solar
Call 0800 064 790 for stockists
Lighting

CANADA

Avant Gardener
1460 Marine, West Vancouver, BC
Tel (604) 926-8784
www.canadaplus.ca

GetSet! to Garden
203–20475 Lougheed Hwy,
Maple Ridge, BC V2X 9B6
Tel (604) 465-0037
General garden supplies

Gisela's Nursery & Hydroponics
11570 Kingston, Maple Ridge, BC
Tel (604) 465-0929

Greenleaf Garden Supplies
1050 Riverside, Abbotsford, BC,
Tel (604) 850-3209

Otter Co-Op
3600–248th St, Aldergrove, BC
Tel (604) 856-2517

FRANCE

Les Jardins du Roi Soleil
Showroom 32, bd de la Bastille,
75012 PARIS
Tel (33) 01 43 44 44 31
jrs@jardinsroisoleil.com
www.jardinsroisoleil.com
*Treillage, garden furniture,
planters and containers*

NEW ZEALAND

Colenso Tree and Landscape
PO Box 165, Whitford, Auckland
Tel (09) 530 9120
*Paving, pergolas, decks and
water features*

Exotic Earth
92 Eastdale Road
Avondale, Auckland
Tel (09) 828 6876
Garden design

Kiwi Art Designs Ltd
66 Gulf View Road, Rothesay Bay,
North Shore, Auckland
Tel (09) 478 4792
www.kiwiartdesigns.co.nz
Sculptures

Lighting Pacific Ltd
130 Felton Mathew Ave
Glen Innes, Auckland
Tel 0800 707270
www.lightingpacific.co.nz
Outdoor lighting

Dyers Road Landscape & Garden Supplies
183 Dyers Road, Bromley
Christchurch City
Canterbury 8062
Tel (03) 3846540
www.dyersroadlandscape.co.nz

Luijten Landscaping
PO Box 72-698
Papakura, Auckland
Tel (09) 294 6620
www.luijten.co.nz
Landscapers

SOUTH AFRICA

Paradise Landscapers
299 Edwin Swales VC Drive,
Rossburgh, Durban
Tel (27) 79 111 9902
www.paradiselandscapers.co.za

Smart Yards
PO Box 72658
Lynnwood Ridge, Pretoria 0040
Tel (27) 12 667 4014
www.smartyards.co.za

Tidy Gardens
LM Mangope Highway
Ga-Rankuwa 0208
Tel (27) 73 078 1666
info@tidygardens.co.za

Ubuhle Garden Décor
Tel (27) 83 276 1288
www.ubuhlegardendecor.co.za

UNITED KINGDOM

Agriframes Tildenet Ltd
Hartcliffe Way, Bristol BS3 5RJ
Tel 0845 260 4450
info@agriframes.co.uk
www.agriframes.co.uk
*Fruit cages and plant supports
(see example on p134, top)*

Alan Gardner
Tel 0121 313 0027
www.alangardnerdesign.com
Garden designs and installations

Anthony de Grey Trellises
Broadhinton Yard
77a North Street
London SW4 0HQ
Tel 020 7738 8866
Fax 020 7498 9075
www.anthonydegrey.com

Bamboostyle
Unit 2, Low Cocken Farm
Plawsworth, Durham DH3 4EN
Tel 0845 652 6530
sales@bamboostyle.co.uk
www.bamboostyle.co.uk
Bamboo furniture and screens

Chilstone
Victoria Park
Fordwood Road
Langton Green
Tunbridge Wells, Kent TN3 0RE
Tel 01892 740866
ornaments@chilstone.com
www.chilstone.com
*Garden ornaments and
architectural stonework*

Finnforest UK Ltd
46 Berth
Tilbury Docks, Tilbury
Essex RM18 7HS
Tel 01375 812737
*Decorative fencing, screens (see
example featured on page 185),
arbours, pergolas and gazebos*

Franchi Sementi Seeds of Italy
C3 Phoenix Industrial Estate
Rosslyn Crescent, Harrow
Middlesex A1 2SP
Tel 020 8427 5020
grow@italianingredients.com
www.seedsofitaly.com
Vegetable seeds

Garden & Security Lighting
39 Reigate Road, Hookwood,
Horley, Surrey RH6 0HL
Tel 01293 820821
Lighting

Gaze Burvill
Newtonwood Workshop
Newton Valence, Alton
Hampshire GU34 3EW
Tel 020 7471 8500
webenquiries@gazeburvill.com
www.gazeburvill.com
Furniture

Giles Landscapes Ltd
Bramley House
Back Drove, Welney
Cambridgeshire PE14 9RH
Tel 01354 610453
Fax 01354 610450
info@gileslandscapes.co.uk
www.gileslandscapes.co.uk
Contemporary garden designers

Grand Illusions
PO Box 81
Shaftesbury, Dorset SP7 8TA
Tel 01747 858300
www.grandillusions.co.uk
*Garden accessories and
ornaments*

Indian Ocean Trading Company
2527 Market Place
London NW11 6JY
Tel 020 8458 5252
Also in Norwich
Tel 01508 492285
www.indian-ocean.co.uk
Furniture

Italian Terrace
Pykards Hall, Rede, Bury St
Edmunds, Suffolk IP29 4AY
Tel 01284 789666
Fax 01284 789299
www.italianterrace.co.uk
Containers

Natural Driftwood Sculptures
Sunburst House
Elliott Road
Bournemouth BH11 8LT
Tel 01202 578274
info@driftwoodsculptures.co.uk
www.driftwoodsculptures.co.uk
Sculpture

Redwood Stone
The Stoneworks
West Horrington, Wells
Somerset BA5 3EH
Tel 01749 677777
Fax 01749 671177
www.redwoodstone.co.uk
Ornamental stonework

Stuart Garden Architecture
Burrow Hill Farm
Wiveliscombe
Somerset TA4 2RN
Tel 01984 667458
Fax 01984 667455
sales@stuartgarden.com
www.stuartgarden.com
Trellis and garden furniture

Sunny Screen
36 Udney Park Road
Teddington
Middlesex TW11 9BG
Tel 0870 803 4149
info@sunnyaspects.co.uk
www.sunnyaspects.co.uk
Screens

Richard Sutton
Tel 02476 616891
Coventry-based builder

Terre de Semences
Ripple Farm
Crundale, Canterbury
Kent CT4 7EB
Tel 01227 731815
contactus@organicseedsonline.
com
www.terredesemences.com
Vegetable seeds

The Modern Garden Company
Millars 3
Southmill Road
Bishops Stortford
Hertfordshire CM23 3DH
Tel 01279 653 200
info@moderngarden.co.uk
www.moderngarden.co.uk
Furniture

The Stewart Company
Stewart House
Waddon Marsh Way
Purley Way, Croydon
Surrey CR9 4HS
Tel 020 8603 5700
info@stewartcompany.co.uk
www.stewartcompany.co.uk
Containers and plant pots

Topiary Art Designs Ltd
Millers Meadow
Grimstone End, Pakenham
Bury-St-Edmunds
Suffolk IP31 2LZ
Tel 01359 232303
www.topiaryartdesigns.com
Topiary

Vivienne Palmer
Tel 01244 370360
vivpalmer@btinternet.com
*Chester-based ceramic and
mural artist*

UNITED STATES
Bear Creek Lumber
495 East County Road
Winthrop, Washington 98862
Tel (800) 597 7191
customerservice@bearcreek
lumber.com
www.bearcreeklumber.com
Wood distributor

Earth Products
515 Cobb Parkway
Marietta, Georgia 30062
Tel (770) 424 1479
Fax (770) 421 0842
www.earthproducts.net
Garden materials and décor

Gardener's Supply Company
128 Intervale Road
Burlington, Vermont 05401
Tel (888) 833 1412
Fax (800) 551 6712
www.gardeners.com
General garden supplies

Garden Expressions
22627 State Route 530 NE
Arlington
Washington 98223
Tel (888) 405 5234
International (360) 403 9532
steve@gardenexpressions.com
www.gardenexpressions.com
Garden accessories

Garden Oaks Specialities
1921 Route 22 West
Bound Brook
New Jersey 08805
Tel (800) 590 7433
Fax (732) 356 7202
Gardenoaks@aol.com
www.gardenoaks.com
Wooden furniture

High Plains Stone
8084 Blakeland Drive
Littleton
Colorado 80125
Tel (303) 791 1862
Fax (303) 791 1919
info@highplainsstone.com
www.highplainsstone.com
Natural building stone

The Home Depot
Stores available throughout
the USA
www.HomeDepot.com
General garden supplies

**Lowe's Home Improvement
Warehouse**
Stores available throughout
the USA
www.lowes.com
General garden supplies

Mother Nature Lighting
1353 Riverstone Parkway Suite
120-269 Canton
Georgia 30114
Tel (888) 867 2770
www.mothernaturelighting.com
Lighting

Trellis Structures
25 North Main St.
East Templeton
Massachusetts 80408
Tel (888) 285 4624
sales@trellisstructures.com
www.trellisstructures.com
Arbours, trellis and pergolas

INDEX

PLANT HARDINESS ZONES

Each of the plants in the Plant Directory has been given a plant hardiness rating for European readers (see text right) and a zone range for readers in the United States (see map and key to zones below).

When applied to the United States, plant entries in this book have been given zone numbers, and these zones relate to their hardiness. The zonal sytem used, shown below, was developed by the Agricultural Research Service of the U.S. Department of Agriculture (USDA). According to this system, there are 11 zones, based on the average annual minimum temperature in a particular geographical zone. When a range of zones

is given for a plant, the smaller number indicates the northernmost zone in which a plant can survive the winter, and the higher number gives the most southerly area in which it will perform consistently.

This is not a hard and fast system, but simply a rough indicator, as many factors other than temperature also play an important part where hardiness is concerned. These factors include altitude, wind exposure, proximity to water, soil type, the presence of snow or existence of shade, night temperature, and the amount of water received by a plant. Factors such as these can easily alter a plant's hardiness by as much as two zones.

European Hardiness Ratings

Frost tender
Plant may be damaged by temperatures below 5°C (41°F)

Half hardy
Plant can withstand temperatures down to 0°C (32°F)

Frost hardy
Plant can withstand temperatures down to -5°C (23°F)

Fully hardy
Plant can withstand temperatures down to -15°C (5°F)

USDA Zones

Zone 1 Below -45°C (-49°F)

Zone 2 -45 to -40°C (-49 to -40°F)

Zone 3 -40 to -34°C (-40 to -29°F)

Zone 4 -34 to -29°C (-29 to -20°F)

Zone 5 -29 to -23°C (-20 to -9°F)

Zone 6 -23 to -18°C (-9 to 0°F)

Zone 7 -18 to -12°C (0 to 10°F)

Zone 8 -12 to -7°C (10 to 19°F)

Zone 9 -7 to -1°C (19 to 30°F)

Zone 10 -1 to 4°C (30 to 39°F)

Zone 11 Above 4°C (39°F)

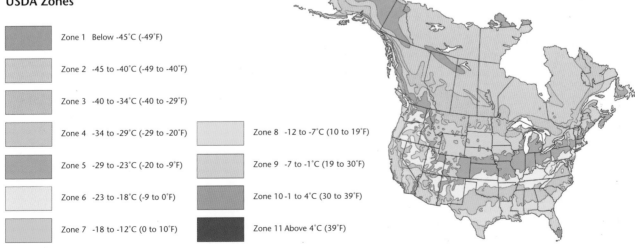

ACKNOWLEDGEMENTS

The publishers would like to thank the following for allowing the use of their gardens for practical photography: Jane and Geoff Hourihan; Peter and Murie Sanders; Leslie Ingram; Jim Austin and Jenny Patel; Martin Faultless; Barbara Williams; Bellamont Topiary; Capel Manor; and the Baron of Cam'nethan. Thanks also to the designer Alan Gardner, who was so generous with his time and introduced us to various locations, some his own garden designs (see Baron of Cam'nethan's garden on pages 168bl and 169tr); also to Vivienne Palmer, who set up and modelled the step-by-step sequences on pages 47, 63, 65, 85 and 183; and to Richard Sutton who set up and modelled the sequences on pages 115, 127, 133 and 185. And grateful thanks to Finnforest UK who gave us the screens to use in the sequence shown on page 185.

The publishers would also like to thank the following designers and institutions for allowing their gardens to be photographed for this book: **New Zealand** p30m and p120t Gordon Collier's garden; p46bl Karaka Point Vineyard; p74br Hamilton Botanic Gardens; p86–87 Eden House; p96tr Monterey House; p103 design by Tim Durrant; p121t Sarah Frater; p124m Neudorf Vineyard; p130bl Larnach Castle; p140, 141, 142, 143tl, tm and tr Liz Morrow,; p156t Bibby garden; p158tr Mincher; p163tr Waitati Garden; p164bm Rapaura Water Gardens; p187br Otari-Wilton's Bush. **The Hannah Peschar Sculpture Garden** p45tr Black and White Cottage, Ockley, Surrey, Garden Design Anthony Paul, stoneware design by Jennifer Jones. **Chelsea Flower Show 2004** p156bl Shizen – The Japanese Way, The Japanese Garden Society, designer Maureen Busby. **Chelsea Flower Show 2007** p1 Realistic Retreat, Adam Frost Landscapes, designer Adam Frost; p2 600 Days with Bradstone, designer Sarah Eberle; p4tl Celebrating 100 years of Hidcote Manor, designer Chris Beardshaw; p5tr and p29 The Fortnum and Mason Garden, designer Robert Myers; p28b Moving Spaces Moving On…, Warner Breaks, designers: Teresa Davies, Steve Putnam and Samantha Hawkins; p58b and 68t Casa Forte – A Mediterranean Retreat, designers: Stephen Firth and Nicola Ludlow-Monk; p107t The Fleming's and Trailfinder's Australian Garden, Fleming's Nurseries, designer Mark Browning; p174–5 The Amnesty International Garden for Human Rights, designers Paula Ryan and Artillery Architecture and Interior Design; p179b The Westland Garden, designers Diarmuid Gavin and Stephen Reilly. **Chelsea Flower Show 2008** p4tr and p121br Real Life by Brett, Brett Landscaping, designer Geoffrey Whiten; p5 (second from bottom) and p147 The Marshalls Garden that Kids Really Want, designer Ian Dexter; p22bl A Cadogan Garden, Cadogan Estates, designer Robert Myers; p74bl Spana's Courtyard Refuge, designer Chris O'Donoghue; p102bl The Children's Society Garden, designer Mark Gregory; p116–117, p127tr, p130t and p191bl The Dorset Cereals Edible Playground, designer Nick Williams-Ellis; p124br and p128m The Summer Solstice Garden, Daylesford Organic, designer Del Buono Gazerwitz; p134br Motor Neurone Disease – Shetland Croft House Garden, designer Sue Hayward; p144–145 Traveller's Retreat, Lloyds TSB, designer Trevor Tooth; p169t Garden in the Silver Moonlight, designers Haruko Seki and Makoto Saito; p5 (bottom) and p177 Urban Rain by Bamboo, designer Bob Latham; p182br The Pemberton Greenish Recess Garden, designers Paul Hensey and Neil Lucas; p186m The Gavin Jones Garden of Corian, designer Philip Nash; p190m The LK Bennett Garden, designer Rachel de Thame; p192m Fleming's and Trailfinder's Australian Garden, designer Jamie Durie. **Hampton Court Palace Flower Show 2007** p7t The Twain Shall Meet, The Bottom Drawer, designers Lorna Thomas and Davinia Wild; p50bm The Ruin on the Corner, Martinspeed, design by Keppel Designs; p61tl Learning to Look After Our World, Alton Infant School; p62b Silver Glade, The Down to Earth Partners, designers Chris Allen and Dorinda Forbes; p118t The Giving Garden, Country Market Garden Centre, Heronshaw, Blackmoor Nurseries, designer Maurice Butcher; p181tl Full Frontal, Hadlow College, designers Heidi Harvey and Fern Alder; p181tr In Digestion, designer Tony Smith; p194m The Raku Garden, designer Rachel Ewer. **Hampton Court Palace Flower Show 2008** p6 The Shade-loving Garden, designer Jonathan Walton; p12–13 The Anglian Green, Black and White Garden, Anglian Home Improvements, designer Krista Grindley; p14t The Croft Spot Secret Garden, Croft Original Sherry, designer David Domoney; p14b The Porsche Garden, designers Sim Flemons and John Warland; p16mt, p20c and p20cr Mundy's Cottage, design by Winchester Growers; p21tr The Homebase Room with a View, designer Philippa Pearson; p23tr Branching Out With Copella – The Apple Juice Garden, designer Sadie May Stowell; p23b The Sadolin Four

Seasons Garden, designer Helen Williams; p94b Living on the Ceiling, Warwickshire College; p102br and p152 Holiday Inn Green Room, designer Sarah Eberle; p104t Formal Elements, Cambourne Homes, Design Build International, Go Modern Furniture, Tobermore, designer Noel Duffy; p108b The Burghbad Sanctuary, Burghbad Bathrooms, designers David Cubero and James Wong; p148m The Widex Hearing Garden, designer Selina Botham; p155t Three in One Garden, Adrian Hall Garden Centre, Barbed, Elmwood Fencing, designer Lesley Faux.

The publishers would also like to thank the following for permission to reproduce their images. **Agriframe:** p134t. **Alamy:** p8tr dbimages; p8br The Print Collector; p50br JHP Travel; p126tl Elizabeth Whiting & Associates. **Art Archive** p9l Bibliothèque des Arts Décoratifs, Paris. **Bridgeman:** p8bl The British Museum; p10b British Library Board. **Amy Christian:** p96tl. **Corbis:** p126b Eric Crichton; p168bl Arcaid. **Felicity Forster:** p1; p101t; p107t; p127tl; p148t; p179b; p181tl; p181tr; p194m. **Garden Picture Library:** p49bl Clive Nichols; p51b Steven Wooster; p64m and p84bl Juliet Greene; p66bl Lynne Brotchie; p71r Janet Seaton; p72b Philippe Bonduel; p73t Mark Bolton; p73b Juliette Wade; p97t Botanica; p104br Dominique Vorillon; p161t David Dixon; p214bl Michele Lamontagne; p214m Lynn Keddie; p215r Anne Green/Armytage; p222l and p230m John Glover; p223r Mark Turner; p232t Kate Gadsby; p234l Adrian Bloom; **John Feltwell/Garden Matters:** p91tl, p91tm, p91tr; **Garden World Images:** p34b J. Need; p67b A. Graham; p90br Mein Schoener Garten; p109b P. Smith (Peter Tinsley Landscaping). **Harpur Garden Images:** p43t; p72m; p100bl; p110b; p162 br. **Istock:** p10t; p100br. **Les Jardins du Roi Soleil:** p36tr. l = left; r = right; t = top; b = bottom; m = middle.